MW00987711

Mid-Century Modern Architecture Travel Guide

West Coast USA

Mid-Century Modern Architecture Travel Guide

West Coast USA

Written by Sam Lubell

Photographs by Darren Bradley

Mid-Century Modern Architecture Travel Guide

West Coast USA

Contents

Few destinations on the planet are as fabled, hyped and dreamed about as the West Coast of the United States. With its gorgeous, sun-kissed beaches, dazzling landscapes, endlessly chronicled culture and storied cities, it's long been one of the most fertile travel destinations in the world. But the West Coast has an unparalleled resource that rarely surfaces in most itineraries; nor is it even on the mental map of most of those who live here. A spectacular secret hidden in plain sight.

From Seattle in the north to San Diego down south right near the Mexican border, the West Coast came into its own during the middle of the twentieth century, fostering endless opportunities for an explosion of talented designers, who in turn blessed it with an extraordinary legacy of Mid-Century Modern architecture. Many of the European-born Modern movement's most revolutionary pioneers settled along the West Coast, not just for its benevolent climate, but also for the unprecedented chance to escape the rigid architectural orthodoxies further east. These pioneers left their mark on the West Coast and have become fixtures in any architectural education: Rudolph Schindler, Richard Neutra,

Introduction

Eames House Charles and Ray Eames (page 158)

Frank Lloyd Wright, Gregory Ain, John Lautner, Craig Ellwood, A. Quincy Jones, Pierre Koenig, Raphael Soriano, Ray Kappe, Pietro Belluschi, Joseph Esherick, Charles Moore, Skidmore, Owings & Merrill, Minoru Yamasaki and Victor Steinbrueck, to name just a very few. They stood on the shoulders of a previous generation of West Coast pre-Modernists and early Modernists like Irving Gill, Greene and Greene, Bernard Maybeck, Julia Morgan, Robert Reamer and J. Lister Holmes and created a revelation: an industrial-inspired, accessible style of architecture that was lighter, simpler and more appropriate to its time and place.

This idyllic edge of the world became the perfect testing ground to replace hefty, ornament-filled buildings with new, fresh, utterly optimistic and stripped down expressions of glass, steel, wood and concrete. The Mid-Century Modern architects opened these novel edifices to stunning landscapes through sliding glass doors, clerestory windows, internal and external courtyards and seamless porches and balconies, merging indoor and outdoor lifestyles into a revolutionary whole. They experimented with new materials like steel-reinforced concrete, wood composite and larger and larger

Case Study House #21 Pierre Koenig (page 169)

expanses of clearer and clearer glass. They explored structural systems like long-span cantilevers, bundled steel tubes, prefabricated components and steel truss systems and space frames, embodying the future-obsessed ideal that nature's hardships, social ills and even human suffering could be overcome through gleaming technologies. They invented or reinvented spatial techniques like open plans, pinwheel sites, decentralized structures and circulation sequences, revolutionizing human dynamics and jettisoning stodgy traditions.

This group of earnest, innovative designers – most of them white men – were woefully lacking in diversity themselves, but they worked in a kaleidoscope of sub-styles under the Modernist umbrella. Their work comprised the glass and steel International Style cubes of Craig Ellwood and the architects of *Art&Architecture* magazine's fabled Case Study House Program; the populist, space-age 'Googie' architecture of Armet & Davis as well as Powers, Daly and DeRosa, with its sharp jutting rooflines, integrated signage and giant plate-glass windows; the wild, daring experimentation of structural expressionists like Bruce Goff and William Pereria, whose inverted ziggurat Geisel Library at the University of California,

Schindler House Rudolph Schindler (page 166)

San Diego, stands as an engineering wonder even today (page 304); the minimal Brutalism of Louis Kahn, whose Salk Institute embodies his juxtaposition of raw solidity and surreal purity (page 300); the curving, land-inspired organic architecture of Frank Lloyd Wright and John Lautner, as well as the classically-inspired, unapologetically ornamented New Formalism of Edward Durell Stone and his compatriots.

Within this vast array of sub-genres came more variation still, drawing on regional culture, climate and geography. Each area had its exceptions and commonalities are frequent, but in a broader sense Southern California, with its incessant sun-shine, developed a lighter, more industrial-inspired style, fusing with the natural world, both shielding and embracing the constant sunlight and nodding to nearby Asian and Latin American influences. Northern Californian masters more often incorporated rustic materials like timber and stone, taking advantage of the redwood forests and adapting to a more diverse climate. In the Pacific Northwest, reactions to inclement weather and to an abundance of natural resources, became even more pronounced, with an embrace of natural materials unmatched almost anywhere in the world

Art Center College of Design Craig Ellwood (page 195)

of Modernist architecture. Exploring work from the legends of Mid-Century Modern architecture along the West Coast demonstrates how its spirit of innovation and democratization were a perfect match for this place: a style that was all about starting over in a place that was ready, willing and able to embrace the new. Yes, the area's utopian dreams have in many places been tempered in more recent decades by congestion, decay and a disregard for architectural treasures, but the best of these Mid-Century buildings evoke uplifting feelings of release and optimism.

Take a turn onto a winding street anywhere along the West Coast and the air gets stiller, your pulse gets slower and there's a chance that the building you're looking at is not just a piece of revolutionary architecture – it's a sublime escape. Lifting your spirit with its beauty and ingenuity, yes, but also transporting you to another time and place. Architecture is a technical art form. But it's also a habitable one, inseparable from its context.

Visit the Eames House, a monument to simple, off-the-shelf beauty in Los Angeles' Pacific Palisades and you can commune

Salk Institute Louis Kahn and Luis Barragan (page 300)

with the gridded, trussed structure or sit on a rope swing, hanging from a tree overlooking the Pacific Ocean (page 158). Take a tour of the Stahl House in the Hollywood Hills, perhaps the most famous Modernist house of all and you're enveloped by glass and, more importantly, Los Angeles (page 178). As day turns into night you watch the lights slowly flickering on and the basin of the sprawling metropolis turning hazier and more mystifying. The city's energy and chaos are spread out before you and become part of the house. This is not merely architecture. It is architecture as a metropolis. Walk through Harwell Hamilton Harris' Weston Havens House on Panoramic Way in Berkeley, made famous by Man Ray's bold black-and-white snapshots and you become part of the picture, staring at the Berkeley clock tower from an extraordinary ship-lapped balcony that feels like the edge of possibility (page 74). Drive into the hills above Berkeley and you'll discover Beverley David Thorne's Brubeck House, built for jazz musician Dave Brubeck, hovering on stilts, literally jutting over the street (page 76). As day becomes night it looks more and more surreal – how could this bridge through the trees be real? As iconic as they are in the insular architecture world, these are special, often unrecognized places to most and

St. Mary's Cathedral Belluschi & Nervi (page 92)

as a visitor you've got them to yourself in a way that you never will when checking out a famous monument or following a well-traveled tourist itinerary. You're off the beaten path, in another time, on a trip that captures the sense of freedom and possibility that infused this architecture when it was built. You've hit the road in a place that, for a time anyway, was the end of the road. The new frontier. It's about new discoveries. So it's natural that once you're versed in the most iconic buildings of this era – the immaculate Case Study Houses projecting off cliffs; the futuristic parabolic arches of 'Googie' Los Angeles; the rat pack-era butterfly roofs of Palm Springs and the humble, spiritual timber spectacles of Sea Ranch (page 64) – that you would want to explore the hidden surprises.

While a handful of architects from the West Coast are canonized as masters – their work immortalized by photographers like Julius Shulman, Marvin Rand and Ezra Stoller in magazines, books, brochures and films – the sensation of Mid-Century Modernism spawned so many more daring designers. Each region had a much larger crop of equally talented, but now-forgotten architects.

Rainier Tower Minoru Yamasaki (page 35)

You'll be captivated by the confident structural audacity of San Diego architect Ken Kellogg, one of a generation of designers in that city under the spell of Frank Lloyd Wright. His Babcock House in Mission Bay rises above a glassy base, spreading its patinated geometric copper wings over a tightly packed beach community (page 320). In Long Beach you'll discover the impeccable artistry of Killingsworth Brady Smith, whose post-and-beam offices, including the Cambridge Building (page 246) and its own studio (page 245), line many of the area's streets and whose gem-like residences, such as the Triad Homes (page 309), retreat from reflective moats, accessible only via well-spaced, square stepping stones, like three-dimensional paintings. You'll approach the folly of talented Carmel-based architect Mark Mills, whose sand-infused structures such as The Shell (page 112), bordering cliffs and rocky beaches, resemble seashells and even phalluses. You'll get a taste of the subtle, austere brilliance of Anshen & Allen, who brought a maverick's spirit to corporate architecture in California and beyond as seen in their Union Bank of California Tower (page 45); and their colleague Donald Olsen, one of the Bay Area's pure Modernists, creating enchanting

Crown Zellerbach Skidmore, Owings & Merrill (page 86)

glass cubes such as his own home (page 72), in a region then known for anything but. You'll appreciate the many brilliant churches of Seattle architect Paul Thiry who adapted ancient vernaculars for structurally brilliant inventions that feel equally old and new, for example, his Agnes Flanagan Chapel (page 52). And revel in the work of Paul Hayden Kirk, who wove light like fabric and inserted mysterious ancient native sculpture into work that was unflinchingly modern – as seen in his University Unitarian Church (page 28). And you are unlikely to forget the sublime work of so many more: Warren Callister, Dale Naegle, Jack Hillmer and Rowan Maiden. And you'll equally appreciate the work of those masters of anonymous Mid-Century Modern buildings – from brilliantly shaped and ornamented supermarkets to carwashes, diners and bowling alleys – whose names were never recorded for posterity.

Of course you'll hit the major cities on the West Coast, but you'll also find yourself exploring a town called Milwaukie right outside of Portland, home to Stearns, Mention and Morris' St. John the Baptist church, whose teardrop shape appears to be carved out of alabaster harvested from J. R. R. Tolkien's Middle Earth (page 51). A few miles away you'll come to a town called Oregon City that contains Stevens and Thompson's Oregon City Municipal Elevator, a baseball cap-shaped concrete structure jutting over the city on a single post, with incredible views at the top (page 54). Also in the vicinity you can tour the Mount Angel Abbey, a convent seemingly pulled out of Umbria, perched on a rocky cliff, home to Alvar Aalto's stunning Mount Angel Library (page 56).

You'll learn the names of so many more unexpected neighborhoods of Mid-Century Modern treasures, like Laguna Niguel in Orange County; Del Mar near San Diego; Pasadena, a town more commonly associated with its Craftsman-style architectural heritage; and Berkeley, a city known for its progressive politics and its Beaux-Arts planned university, not its hillsides brimming with Mid-Century Modern residences. You'll come across sublime housing tracts built by visionary real estate developers the Eichlers and the Alexanders and by cooperatives of artists and architects at places like Crestwood Hills in Brentwood (page 146), Mar Vista Tract on Los Angeles' West Side (page 207) and the Hilltop Community in Bellevue, Washington (page 41). You'll round a bend in the hills above Los Feliz and Lloyd Wright's woefully unknown Samuel-Novarro House will unfold before you –

a cruciform gem of patinated copper and white stucco, whose scale and pure beauty takes your breath away (page 181). When you're traveling the West Coast, stunning architecture will take not just the form of pristine houses and museums, but also of hospitals, churches, banks, offices, stadia, car washes, diners, schools and universities.

The social permissiveness that made California such a destination for hippies, beatniks and other free thinkers in the middle of the twentieth century will bring you to 'The Onion', officially known as Selulveda Unitarian Church, a church supported by glulam beams shaped like, yes, an onion (page 138). And elsewhere, you'll be transfixed by homes that are molded like eagles, seashells, waves and ski jumps. Jones & Emmons and Eliot Noyes' IBM Building resembles a computer punch card (page 230). Frank Lloyd Wright's spired and domed Marin County Civic Center resembles – and in fact inspired – the architecture of the planet Naboo in *Star Wars* (page 66). Unsung master Welton Becket's famed Capitol Records Building looks like a record player (page 180), while his Cinerama Dome is a concrete version of a Buckminster Fuller geodesic dome (page 177).

Marin County Civic Center Frank Lloyd Wright (page 66)

Of course, uncommon architectural adventure is not always easy, nor fruitful. A number of buildings had to be – sadly – omitted from this guide because they are, in fact, impossible to view from the street: hiding behind walls or perched above private or inaccessible canyons. Often Mid-Century Modernism's wonderful transparency was achieved by closing a building's public face and opening up the building behind it, either by fences or natural barriers like berms or hillsides, making the building impossible to view from a public space, one of the criteria for inclusion in this guide. That's a great thing if you're a family, but not if you're a visitor. Many are behind high gates or hedges, the property of wealthy celebrities or visitor-weary individuals. Beverley David Thorne's masterpiece, the floating Case Study House #26 in San Rafael, is impossible to see from the street, as it dips down below its long driveway. The same applies to Raphael Soriano's bar-shaped, landscape-enveloped home for legendary Mid-Century architectural photographer Julius Shulman in the Hollywood Hills, Rodney Walker's Transparent House in Ojai, Jack Hillmer's Hall House in Kentfield, Lutah Maria Riggs' Erving House in Santa Barbara, John Lautner's Elrod House and Silvertop Houses in Palm Springs

Kaufman House Richard Neutra (page 273)

and Silver Lake, Richard Neutra's Singleton House on Mulholland Drive in Los Angeles – and the list goes on and on.

Visiting some of these now-fragile Mid-Century edifices, most of them more than half a century old, sometimes delivers heartbreak. The slings and arrows aimed at an architectural movement that has only regained respect in the last decade or so are clear, as hundreds of noted Mid-Century Modern buildings have been horribly altered, destroyed, defaced or left for dead at the hands of neglect. Once John Carl Warnecke's Oakland International Airport was fronted by a mesmerizing array of rolling exposed concrete arches. Now it's hidden behind an unsympathetic facade. Paul Thiry's Mercer Island Presbyterian church used to be a floating, singular, geometric concrete marvel. Now it's covered with a horrible standing seam rain screen, making the Herculean structural effort for naught. Mario Ciampi's glorious Berkeley Art Museum, with its fanning, cantilevered bays and glowing central atrium, was structurally compromised and has since been closed, its fate uncertain. Rudolph Schindler's Bethlehem Baptist Church in Compton, while a fascinating detour from his usual work, is in such poor condition it's almost impossible to appreciate

Kappe Colony, Benedict Canyon Ray Kappe (page 154)

from the outside and now the inside is closed to the public. And Richard Neutra's Connell House in Pebble Beach was, at the time of publication, surrounded by green barriers, destined for the wrecking ball.

And yet despite these necessary omissions, this is a thoroughly expansive and representative architectural travel guide, packed not just with histories, descriptions and first-hand anecdotes, but also with useful visitor information on more than 250 buildings. But it is not exhaustive, nor could it ever be. Besides the fact that many of these buildings are impossible to visit, the Mid-Century Modern movement was so deep and widespread on the West Coast that any attempt to comprehensively catalog its achievements will always fall short. What this book will do, however, is set you on a path of discovery that will transport you from old sun-bleached Kodachrome photographs and vague memories into a world of spectacular reality; a 2,000-mile (3,200-kilometer) road trip from Seattle to San Diego that for some exhilarating moments will recapture the sense of liberation that infused Modernism in its Mid-Century heyday. It will not just introduce you to splendid architecture, but also transport you from the banality that surrounds the world we've since created.

Architecture seen through the eyes of architects can sometimes be a rather dry exercise in structure, geometry and technical achievement. Architecture seen through the eyes of explorers, however, is about architectural drama, to be sure, but it's just as much about the visceral experience of the building, its site, its history and the raw emotions that it can elicit. It all stays with you. Even after you've left the West Coast, Mid-Century Modernism will pop up everywhere, in your periphery vision and in your mind's eye. You'll begin to notice and appreciate the lasting imprints of a visionary movement that was so widespread it touched every corner of the earth. You'll grasp how architecture – Mid-Century Modern or otherwise – has a singular ability to lift us to primal and spiritual heights we never thought possible. In the middle of the twentieth century, in this special part of the United States, in a few gleaming instances, the *experience* of architecture was honed to a near perfection that it rarely had before and rarely has had since.

Notes

The buildings in the *Mid-Century Modern Architecture Travel Guide* are organized geographically from north to south into five regional chapters – Pacific Northwest, San Francisco (and the Bay Area), Los Angeles, Palm Springs and San Diego. Each chapter is identified with its own color and shape code: a green diamond for the Pacific Northwest, a yellow circle for San Francisco, a red square for Los Angeles, an orange hexagon for Palm Springs and a blue triangle for San Diego. The buildings are generally presented in geographical sequence from north to south, as indicated on the regional map at the beginning of each chapter. The regional maps in this book are intended as a guide to the general location and to indicate the spread of Mid-Century Modern architecture in each region or city. I trust that readers will avail themselves of the appropriate maps, whether analog or digital, for accurate way-finding.

Each building entry is presented with its full street address to allow navigation directly to the property, as well as the name of the building, the architect, the year in which the building was completed and a brief description. The building entry also includes detailed information on the facilities you can expect to find at each property, including whether or not the building is open to the public, whether it has a cafe or restaurant, a shop and whether it offers overnight accommodation.

It should be noted that the majority of the buildings featured in this book are private property. While I have restricted inclusion in the main part of the book to buildings that are visible from either the street or other public property, I ask you to respect the privacy of every building owner.

In the back of the book can be found more detailed information about properties, including website addresses and opening times for buildings that are open to the public – whether as tourist attractions, in the case of some, or as businesses such as shops, restaurants, or banks in others. It should be noted that while every care has been taken to ensure accuracy throughout the book, opening times and dates are subject to change and therefore it is advisable to check the times and opening details prior to visiting or arranging travel.

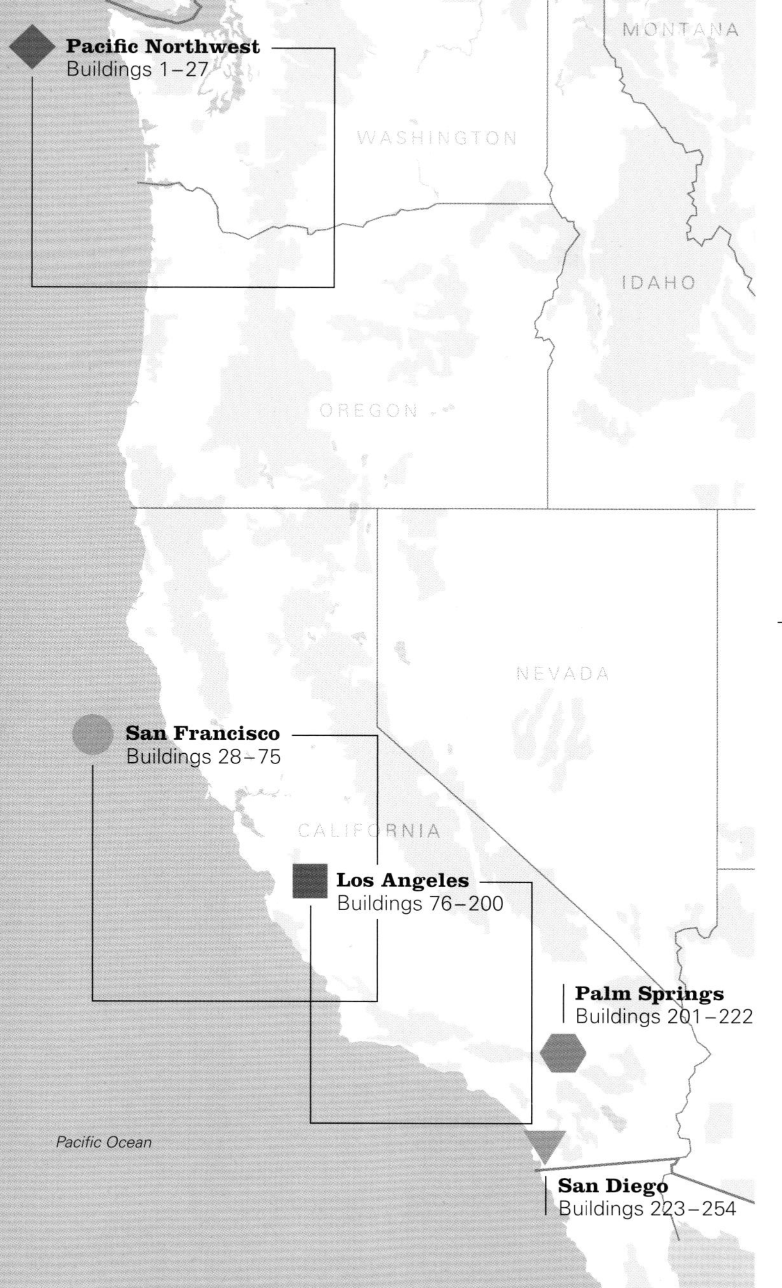

West Coast USA

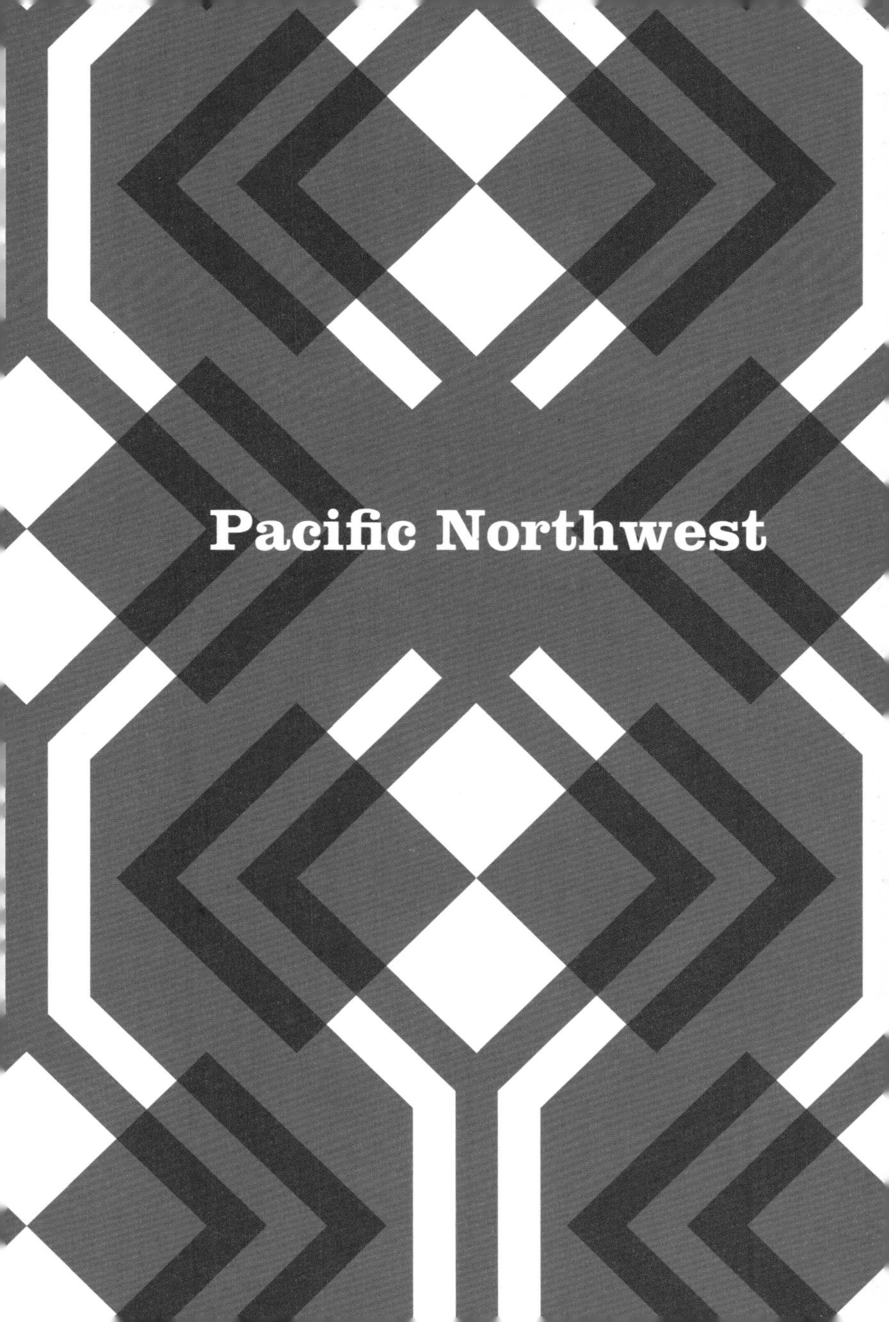

Pacific Northwest

1 University Unitarian Church **2** University of Washington Faculty Club **3** Canlis Restaurant **4** St. Paul's Episcopal Church **5** Space Needle **6** Pacific Science Center **7** Rainier Tower **8** Plymouth Congregational Church **9** IBM Building **10** Safeco Plaza **11** King County Administration Building **12** Chopp House **13** Hilltop Community **14** St. Charles Borromeo Catholic Church **15** St. Joseph's Hospital **16** Veterans Memorial Coliseum **17** Union Bank of California Tower **18** Wells Fargo Center **19** Equitable Building **20** Watzek House **21** Zidell House **22** Feldman House **23** St. John the Baptist Catholic Church **24** Agnes Flanagan Chapel, Lewis and Clark College **25** Oregon City Municipal Elevator **26** Gordon House **27** Mount Angel Library

Pacific Northwest

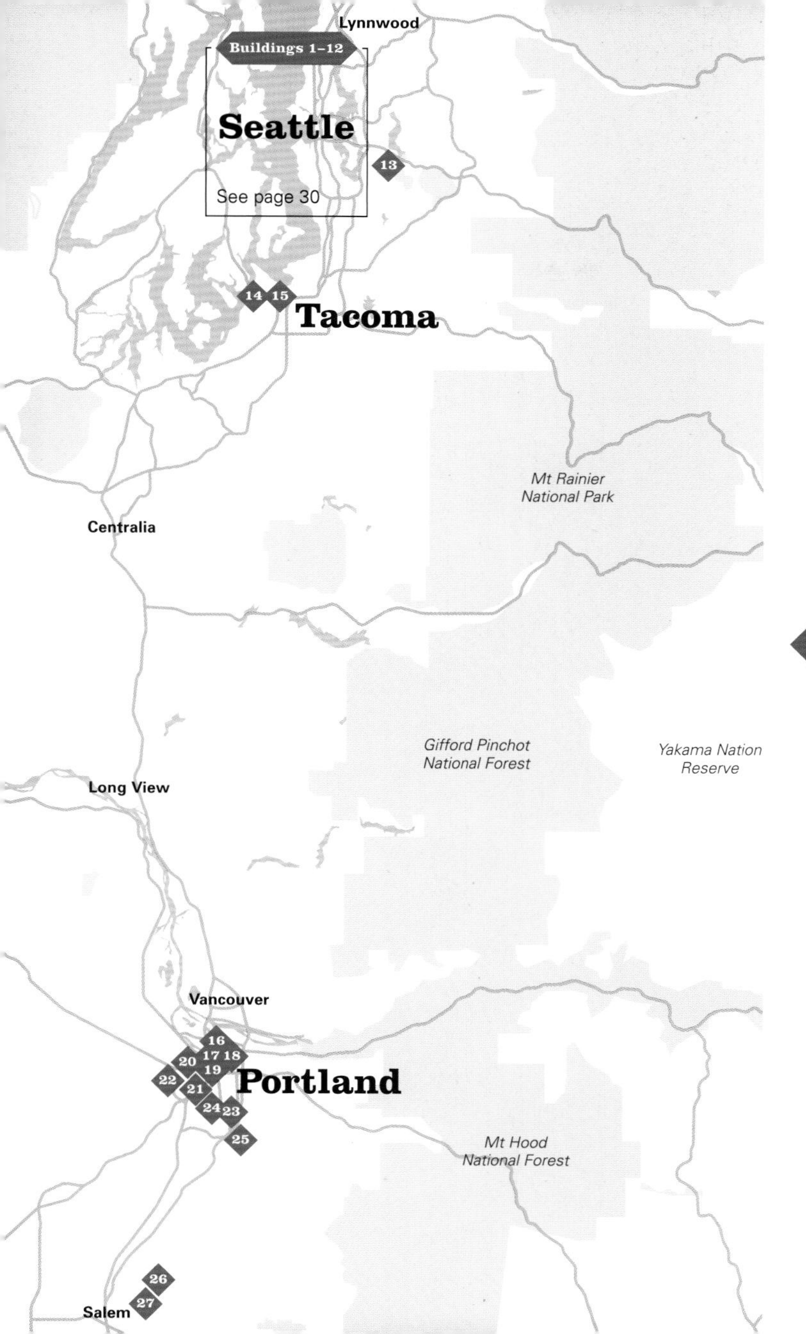

Sunset Hill

Ballard

Phinne Ridge

Shilshole Bay

Lawntonwood

Old Ballard

West Woodland

Discovery Park

North Queen Anne

Magnolia

Queen Anne

Elliott Bay

Northeast Seattle
Pontiac
Green Lake
Ravenna
Ravenna Park
Meridian
Bryant
Windermere
University District
Wallingford
Wolf Bay
Union Bay
East Lake
Montlake
Lake Union
Washington Park
Madison Park
West Lake
Volunteer Park
Capitol Hill
Hilltop
Madrona
Pike/Pine
Lake Washington
Mann
Seattle
Downtown
Leschi
Atlantic
Mt. Baker

University Unitarian Church

Pacific Northwest **Architect** Paul Hayden Kirk **Year** 1960
Address 6556 35th Avenue NE, Seattle, WA 98115

Open to Public Yes **Free Entrance** Yes **Café/Restaurant** No
Overnight Accommodation No **Gift/Bookshop** No

Any church with Eames chairs as pews wins the Mid-Century Modern stamp of approval. It doesn't hurt that Paul Hayden Kirk's University Unitarian Church, in Northeast Seattle's Ravenna-Bryant neighborhood, is a stunner even without the furnishings. The building is designed as an architectural mixing bowl, bringing together sublime, modulated light, Pacific native culture and Mid-Century Modern simplicity in an utterly unique form. Critical of the severity of the International Style, Kirk admired Japanese and Scandinavian architecture, with their embrace of warm, natural elements, sophisticated joinery, large windows, subtle screening and the integration of the exterior. The building, abutting a narrow courtyard, is screened by a long wall of amber colored stained glass and primitive steel sculpture, held away from the building by a series of exposed wood frames to create light and shadow patterns. Inside, indirect light enters through a long clerestory window. Colored light filters through the stained glass, adding yet another layer of illumination. Look up to see a skeleton of exposed, intersecting beams. Look forward to seeing a building that unfolds like origami, culminating in a slatted wood-screened altarpiece. The sanctuary connects to a series of offices and classrooms, interspersed with interior courtyards. ◆

1

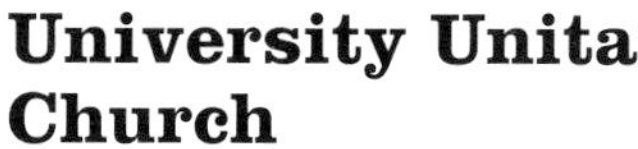

University Unitarian Church

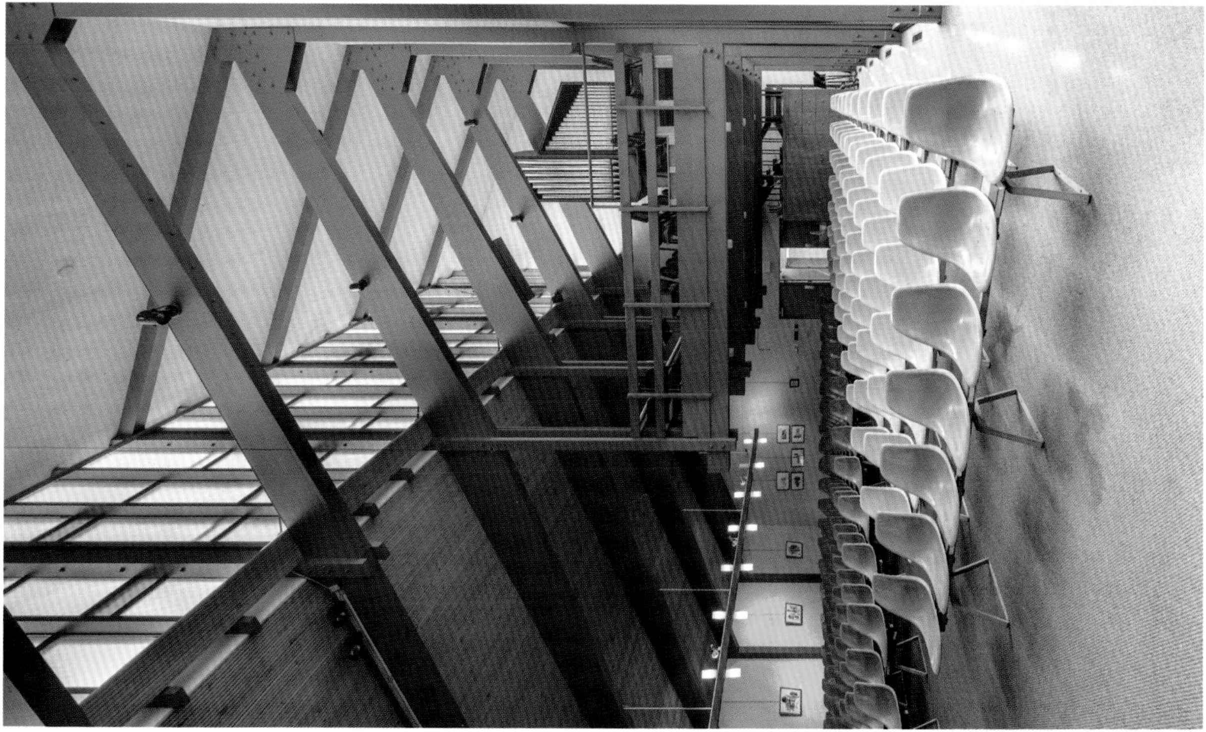

University of Washington Faculty Club

Pacific Northwest **Architect** Paul Hayden Kirk and Victor Steinbrueck **Year** 1960
Address University of Washington, 4020 E Stevens Way, Seattle, WA 98195

Open to Public No **Free Entrance** No **Café/Restaurant** No
Overnight Accommodation No **Gift/Bookshop** No

Sure, universities revolve around students, but their best buildings often belong to the professors. Designed by two of Seattle's Mid-Century Modern architecture stars, Paul Hayden Kirk and Victor Steinbrueck, the University of Washington Faculty Club is no exception. It's one of several notable Modernist buildings on this rolling Gothic campus, located due north of downtown Seattle. The simple steel and white stucco building, reminiscent of the work of Craig Ellwood and Mies van der Rohe, resembles a residence more than an institutional structure. It consists of a series of rectangles, connected by raised walkways and interior courtyards, floating on steel stilts above a downhill parking lot and stretching east toward Union Bay, its large glass expanses protected by deep overhangs. Inside, gentle wood surfaces, elegant furniture and an exposed structure offset the exterior's quiet but bold coolness. 'If you're going to defy a context, defy it strongly', wrote the *Seattle Times*' Lawrence Cheek about the building, which was one of the first Modernist structures on campus. But at the same time, wrote Cheek, 'its presence is quiet, not blustery or self-aggrandizing. It's like the student who sits unnoticed in the back, seldom speaking or doing anything to attract notice and one day she turns out to be the valedictorian.' ◆

If you like good food, views and Mid-Century Modern architecture, then Canlis is the right place. Opened in 1950 by Hawaiian restaurateur Peter Canlis, and designed by Seattle master architect Roland Terry, the restaurant, located about three miles (five kilometers) north of Downtown Seattle, combines a sense of Pacific warmth and openness with the rustic charm of the Northwest. The building, which seems to float over a bluff above Lake Union, provides panoramic vistas through huge expanses of glass, supported by equally large lengths of timber. Inside, the tall, open-planned space is warmed with rugged stone walls, indoor plantings and even a central stone fireplace and chimney. The restaurant's eastern windows angle sharply outward to reduce ceiling light reflections and to draw views from even further out. Beneath it vigorous landscaping adds to a sense of Pacific-Northwest fusion. The building turns its back on its western side, where there is a busy road. Terry, who became known as one of the primary definers of the Northwest School of architecture, made his mark with homes, shops, hotels and restaurants utilizing local wood, stone and other natural materials. ◆

Pacific Northwest **Architect** Roland Terry and Peter Wimberly **Year** 1950
Address 2576 Aurora Avenue N, Seattle, WA 98109

Open to Public Yes **Free Entrance** No **Café/Restaurant** Yes
Overnight Accommodation No **Gift/Bookshop** No

Canlis Restaurant

St. Paul's Episcopal Church

Pacific Northwest **Architect** Steinhart, Theriault and Anderson **Year** 1962
Address 15 Roy Street, Seattle, WA 98109

Open to Public No **Free Entrance** No **Café/Restaurant** No
Overnight Accommodation No **Gift/Bookshop** No

The steep roof of this bulky, shingled A-framed church (actually, there are six A-frames), which is on a mid-block lot on the scruffy downhill edge of Seattle's upscale Queen Anne neighborhood, looks like the pleated bellows of an accordion. Its roofline rises from close to the ground, covering the structure almost completely and giving it the feel of a vaguely mystical, other-worldly structure. An enclosed plaza to the east contains a garden, a paved labyrinth and a fountain. Designed by one of the region's premier sacred space architects, Steinhart, Theriault and Anderson, the tall building's interior reveals a structural system of angular laminated beams, branching out like tree limbs. When inside, be sure to turn around and enjoy the floating Spaeth organ, hanging from steel rods above a balcony near the entryway. A renovation completed in 2011 by local firm atelierjones stripped away past accumulations, installed new colorful laminated glazing along the lower sides of the sanctuary and created a new glass entryway on Roy Street, opening the building to the outside – although perhaps bringing more distractions inside than the original designers would have wanted. The renovation also included the addition of a new organic altar and baptismal font, both by artist Julie Speidel. ◆

Many out-of-towners visiting Seattle think this landmark, seen in basically every movie, television show and advertisement that has ever involved the city, is in the heart of downtown. But it is actually just north, soaring 605 feet (184 meters) above the Seattle Center in the Lower Queen Anne neighborhood. When the hourglass-shaped tower, with its massive steel beam legs and flying saucer-shaped observation space and rotating restaurant, opened in 1962, it was the tallest building west of the Mississippi. Yet its design origins are sketchy at best. In one version, Seattle hotel owner Edward E. Carlson, inspired by the Stuttgart Television Tower in Germany, sketched an early design – which resembled a tethered balloon – on a napkin in a coffee shop. Architect John Graham refined it, bringing in the restaurant and observatory. Architect Victor Steinbrueck added its curved form. Investors bought the land beneath the Space Needle in 1961 for just $75,000. The small footprint necessitated a 30-foot-deep (9-meter) concrete foundation and required 467 trucks to pour over 5,000 tons (4,535 tonnes) of cement. The elevator trip to the top traveling at 10 mph (1.6 kph) takes 43 seconds. The view is, not surprisingly, extraordinary in all directions, as long as the gray Seattle weather and the unpredictable Mount Rainier, cooperate. ◆

Pacific Northwest **Architect** John Graham and Victor Steinbrueck **Year** 1962
Address 400 Broad Street, Seattle, WA 98109

Open to Public Yes **Free Entrance** No **Café/Restaurant** Yes
Overnight Accommodation No **Gift/Bookshop** Yes

Pacific Science Center

Seattle-born Minoru Yamasaki's visionary architecture was perfectly at home during the city's 1962 World's Fair, otherwise known as the Century 21 Exposition, which saw the construction of, among other famed structures, the iconic Space Needle (page 33). Yamasaki's no less visionary contribution was the United States Science Pavilion, now called the Pacific Science Center. Located in the city's Lower Queen Anne quarter, Yamasaki's 'virtual cathedral of science' was a vital part of an effort to showcase America's scientific prowess during the Cold War. It featured models of satellites and space capsules, exhibits on the history of science and a 'spacearium' taking crowds on a simulated voyage through the solar system. The building itself, almost completely windowless by necessity, was saved from dull blankness through intricate walls of precast concrete, forming a lacy, arched filigree. Its Modernist courtyard is highlighted by giant white sculpted arches that continue this 'Modern Gothic' language and includes concrete platforms hovering over large, fountain-filled reflecting pools. The structure is one of the highlights of the former fairgrounds, which have become the Seattle Center, a 74 acre (30 hectare) park containing museums, performance halls and sports complexes. Other remaining fair pieces include the International Fountain, the Key Arena, the Seattle Armory (now home to the Seattle Children's Museum) and, of course, the needle and the monorail. ◆

Pacific Northwest **Architect** Minoru Yamasaki **Year** 1962
Address 200 Second Avenue N, Seattle, WA 98109

Open to Public Yes **Free Entrance** No **Café/Restaurant** Yes
Overnight Accommodation No **Gift/Bookshop** No

Pacific Northwest **Architect** Minoru Yamasaki **Year** 1977
Address 1301 5th Avenue, Seattle, WA 98101

7

Rainier Tower

Open to Public No **Free Entrance** No **Café/Restaurant** No
Overnight Accommodation No **Gift/Bookshop** No

With an eleven-story tapered solid concrete base that resembles a beaver-felled tree beneath twenty-nine office floors, Rainier Tower is hard to miss if you are in downtown Seattle. The building was designed by Minoru Yamasaki, who worked on projects ranging from the nearby Pacific Science Center (opposite), to the infamously demolished Pruitt-Igoe in St. Louis, to, of course, the former World Trade Center in New York City. Locals say that the tower, clad above its amazing base with vertical stripes of glazing and aluminum cladding (similar to both the Twin Towers and Yamasaki's Century Plaza Towers on page 162), is one of the safest places to be inside during an earthquake, as it reportedly has one of the lowest centers of gravity of any skyscraper in Seattle. A raised, hidden terrace behind the building allows for a peaceful retreat and an uninterrupted and dizzying view up the building's massive facade, but reports say that it and the covered mall below, will be replaced by a fifty-eight-story tower by NBBJ. Either way, the best views of the tower come from diagonally across the street, from the plaza of yet another Yamasaki building, the IBM Building (page 37). ◆

Plymouth Congregational Church

Pacific Northwest **Architect** Naramore, Bain, Brady and Johanson (NBBJ)
Year 1968 **Address** 1217 6th Avenue, Seattle, WA 98101

Open to Public Yes **Free Entrance** Yes **Café/Restaurant** No
Overnight Accommodation No **Gift/Bookshop** No

The third piece of the Modernist triumvirate at Seattle's Olympic Tract, NBBJ's Plymouth Congregational Church, replaced the parish's ornate neoclassical structure, whose salvaged fluted columns now stand, rather oddly, at Plymouth Pillars Park, a small island of land adjacent to one of the city's freeways. This white, quirkily adorned complex, with its concave and flat walls, wraps a site raised above the adjacent IBM Plaza. It consists of blocky, rounded volumes inlaid with small, dove-inspired glass blocks. Its centerpiece is the pill-shaped sanctuary, a tall but intimate space infused with glowing light, piercing those bird-like blocks. A smaller chapel to the south contains similar elements, but in a much more compressed, circular area. Other zones are less profound, but provide great views to the downtown core. It's a miracle the church has remained on this spot in the dense core of such a booming city. While here, make sure to walk across the street to Lawrence Halprin's Freeway Park, the first public space built over a highway in the world. The 5.5 acre (two hectare) green, which bridges Interstate 5, consists of irregular, linked plazas and is famed for its stacked, exposed concrete 'canyons' and 'waterfalls', which are best to explore during the day, as the park can attract unsavory characters at night. ◆

One of a trio of remarkable Modernist buildings on the Olympic Tract, a downtown plot that used to contain the University of Washington, Minoru Yamasaki's twenty-story IBM Building possesses many of the same characteristics as his Rainier Tower, across the street and of the architect's fallen Twin Towers in New York City. Particularly similar are the long stripes extending up the length of the building, formed by exterior precast pipe columns over a glass and steel base. The World Trade Center's version had a lighter metallic skin, to avoid imposing too much load on the 110-story structure. The building – a collaboration between Yamasaki and NBBJ – floats on a glass base supported by classically rounded concrete arches. Its small, semi-circular lobby is a time capsule: with a mirrored ceiling, terrazzo cladding, Modernist sculpture and a small spiral stair. Another notable element is its multi-level concrete plaza, containing a five-thousand-pound (2,270 kilogram) bronze fountain by Seattle artist James Fitzgerald and charming umbrella frame lampposts. Yamasaki, the son of Japanese immigrants, was born in Seattle and completed his undergraduate studies in architecture at the University of Washington. While he went on to establish his office in Michigan, he left a strong mark on Seattle with this building, the Pacific Science Center (page 34), and the Rainier Tower (page 35). ◆

Pacific Northwest **Architect** Minoru Yamasaki **Year** 1963
Address 1200 Fifth Avenue, Seattle, WA 98101

Open to Public No **Free Entrance** No **Café/Restaurant** No
Overnight Accommodation No **Gift/Bookshop** No

IBM Building

Safeco Plaza

10

Pacific Northwest **Architect** Naramore, Bain, Brady and Johanson (NBBJ)
Year 1969 **Address** 1001 4th Avenue, Seattle, WA 98154

Open to Public No **Free Entrance** No **Café/Restaurant** No
Overnight Accommodation No **Gift/Bookshop** No

Built by NBBJ, a firm often called the Skidmore, Owings & Merrill of the Northwest, Safeco Plaza is sometimes called the Seagram Building of Seattle. Despite these unfair comparisons, the tower, originally known as the Seattle First National Bank Building, is a remarkable achievement, rendered an afterthought for most tourists in favor of Rem Koolhaas' sexy Seattle Public Library, right across the street. Similar to Seagram, the fifty-story Safeco Plaza is clad in a brown glass and anodized aluminum curtain wall. But unlike that New York landmark, these curtain walls – divided into three sections by mechanical vents – are also Vierendeel trusses, transferring loads to the corners of the building, so interiors can be further opened. The most open space of all is the tall, glassy lobby, above which the rest of the edifice floats. Its only structural elements are the elevator core and four thin corner columns. A peaceful corner courtyard and underground shopping complex flow through the gained space and a stepped plaza containing modern sculpture fronts the building. NBBJ is still quite active filling out Seattle's skyline. Among other ventures, the firm recently completed the Bill and Melinda Gates Foundation in Lower Queen Anne and it's now working on the expansive new downtown headquarters for Amazon, including three large domes that resemble glass soccer balls. ◆

Seattle-based Harmon, Pray & Detrich was one of the few architecture firms known for creating adventurous buildings for large corporations and governments. Probably its most famous work is the nine-story King County Administration Building, on the southern edge of downtown. The cube-shaped structure is hard to miss, with its three-dimensional, gold and tan diamond and honeycomb metal walls and hexagonal windows. Like many high profile Modernist buildings, the structure is widely hated. Former Seattle Deputy Mayor Tim Ceis said, 'I think everybody acknowledges it may be the ugliest building in Downtown Seattle.' But that difficult beauty is one of the things that makes this metal-panel-walled building so wonderful. Go ahead and love it, even if the masses turn their backs. You enter through a truncated triangular entryway, topped with a small metal canopy and fronted by a wormlike stainless-steel sculpture. Located on a fairly steep slope, the building's downhill sides abut large raised plazas, exposed as the building is lifted on triangular legs. If you can't get enough, check out the firm's City Light Power Control Center (157 Roy Street), an octagonal precast concrete building that is entirely without windows. ◆

Pacific Northwest **Architect** Harmon, Pray & Detrich **Year** 1971
Address 500 4th Avenue, Seattle, WA 98104

Open to Public No **Free Entrance** No **Café/Restaurant** No
Overnight Accommodation No **Gift/Bookshop** No

King County Administration Building

Chopp House

12

Pacific Northwest **Architect** Frank Chopp Jr. and Frank Chopp Sr. **Year** 1970s
Address 2402 E Yesler Way, Seattle, WA 98122

Open to Public No **Free Entrance** No **Café/Restaurant** No
Overnight Accommodation No **Gift/Bookshop** No

Interesting structures come from interesting people, like Frank Chopp, Jr., Speaker of the House of the Washington House of Representatives. In the 1970s he partnered with his dad, Frank Chopp Sr., to hand-build two highly unusual structures on a grassy lot on the corner of East Yesler Way, in Seattle's Garfield neighborhood, east of downtown. Now nicknamed the 'urban cabins', they're hybrid structures: a studio property combining a wood-paneled A-frame with a severely angled barn and a wooden shed pierced by an A-shaped opening, filled with glass blocks. Inside they feel like cozy, rustic cabins, with exposed, reclaimed wooden rafters and horizontal cedar panels. The buildings are now used as rentals, but considering the value of the property, don't be surprised if they disappear. Chopp has said he might someday use the land for a community center or low-income housing. For now they're a strange surprise in the middle of a leafy, otherwise traditional neighborhood. If you enjoy strangely angled, glassy rustic buildings like this, you should consider taking the ferry to Bainbridge Island to see Paul Hayden Kirk's Bloedel Guest House at the Bloedel Reserve (7571 NE Dolphin Drive, Bainbridge Island). With its soaring A-frame windows and wing-like roofline, the cedar building combines Japanese and Northwest styles in a unique way. ◆

Hilltop Community

13

After crossing the Homer M. Hadley and East Channel Bridges from Seattle and winding into the slopes southeast of downtown Bellevue, you enter Hilltop, a legendary Modernist community that blends as well with its natural environment as any on the West Coast. Consisting of forty houses on sixty acres (twenty-four hectares), the neighborhood was cooperatively planned by a progressive group of artists, architects, builders, engineers and professors between 1947 and 1950. Its homes, showcasing exposed structure; exotic woods; low-pitched, flat, or shed roofs; and expansive use of glass, are sited away from the street and surrounded by luxuriant natural landscaping; the houses disappear among the (many) trees. Curved streets follow the natural topography and undulating lots are carefully arranged to preserve privacy and enhance views to the lakes below. A natural greenbelt was retained along the perimeter, providing, along with a central green, about 17 acres (9 hectares) of parkland. Houses were custom-designed by some of Seattle's top architects, including Perry B Johanson, Fred Bassetti, Paul Hayden Kirk (pictured) and Lee McRae. While there are many lovely homes to explore, a stop here wouldn't be complete without examining Kirk's house at Hilltop, a sharply angled (and oddly space-aged) wood and steel pavilion that opens completely to Lake Sammamish on one side and the neighborhood on the other. ◆

Pacific Northwest **Architect** Paul Hayden Kirk among others **Year** 1946
Address 5264 148th Avenue SE, Hilltop, Bellevue, WA 98006

Open to Public No **Free Entrance** No **Café/Restaurant** No
Overnight Accommodation No **Gift/Bookshop** No

St. Charles Borromeo Catholic Church

14

Pacific Northwest **Architect** Nelson, Krona & Ziegler **Year** 1969
Address 7112 S 12th Street, Tacoma, WA 98465

Open to Public No **Free Entrance** No **Café/Restaurant** No
Overnight Accommodation No **Gift/Bookshop** No

Sometimes architectural tourism takes you to places you would never visit, by architects you have never heard of. That's the fun of it. Certainly St. Charles Borromeo Catholic Church in the faceless outskirts of working-class Tacoma is a case in point. Set back from a large surface parking lot, the church was one of many built in the area after World War II to accommodate the area's large, quickly forming new housing tracts. Floating behind an ugly stucco pedestal is a brick building, topped by a white zigzag roof and an oversized yellow glass truncated cone, which resembles a sort of holy thimble. Is it pretty? No. Is it fascinating? Yes. Inside, the spacious sanctuary is flooded with amber light from the cone, sited above the altar. The roofline fans out from here, its timber beams allowing for a column-free space below. Other interior materials include birch and cedar paneling, Italian marble and mosaics and large glass windows and doors. The area is a great place to explore unusual Modernist sacred spaces, including Temple Beth El (5975 S 12th Street), with its pilgrim hat roof and Christ Episcopal Church (310 N K Street) an unapologetically Brutalist landmark by local legend Paul Thiry. ◆

Anyone familiar with the zany, amazing constructions of Bertrand Goldberg (he designed, for instance, the cylindrical Marina City Towers in Chicago, with their endless clamshell balconies) would be excited to know he built a typically adventurous hospital in the Pacific Northwest. The St. Joseph's Hospital, a hilltop structure overlooking Commencement Bay in Tacoma, looks like a mash-up of rocket ships, grain silos and cake icing tubes, dotted with amazing oval-shaped windows – similar to boat portholes – that frame unique views from the rooms inside. The building's curved shell reinforced-concrete walls, smoothed with a white fiberglass finish, help create the building's organic form, which wraps like fabric around nine towers, all propped on thin columns, floating above a two-story base building. Each floor of the nine-story building is organized into four quadrants, or 'villages', each containing ten beds and its own nurse's station. But while the exterior is breathtaking, the interior, like that of many hospitals, is not remarkable. The self-supporting thin shell construction allows the building to have no interior columns, to manage its seismic load and, perhaps most importantly, look like a science-fiction treatment center from the twenty-second century. ◆

Pacific Northwest **Architect** Bertrand Goldberg **Year** 1975
Address 1736 S I Street, Tacoma, WA 98405

Open to Public No **Free Entrance** No **Café/Restaurant** No
Overnight Accommodation No **Gift/Bookshop** No

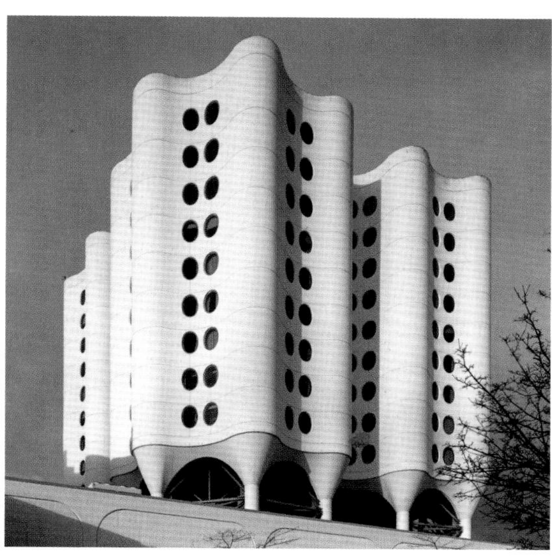

Veterans Memorial Coliseum

16

Pacific Northwest **Architect** Skidmore, Owings & Merrill **Year** 1960
Address 300 N Winning Way, Portland, OR 97227

Open to Public Yes **Free Entrance** No **Café/Restaurant** No
Overnight Accommodation No **Gift/Bookshop** No

Some projects are an acquired taste, necessitating some investigation before you like them. Such is Portland's Veterans Memorial Coliseum, located on the eastern edge of the Willamette River, overlooking the Pearl District and much of downtown. The square, Miesian building, 360 feet (110 metres) long on a side, is clad with grids of gray tinted glass, supported by thin concrete columns and steel trusses. Inside that shell Skidmore, Owings & Merrill placed a curving, terraced seating bowl made of free-standing concrete. The juxtaposition of the rectangular exterior and the fluid interior is what distinguishes this building, which is unlike any stadium you've likely ever visited. Other unusual elements include the sunken courtyards along the corners, which enhance the floating quality of the building, the massive blackout curtain to cover the windows when necessary and the curving thin shell concrete canopy in front. The composition can be off-putting at first, especially during the day, when light doesn't emanate from within and the mass seems monolithic. But walk into the concourses to take in the stepped undersides of the bleachers, the mid-century signage and, most significantly, the panoramic views of the river and the city beyond. It's this peerless (and potentially lucrative) location that continually puts the building at risk and is perhaps why the city seems to have dedicated few resources to its upkeep. ◆

17 Union Bank of California Tower

There's something about an elegant Modernist tower. Maybe it's all that marble or the serene austerity. But they exude the confidence and panache that was the hallmark of the *Mad Men* era corporate world, back when 'corporate' wasn't a catch phrase for banality. Portland's classiest variant on this theme is Anshen & Allen's Union Bank of California, a fifteen-story International Style tower in the heart of downtown. The proud structure, faced in long vertical bands of glass, steel and tapered concrete, floats over a rectangular pedestal (with even more deeply tapered columns that take on the appearance of fins) and contains two exposed service cores, clad in light-gray Elterwater slate with a greenish tint. These mosaic-like cores are a late-Modern variation on those found in San Francisco's Crown Zellerbach building (page 86). Inside, the double-height lobby boasts an exposed waffle slab ceiling, green marble floors and gridded wood-panel walls. Another of Anshen and Allen's notable corporate towers outside of Portland is San Francisco's International Building (601 California Street), featuring boldly cantilevered floor plates that produced more corner offices than had ever been possible. The Mad Men would be pleased. ◆

Pacific Northwest **Architect** Anshen & Allen **Year** 1972
Address 707 SW Washington, Portland, OR 97205

Open to Public No **Free Entrance** No **Café/Restaurant** No
Overnight Accommodation No **Gift/Bookshop** No

Wells Fargo Center

The tallest and perhaps least-liked building in Portland is Charles Luckman's Wells Fargo Center, a forty-story office tower on the southern side of downtown, right around the corner from Michael Graves' infamous postmodern Portlandia Building. Originally named First National Bank Tower, the edifice consists of a grid of bronze-tinted glass and anodized aluminum mullions and spandrels, overlaid with blade-like stripes of white Italian marble – the building contains a whopping sixty-thousand square feet (5,570 square meters) of marble – giving it the profile of a menacing rocket ship when you look up its face. A related five-story building, connected via a raised bridge, floats on wide, fin-like columns, creating gathering spaces underneath it and resembling, perhaps, the rocket ship's Brutalist launching pad. Like many hated Modernist icons, this one has a lot to like if you keep an open mind, not least its formal audacity and flared, bell-bottom-ish base. In its lobby the center contains a Wells Fargo History Museum, containing authentic Wells Fargo stage-coaches and memorabilia. Just down the street you might want to explore the Unitas Center, another floating pavilion, this one blond in color and Brutalist in style, with rows of punched, rounded rectangle windows. ◆

Pacific Northwest **Architect** Charles Luckman **Year** 1972
Address 1300 SW 5th Avenue, Portland, OR 97201

Open to Public Yes **Free Entrance** Yes **Café/Restaurant** Yes
Overnight Accommodation No **Gift/Bookshop** No

23 St. John the Baptist Catholic Church

Pacific Northwest **Architect** Stearns, Mention & Morris **Year** 1966
Address 10955 SE 25th Avenue, Milwaukie, OR 97222

Open to Public Yes **Free Entrance** Yes **Café/Restaurant** No
Overnight Accommodation No **Gift/Bookshop** No

I bet you didn't know there was a city called Milwaukie (named in honor of Milwaukee, Wisconsin) just outside of Portland. I also bet you didn't know it contains one of the most otherworldly buildings on the West Coast: St. John the Baptist Catholic Church. The flat, red stone building, connected to offices and a school by thin covered walkways, is topped by a steeply curving, pointed roof, resembling an edifice from *The Lord of the Rings* or a white chocolate Hershey's Kiss with its tag standing straight up. The textured lower walls represent man's roughness, while the smooth white roof symbolizes the purity and mountainous immensity of God. The tower was set in place via crane, while the pointed lightning rod at its tip was lowered in via helicopter. Glass doors and clerestory windows along the lower edges of the roof allow light into the cavernous sanctuary, whose banks of pews radiate from a central altar. The building was designed by Oregon-based architecture firm Stearns, Mention & Morris, whose body of work has been all but lost to time. But this place remains a wonderful diamond in the rough, an example of the Modern treasures waiting to be found off the beaten path. ◆

Agnes Flanagan Chapel, Lewis and Clark college

24

Pacific Northwest **Architect** Paul Thiry **Year** 1968
Address 0615 SW Palatine Road, Portland, OR 97219

Open to Public Yes **Free Entrance** Yes **Café/Restaurant** No
Overnight Accommodation No **Gift/Bookshop** No

Paul Thiry, widely credited as the first Seattle architect to manifest the influence of European Modernism, was best known for his ethereal houses and churches that combined the style with his unique brand of regionalism based resolutely in history, culture and landscape. His Agnes Flanagan Chapel at Lewis and Clark college – a wooded campus in the hills south of Portland – exemplifies the uniqueness of Thiry's vernacular. The building looks like nothing else you'll see this side of a hobbit's village, its shingle-clad, upside-down funnel roof inspired, reportedly, by a Tlingit ceremonial rain hat. (The Tlingit are an indigenous people of the Pacific Northwest). Students call it the 'Hershey's Kiss'. Its bridged entrance is flanked by bulky, sculpted figures of the four evangelists, designed by Chief Lelooska of the Cherokee tribe. The 460-seat interior, lined with horizontal timber slats and supported by arching laminated beams, features a circular five-thousand-pipe Casavant organ, hanging from the ceiling like the display in the center of a sports arena. A circular band of stained-glass clerestory windows, designed by Gabriel Loire of Chartres, France, depicts the creation story in the book of Genesis. Enter here and your eyes shoot up to the heavens. You've escaped this world and entered a place of calm and retreat. A small addition, a pyramidal structure known as the Diane Gregg Memorial Pavilion, was added in 2011. ◆

24

Agnes Flanagan Chapel, Lewis and Clark college

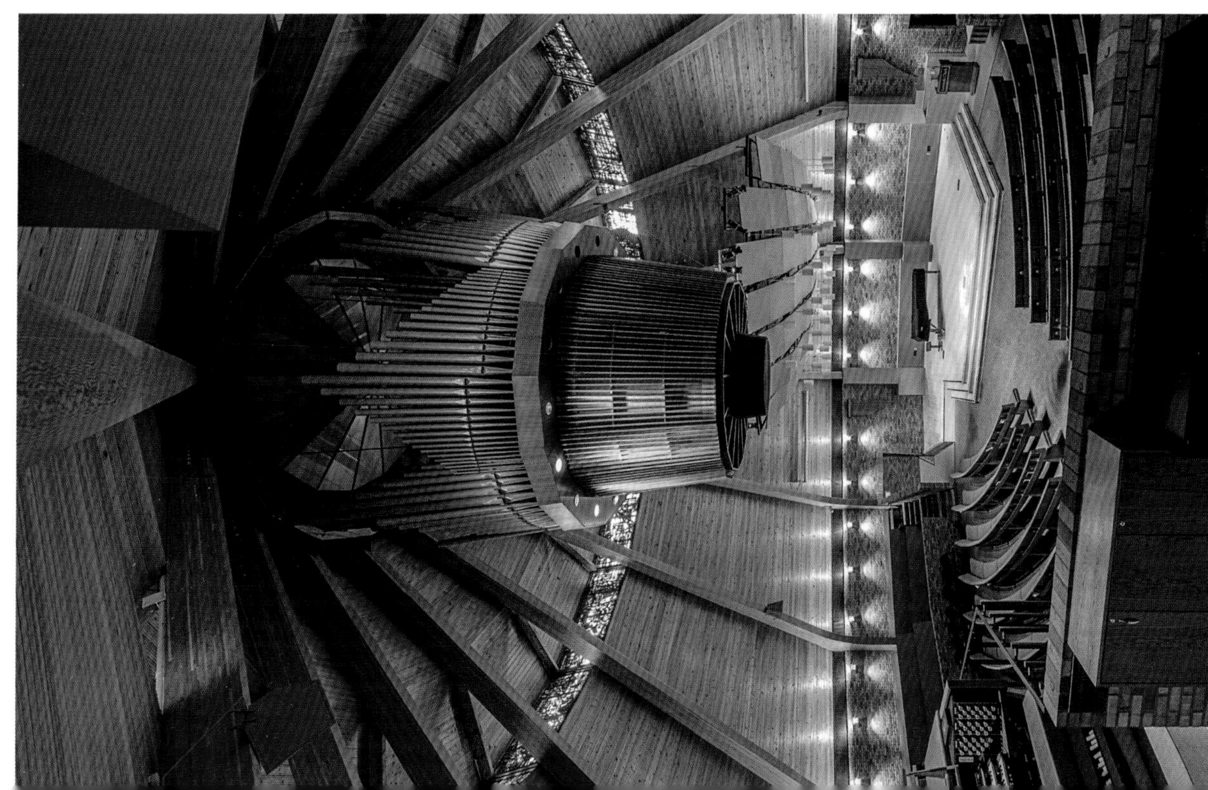

Oregon City Municipal Elevator

25

Pacific Northwest **Architect** Stevens and Thompson **Year** 1955
Address 6 Railroad Avenue, Oregon City, OR 97045

Open to Public Yes **Free Entrance** Yes **Café/Restaurant** No
Overnight Accommodation No **Gift/Bookshop** No

It's not easy to navigate a city divided in half by railroad tracks and a tall cliff. Officials in Oregon City, about thirteen miles (48 kilometers) south of Portland, understood that and by 1915 had installed a steel and wood elevator connecting the city's lower portions to the bluffs above. By the 1950s break-downs had become so common that the city voted to install a modern version. Designed by Stevens and Thompson, the 130-foot-tall (40-meter) structure, accessible via a thirty-five-foot-long (ten-meter) tunnel under the tracks, took 751 tons (681 tonnes) of concrete and steel to construct. It's difficult to believe the structure, which is the only municipal elevator in the United States and one of only four in the world, is real. It looks like a UFO that has landed on a massive column, sliding about a fifth of the way down. Its shaft is clad in light-colored concrete panels, while the cantilevered, window-lined, gray concrete observatory above is shaped like a boat; or a duck bill; or a horseshoe; or the brim of a baseball cap. It takes about fifteen seconds to make your way up to the top of the basalt cliffs, from where you get a clear view of the industrial town and the Willamette River. Walk on the public pathway over the bluffs, enjoying not just the views, but also the eclectic houses lining its length. ◆

Frank Lloyd Wright's sole house in Oregon, the Gordon House, is a rare two-story Usonian (Wright's low-priced family dwellings), picked up and moved from its original location on a farm on the banks of the Willamette River to Silverton's picturesque Oregon Garden in 2001. Wright designed the 2,100-square-foot (195-square-meter) house (completed after his death) for Conrad and Evelyn Gordon so they could commune with their natural surroundings and it does this expertly through an open floor plan, floor-to-ceiling glass doors opening onto terraces and strong horizontal lines that draw your eye outward. The flat wooden roof, changing heights at various points, wraps around the entire home and extends over the external walls to protect all this openness. The house is clad inside and out with board-and-batten patterned western red cedar and raked masonry, a surface that makes this building rare for Wright, who generally preferred brick or concrete block. The abstract patterns carved into wood overlaying the home's horizontal glazing seem to resemble flowers and other natural forms. These patterns, as well as perforations in the roof canopy, create poetic shadows that move as the sun changes, which happens often in this region. Just up the road, be sure to visit Pietro Belluschi's Immanuel Lutheran Church (303 N Church Street), another example of expertly modulated Pacific Northwest light. ◆

Pacific Northwest **Architect** Frank Lloyd Wright **Year** 1964
Address 869 W Main Street, Silverton, OR 97381

Open to Public Yes **Free Entrance** No **Café/Restaurant** No
Overnight Accommodation No **Gift/Bookshop** Yes

Mount Angel Library

27

Pacific Northwest **Architect** Alvar Aalto **Year** 1970
Address 1 Abbey Drive, Saint Benedict, OR 97373

Open to Public Yes **Free Entrance** Yes **Café/Restaurant** Yes
Overnight Accommodation No **Gift/Bookshop** Yes

Few side trips are as exhilarating as a drive from Portland to Alvar Aalto's Mount Angel Library in Saint Benedict. First there's the location, a Benedictine monastery resting on a wooded butte that looks like it's been transplanted from an Italian hill town. Then there's the library itself, created by Finland's master architect, Alvar Aalto. From the outside its flat brick form, lightened with protruding, redwood grilled windows, betrays no hint of the glory inside. But once you enter you experience a space suffused with wondrous light and an exceptional progression of spaces. Aalto, handpicked by abbey friar Barnabas Reasoner, initially refused. So Barnabas traveled to Europe to convince him. Aalto's semi-circular building, wrapped in strips of glass, changes remarkably as you move through, its center stepping down to reveal fan-shaped book stacks below and an angled band of curved skylights providing soft, even light above. The carved, stepped, floating curves look like hovering spaceships from below. Continuous reading desks ringing the mezzanine are fitted with lines of white, Aalto-designed lamps. It's wonderful to sit on an Aalto stacking stool or chair and watch natural light fill the space and change its character completely. You have a primal reaction to the simultaneous sensations of enclosure, expansion and wonderment. ◆

Mount Angel Library

San Francisco

28 Sea Ranch **29** Marin County Civic Center **30** Pence House **31** Currey Lane Colony **32** Taves House **33** Hahn House **34** Olsen House **35** Greenwood Common **36** Weston Havens House **37** Cagliostro House **38** Brubeck House **39** Oakland Museum of California **40** Mills College Chapel **41** San Lorenzo Community Church **42** Schiff Duplex **43** Russell House **44** Larsen House **45** Kahn House **46** Alcoa Building **47** Crown Zellerbach Building **48** V.C. Morris Shop **49** Embarcadero Center & Hyatt Regency **50** Darling House **51** 2 Clarendon Avenue Residence **52** St. Mary's Catheral **53** San Francisco State University Student Union **54** Vista Mar Elementary School **55** Ascension Chapel, Holy Cross Catholic Cemetery **56** College of San Mateo Library **57** Life House, The Highlands **58** Midglen Way House **59** Nail House **60** Sunset magazine Headquarters **61** First United Methodist Church of Palo Alto **62** Hanna House **63** Foothill College **64** Sunnyvale Bank of the West **65** Tan's Touchless Carwash **66** Center for the Performing Arts **67** University of California Santa Cruz Theater Arts Center **68** Community Hospital of the Monterey Peninsula **69** The Shell **70** Walker House **71** Hass House **72** Johnson Riebe House **73** Nepenthe Restaurant **74** Wild Bird **75** Kundert Medical Clinic

Sacramento
Santa Rosa
Buildings 29–66
Stockton
San Francisco
Modesto
See page 70
Henry W Coe State Park
67 Santa Cruz
Pacific Ocean
Monterey
69
68
70
72
71
Los Padres National Forest
73
74
Paso Robles
San Luis Obispo
75

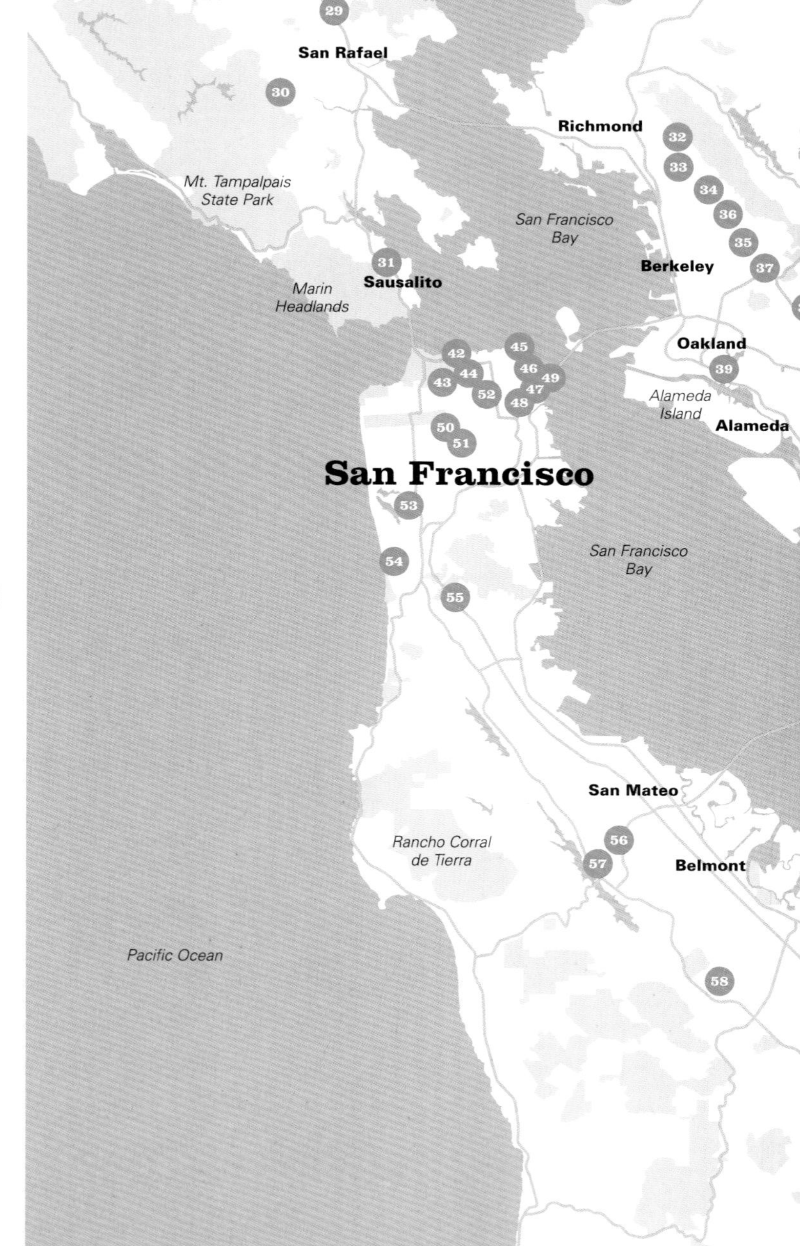
29
San Rafael
30
Richmond
32
33
34
36
35
37
Mt. Tampalpais
State Park
San Francisco
Bay
31
Sausalito
Berkeley
Marin
Headlands
45
42
44
46
49
43
47
52
48
Oakland
39
Alameda
Island
Alameda
50
51
San Francisco
53
54
San Francisco
Bay
55
San Mateo
56
Rancho Corral
de Tierra
57
Belmont
Pacific Ocean
58

Concord
Briones Regional Park
Walnut Creek
Diablo State Park
Anthony Chabot Regional Park
San Leandro
41
Hayward
Livermore
Fremont
Sunol Regional Wilderness
Ohlone Regional Wilderness
60
61
Palo Alto
62
64
63
65
San Jose
66
Joseph D. Grant County Park

Sea Ranch

28

San Francisco **Architect** Moore, Lyndon, Turnbull & Whitaker (MLTW)
Year 1965 **Address** 110–128 Sea Walk Drive, Sea Ranch, CA 95497

Open to Public Yes **Free Entrance** Yes **Café/Restaurant** No
Overnight Accommodation Yes **Gift/Bookshop** No

Of all the architectural pilgrimage spots in this book, none is as spiritually significant as Sea Ranch, a community of Bay Modernist homes perched on a ten mile (sixteen kilometer) stretch of rugged cliffs, about three hours north of San Francisco. Straddling both sides of the Pacific Coast Highway, it extends about a mile (1.6 kilometers) inland, creating a linear form consisting of clusters of houses marked by cypress and pine hedgerows that form enclaves of grassy meadows. The tiny town was founded by developer Oceanic California, whose planning director, Al Boeke, assembled a group of architects, landscape architects and planners to create a place where all buildings recognize and reinforce the natural topography, placed 'within it, not upon it.' Lawrence Halprin led the landscape development, while prototype buildings – angular, modern structures clad in vertical wood siding, – were created by Moore, Lyndon, Turnbull & Whitaker, Joseph Esherick and others. The most famous is the ten-unit Condominium One, Charles Moore's first major work. The shed-style building, with its mono-pitched roof, comprises intimate spaces containing 'saddlebags', small projections that provide views and contemplative space. There are so many places to explore at Sea Ranch and you can rent a number of units. Most share the original spirit of rustic simplicity, but newer homes to the north feel more suburban, less special. ●

Sea Ranch

San Francisco **Architect** Frank Lloyd Wright **Year** 1962
Address 3501 Civic Center Drive, San Rafael, CA 94903

Open to Public Yes **Free Entrance** Yes **Café/Restaurant** No
Overnight Accommodation No **Gift/Bookshop** No

One of the most dramatic sights you'll see from your car is Frank Lloyd Wright's Marin County Civic Center rising from beyond the 101 Freeway in San Rafael. The massive complex, Wright's last work, consists of a string of long, horizontal buildings, topped with curved blue roofs, bridging the tops of three hills. The slender structures are connected by circular domes – one fitted with a jagged spire – evocative of both Middle Eastern design and *Star Wars*. Wright died in 1959, before the center's completion and it's a prime example of his late turn toward a more futuristic style. The edifice consists of an Administration Building and Hall of Justice. You're immediately drawn to the glowing ceilings, the gold spheres outlining the rooflines, and the impossibly long, plant-filled corridors. Low, curved railings evoke those of Wright's Guggenheim Museum in New York and bands of windows, articulated by arches of varied sizes, permit views to the landscapes around you. To get the best sense of the site, look over the balcony of the patio outside the cafeteria. It's all a bit much, but Wright has transported you to a different world. Also visit the adjacent Marin Veterans' Memorial Theater, another domed, futuristic vision designed by Wright's successor firm, Taliesen Associated Architects. ●

Pence House

30

San Francisco **Architect** Marquis & Stoller **Year** 1965
Address 4 Walden Lane, Mill Valley, CA 94941

Open to Public No **Free Entrance** No **Café/Restaurant** No
Overnight Accommodation No **Gift/Bookshop** No

Located on an idyllic sliver of land overlooking an alpine valley that resembles the Sierras more than Marin County, the Pence House is truly one of a kind. Accessing the structure, which pops up behind a tall wood fence, takes patience; you journey on several switchback roads through the high hills above Mill Valley until you reach the residence, an irregular line of three interconnected, hip-roofed, Asian-inspired pavilions. The furthest contains a glazed living space lit by a pyramid-shaped skylight and all pavilions take in the surrounding landscape through sliders and large windows. The deep-eaved, red shingle-roofed pieces are organized around a lovely stone-floored courtyard and pool and the elegantly landscaped spaces in between resemble Asian gardens. Robert Marquis and Claude Stoller were in partnership from 1956 to 1973, not just creating memorable residences, but also expanding into educational and larger-scale housing work. Look around the neighborhood and you'll see, among other things, what was once a cantilevered, exposed concrete home by one of Frank Lloyd Wright's apprentices, which, sadly, has been compromised by several orange stucco insertions. ●

When Bay Area developer Bob Rose subdivided Toyon Terrace, a new neighborhood above Sausalito, in the 1950s, he had a smart requirement: all houses must be designed by an architect. Its streets are excellent examples of Mid-Century Modern design, showing off post-and-beam construction, transparency and a seamless connection with the stunning natural environment. Of these fine homes, Warren Callister's 250 Currey Lane is exceptional, elegantly combining wood cladding and Asian influences with modern engineering and bold layouts. The wide, angled-roofed building unfolds aggressively but gracefully toward the exceptional views of the water and the neighborhood, through cantilevered floors and large sheets of glass (mitred at their corners to avoid physical interruption). Open plans, informally divided when necessary and revolving around diamond-shaped cores, maintain your focus on the outside, as do long, relatively low ceilings. Currey Lane Colony is full of other standouts, like 139 (by John Funk), 244 (Roger Lee), 260 (John Hoops) and 290 (Henrik Bull). While in the area, visit nearby Belvedere Tiberon to explore Callister's Church of Christ Scientist (501 San Rafael Avenue). With its angular floating roof and thin, blade-shaped spire, it evokes the prows and masts of boats in the nearby harbor. Its intimate, wooded interior contains a central concrete fireplace and is covered with slitted stained glass, drawing in dappled, colored light. ●

San Francisco **Architect** Warren Callister, John Funk, Roger Lee among others
Year 1951 **Address** 260 Currey Lane, Sausalito, CA 94965

Open to Public No **Free Entrance** No **Café/Restaurant** No
Overnight Accommodation No **Gift/Bookshop** No

Currey Lane Colony

Donald Olsen's love for Bauhaus purity and simplicity – a rare departure from the area's omnipresent Bay Region style – was taken to its logical conclusion with the Taves House, a two-story hilltop residence that he built, appropriately, for a sheet metal worker and his wife in El Cerrito. A town, it should be noted, that is a virtually unknown Modernist stronghold. The home checks every box of the European Modernist movement, which Olsen studied at Harvard under the German emigré architect and founder of the Bauhaus, Walter Gropius. And in the spirit of the Bauhaus, this is 'building as machine.' There are only right angles. There are only industrial materials. All materials and structural members are exposed, including the floating stair and the frames of the all-glass facade, which is protected from the elements only by the entrance canopy and a lot of curtains. A typical Olsen touch. Yet despite all this cool rationalism, the house doesn't feel cold or off-putting. Like most of Olsen's work it feels approachable, low-key and comfortable in its natural surroundings. He employed Modernism as a quiet receptor of its surroundings, not a dogmatic statement shouting over them. ●

San Francisco **Architect** Donald Olsen **Year** 1957
Address 1366 Brewster Drive, El Cerrito, CA 94530

Open to Public No **Free Entrance** No **Café/Restaurant** No
Overnight Accommodation No **Gift/Bookshop** No

San Francisco **Architect** Beverley David Thorne **Year** 1963
Address 779 Balra Drive, El Cerrito, CA 94530

Open to Public No **Free Entrance** No **Café/Restaurant** No
Overnight Accommodation Yes **Gift/Bookshop** No

33

Hahn House

This residence in the hills of El Cerrito, a working-class city north of Berkeley, is a good example of Beverley David Thorne's astonishing ingenuity. The hilly site, overlooking the San Francisco Bay and the Golden Gate Bridge, is split by a stream, with neither side containing enough flat land to build. So Thorne created a steel-framed house that doubled as a bridge, spanning the water. It's imbedded into a curving landscape of thick trees and heavy ivy, accessible via a wooden footbridge. The standing seam metal roof's deep eaves protect an exterior that is essentially all glass. The current owners have installed unfortunate screens, presumably for privacy and sun protection (despite Thorne's intention that the natural setting would take care of that), but it doesn't stop you from seeing straight through the home in places, all the way to the water. Walk around to the waterfront side to observe how the building also cantilevers over a small carport, from where the owners climb a spiral stair (which even contains its own tree, popping above the roofline) to the main level. ●

Olsen House

34

At the top of a small, peaceful hill among the winding roads of Berkeley is a masterpiece: Donald Olsen's own home, the Olsen House. Olsen, who studied with Walter Gropius at Harvard, was a rare pure Modernist in the Bay Area and this floating glass box in the woods was the culmination of his work. The home appears to levitate on thin steel columns above a carport, providing uninterrupted views of the Bay and the Golden Gate Bridge below. Its white spandrels emerge from far into the hillside, representing the only opacity – except for off-white curtains that provide privacy and solar protection – of a continuous glass volume. A solid structure underneath, containing staggered rectangular windows that reveal a white steel stair, is painted black, rendering it almost invisible. Across the street you can visit a spectacular park that winds through a ravine filled with trails, wooden bridges and gnarled, moss-covered trees. To the left of the home is an ivy-covered creek flowing downhill and to the right is Olsen's equally stunning Kip House (775 San Diego Road). Modernism works exceptionally well when fused with nature. ●

San Francisco **Architect** Donald Olsen **Year** 1954
Address 771 San Diego Road, Berkeley, CA 94707

Open to Public No **Free Entrance** No **Café/Restaurant** No
Overnight Accommodation No **Gift/Bookshop** No

San Francisco **Architect** Rudolph Schindler among others **Year** 1955
Address Greenwood Common, Berkeley, CA 94708

Open to Public No **Free Entrance** No **Café/Restaurant** No
Overnight Accommodation No **Gift/Bookshop** No

Greenwood Common

A few Modernist communities perfectly embody the movement's tenets of frugality, simplicity and harmony with nature. The best example in the Bay Area is Greenwood Common, a superb collection of eight rustic modern homes in the Berkeley Hills designed by legends like Joseph Esherick, Harwell Hamilton Harris, Rudolph Schindler, Donald Olsen, Henry Hill, and John Funk. Planned by architect William Wurster, then dean of Berkeley's College of Environmental Design, the development is focused around Lawrence Halprin's rugged landscapes; in particular, a rectangular green that serves as the site's focus. Halprin planted the area around this with flowering plum trees, Japanese maples and junipers and installed small, winding rock paths. Filled with the rough-but-sophisticated spirit of an intellectual bohemian community, the subdivision's timber-clad homes appear simple and downright countrified. But under this skin they reveal hints of bold innovation, from projecting beams and bays to copious built-ins and natural light. Olsen's house floats on thin pilotis, like his own house nearby. Schindler and Wurster's homes, closest to the astonishing bay view, seem to reach out for the city below. The key move was leaving the space between them open to provide vistas to the entire neighborhood. It's part of a communal spirit that's all but lost in today's profit-driven developments. ●

Drive on countless hairpin turns above the Berkeley campus, past enough impressive homes to whet your appetite for something amazing and you'll finally reach the Weston Havens House, architect Harwell Hamilton Harris' masterpiece. Harris designed the home for philanthropist John Weston Havens Jr., the great-nephew of Wells Fargo founder Francis Kittredge Shattuck. Havens, a noted progressive, wanted Harris to design a dwelling that, perhaps paradoxically, offered copious privacy, sheltered his extensive library and opened almost completely to the area's unbelievable views. Made famous by Man Ray's mid-century black-and-white photographs, the residence comes to colorful life on a visit. Huge, angled decks – supported (along with the roof and floors) by timber-covered inverted triangular trusses – frame views, shelter large glass walls and serve as the home's signature. Although flat, the decks seem to tilt upward like airplane wings. Inside, Harris created a seamlessly interconnected series of spaces organized around a large sunken courtyard that once contained (yes, really) a badminton court. As you visit look for the architect's amazing attention to detail. The kitchen's walls unfold to reveal a map of the world; bookshelves angle up like the decks; translucent skylights are indirectly lit via a clerestory system; slats, planters and shades increase privacy. Also enjoy the collection of Breuer, Saarinen, Aalto and other Mid-Century Modern furniture. ●

San Francisco **Architect** Harwell Hamilton Harris **Year** 1941
Address 255 Panoramic Way, Berkeley, CA 94704

Open to Public Yes **Free Entrance** No **Café/Restaurant** No
Overnight Accommodation No **Gift/Bookshop** No

San Francisco **Architect** Jack Hillmer **Year** 1977
Address 49 Vicente Road, Berkeley, CA 94705

Open to Public No **Free Entrance** No **Café/Restaurant** No
Overnight Accommodation No **Gift/Bookshop** No

Cagliostro House

37

There are so many unsung Modernist masters, you start to wonder if any of them got their due. Yet another talented architect to fall into this category is Jack Hillmer, an expert in the use of natural materials, inventive construction and the sophisticated execution of even the most minute details. Hillmer's work at the time won publication in magazines like *Life* and *Architectural Forum* and was displayed in museums like SFMoMA and MoMA New York. But over the years his small but powerful built legacy has been largely lost. One of Hillmer's complex, expressive masterpieces is the Cagliostro House in the Berkeley Hills. The redwood-clad residence was built for NASA engineer Dominic Cagliostro and it tests the limits of levitation. Exposed timber posts and cross-beams support a second story that hovers in three directions over a raised entryway and carport, its syncopated edges extending even further, as if the home were expanding by the minute. Inside, the house is soaked in its green surroundings, with long window bands and clerestories surrounding almost every inch of the open-plan, wood-clad spaces. This starts to explain why the rooflines project so far. Another divine example of Hillmer's ability to test the limits of hovering is his Hall House in Kentfield (405 Goodhill Road). Peer down the curved driveway to spy a super-long first-floor deck, soaring over the canyon like the prow of an impossibly large ship. ●

Beverley David Thorne was another astounding architect who was revered locally but somehow unknown to everybody else, despite his participation in the legendary Case Study House Program for *Arts & Architecture* magazine. His most inspired residence is the Brubeck House, designed on a steep Oakland lot for famed jazz musician Dave Brubeck and his wife, Iola. The couple wanted the view from the top of the hill, but the only buildable area was below, near the road. So Thorne ingeniously thought of cantilevering the project over the site and anchoring it to the stone of the nearby hills. The project is essentially a bridge: a long, narrow bar hovering amid the thick tree canopy on (very) exposed steel beams above a carport. Huge, thin fins shield the large windows from direct sunlight. The bedroom end, closest to the street, cantilevers more than sixteen feet (five meters) in the air, and it's the part of the house you can see the clearest. It's one of those pieces of architecture that you can't believe you're looking at. Come at different times of day to see how the shadows and light change constantly, peeking through the forest. ●

San Francisco **Architect** Beverley David Thorne **Year** 1954
Address 6630 Heartwood Drive, Oakland, CA 94611

Open to Public No **Free Entrance** No **Café/Restaurant** No
Overnight Accommodation No **Gift/Bookshop** No

39 Oakland Museum of California

San Francisco **Architect** Kevin Roche, John Dinkeloo & Associates
Year 1969 **Address** 1000 Oak Street, Oakland, CA 94607

Open to Public Yes **Free Entrance** No **Café/Restaurant** Yes
Overnight Accommodation No **Gift/Bookshop** Yes

The Modernist fascination with merging architecture and landscape is impressively displayed at the Oakland Museum of California, located right between Lake Merritt and downtown Oakland. The museum contains a unique combination of galleries about art, history and science. The stepped, low-level concrete building's terraced gardens, designed by landscape architect Dan Kiley, serve as insulating roofs for each of its three levels. They're united by a complex series of stairs and a central plaza, becoming a sort of village green for the community. It's easy to spend more time wandering here than in the spaces inside. In 1968 the *New York Times* architecture critic Ada Louise Huxtable wrote, 'In terms of architecture and environment, Oakland may be the most thoughtfully revolutionary museum in the world.' This was Roche's first commission after the death of his mentor, Eero Saarinen and indicative of his genius for unique problem-solving. Inside, while heavy, exposed concrete surfaces at first seem off-putting, the rough planes seem to float and move. The way they open to the greenery and, in some cases, water outside enriches the experience. ●

Mills College Chapel

40

San Francisco **Architect** Warren Callister **Year** 1967
Address Mills College, 5000 MacArthur Boulevard, Oakland, CA 94613

Open to Public Yes **Free Entrance** Yes **Café/Restaurant** No
Overnight Accommodation No **Gift/Bookshop** No

Warren Callister's rare combination of daring and subtlety is on display at the Mills College Chapel, located in the heart of this small women's college on the leafy outskirts of Oakland. From the street an Asian-style entry gate forms a somewhat strange approach, but glimpses of architectural magic await just beyond. The drum-shaped exterior, with its repeating concave walls, has the scale and feel of a barn. A lower band of windows allows tempting glimpses inside. Once you walk into the circular chapel, you're surrounded on all fronts by warm-colored cedar ribbon walls, exposed timber rafters and, on the lower levels, strips of gray concrete. Your attention is quickly drawn upward, to a ring of clerestories that reflect light off the gleaming surfaces. The space feels soaring and intimate at the same time, bringing the congregation together – a welcome change from authoritarian church design – and lifting your spirit. Like his stunning built-in furniture, Callister's stepped and angled wood organ, at the back of the space, is artful and unique. Aggregate flooring connects the space to the earth, while primitive symbols evoke raw spirituality. ●

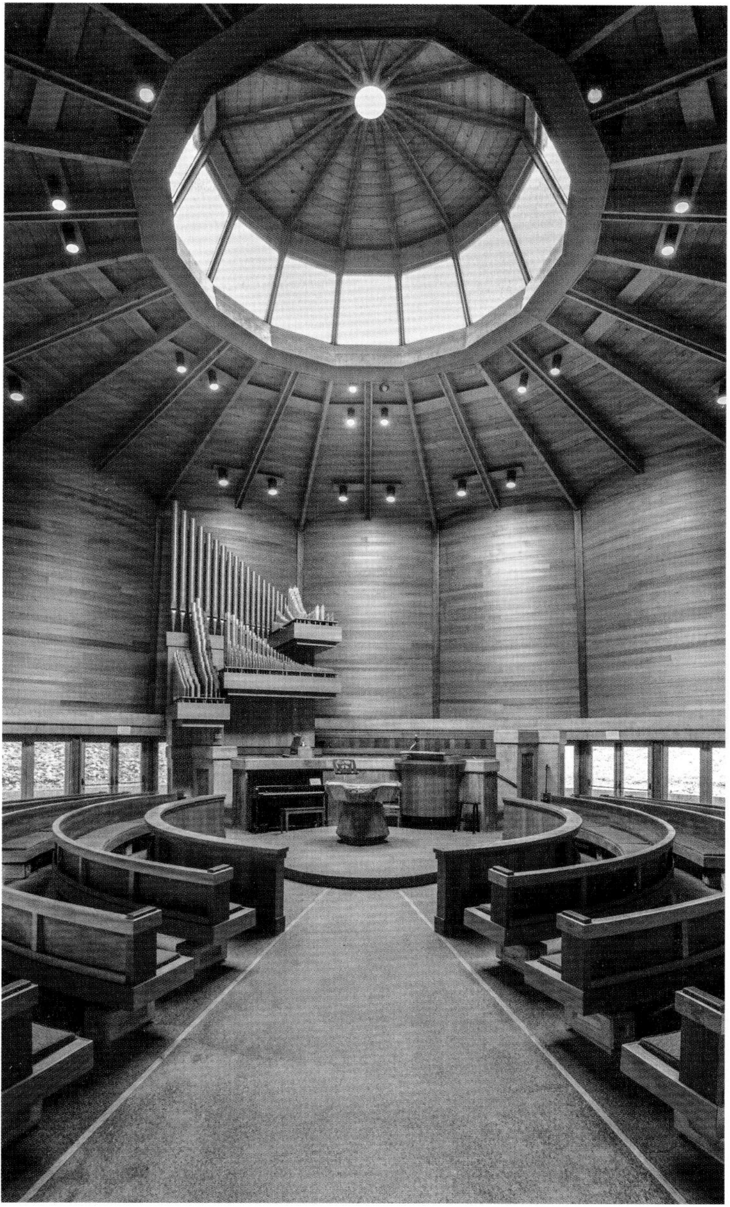

Mills College Chapel

San Lorenzo Community Church

41

If you don't know the work of Bruce Goff, you've been missing out on some of the strangest, most original architecture in the country. The Oklahoma-based architect, who developed a strong bond with Frank Lloyd Wright, designed around five-hundred buildings, but less than a quarter were built. That's how things often go for creative visionaries. Goff originally designed the San Lorenzo Community Church during World War II for the nearby military base Camp Parks, where it was known as McGann Chapel. After the war it was dismantled and moved to this 'new town', one of several low-cost developments constructed to house the exploding post-war population. The building is considered one of the most successful efforts to transform the barrel-vauted Quonset huts that had sprang up in the hundreds of thousands during World War II on military bases and were sold to the public after the war. The design consists of two huts joined to form a massive vaulted space, which Goff adorned with glass panels and acoustical tile, pierced by lightly patterned red brick and redwood walls and rooflines. The insertions, with their horizontal emphasis, layered banding and clerestory glazing, have a distinctly (Frank Lloyd) Wrightian flavor. But the rest is all Goff. And while the structure is now a little long in the tooth, it's still enveloped in colorful landscaping and definitely worth the forty-minute drive from San Francisco. ●

San Francisco **Architect** Bruce Goff **Year** 1946
Address 945 Paseo Grande, San Lorenzo, CA 94580

Open to Public No **Free Entrance** No **Café/Restaurant** No
Overnight Accommodation No **Gift/Bookshop** No

San Francisco **Architect** Richard Neutra **Year** 1938
Address 2056 Jefferson Street, San Francisco, CA 94123

Open to Public No **Free Entrance** No **Café/Restaurant** No
Overnight Accommodation No **Gift/Bookshop** No

42

Schiff Duplex

A stone's throw from San Francisco's spectacular Palace of Fine Arts, Richard Neutra's Schiff Duplex was the home of William and Ilise Schiff, an affluent German Jewish couple who fled Germany during the Holocaust. The three-level home is fronted with a grid of glass and heavy steel windows, with a planter box forming an overhang at the second floor. A third-floor penthouse is set back from the street, while a rooftop terrace still contains window-covered walls, giving it the feel of an outdoor room. The home exemplifies Neutra's early reliance on Bauhaus principles, and it recalls industrial European architecture as much as American residential design. While broken into cells, its large window walls would have seemed even larger in its time. Architect Chad Overway, who purchased the building in 1993, has thoroughly restored the two-story upper unit, where he and his wife now live. While in the area take the time to sit on a bench and stare at the Palace of Fine Arts, a monumental Beaux-Arts complex designed for the 1915 Panama-Pacific Exposition. ●

Russell House

43

San Francisco **Architect** Erich Mendelsohn **Year** 1951
Address 3778 Washington Street, San Francisco, CA 94118

Open to Public No **Free Entrance** No **Café/Restaurant** No
Overnight Accommodation No **Gift/Bookshop** No

It's hard to imagine how striking Erich Mendelsohn's Russell House would have looked upon its completion on a sharply sloping site in San Francisco's Pacific Heights, a wealthy neighborhood dominated by Victorian and Beaux-Arts mansions. Mendelsohn, one of the pioneers of Modernism, fled Germany in the 1930s, eventually settling in San Francisco. He's known for his sinuous Streamline Moderne buildings in Europe, such as the Einstein Tower in Potsdam, Germany (1921), but this project marks his progression into a purer form of Modernism. The L-shaped house, clad in lapped brown siding and protected by several mature trees, is made up of two interlocking wings framing a stepping, densely planted courtyard. The main wing, fronted by long ribbon windows, is raised one story on slender columns. Porthole windows along the other wing recall Mendelsohn's Streamline roots. The visual highlight is the master bedroom's cylindrical bay window, which extends from the main structure, floating on an ultra-thin column. Peeking through the trees it looks from some angles like it's floating on its own, a spaceship hanging off an already remarkable building. Russell House is one of Mendelsohn's last works and his only intact San Francisco project. ●

44

Larsen House

If someone told you that Joseph Esherick's Larsen House – just blocks from the water in Pacific Heights – were built last year, you'd probably believe him. The supremely modern three-story residence, built for Niels and Jeanette 'Tito' Larsen, exemplifies Esherick's work to articulate simple boxes on confined sites. He co-founded both the firm EHDD (Esherick Homsey Dodge & Davis), which was responsible for the Monterey Bay Aquarium and contributed to Sea Ranch (page 64) and Berkeley's College of Environmental Design. On the front facade the architect maintained a smooth white stucco palette and pierced it with artful protruding boxes and windows, softened by small but lovely garden spaces outside. To the bay side the home is set with black steel frames, railings and a fire escape, hinting at a more expressive side to the architect's work. You can peer through massive windows at interlocking, gallery-like fourteen-foot-tall (four-meter) interiors with stark white walls arranged around a floating spiral staircase. Beyond that you can see straight through to the blooming trees in the back. Sliding glass doors open onto large balconies with superb views of the bay. The home is in immaculate condition and fitted with incredible Mid-Century Modern furniture and art. From the outside it feels like a museum or gallery more than a residence. ●

San Francisco **Architect** Joseph Esherick **Year** 1962
Address 2610 Scott Street, San Francisco, CA 94123

Open to Public No **Free Entrance** No **Café/Restaurant** No
Overnight Accommodation No **Gift/Bookshop** No

Kahn House

45

San Francisco **Architect** Richard Neutra **Year** 1939
Address 66 Calhoun Terrace, San Francisco, CA 94133

Open to Public No **Free Entrance** No **Café/Restaurant** No
Overnight Accommodation No **Gift/Bookshop** No

You might not want to walk to this amazing San Francisco landmark, perched over the very top of Telegraph Hill. But once you get there you'll enjoy the surreal views of the skyline and the bay. And once you see the home – hidden among a sea of Victorian and shingled historic homes – you'll be happy you made it. Built for financier Sidney Kahn, the three-story residence, fronted on its bay side with continuous block windows and cantilevered balconies, feels like Neutra's famous Lovell or Kun Houses transplanted to San Francisco. The best view of the glassy side is from the adjacent (steep) stairs. Its street side is partially solid, a smooth white wall pierced by smaller bands of ribbon glazing and a few porthole windows, floating over a recessed entry porch. Looking over the building from back to front, you can see the progression from Streamline to pure Modernism and the home projects a sense of simple, artistic elegance that sums up what European Modernism was all about before being co-opted by the wealthy. ●

46

Alcoa Building

This twenty-five-story tower, wedged between John Portman's Embarcadero Center (page 88) and the Transamerica Pyramid, is remarkable for its glass curtain wall facade and diagonal steel cross bracing, clad in bourbon-colored anodized aluminum. It looks like Chicago's John Hancock Building (1969) with the top chopped off. Its five-story-tall X-braces are placed eighteen inches (five-hundred millimeters) outside the curtain wall. It's more impressive early in the day, before employees start pulling down the ugly white sunshades. The complex's lovely terrazzo plaza and sunken grass roof gardens, which connect via bridge to the raised walkways of the Golden Gateway Center (the city's first redevelopment project) and Embarcadero Center, were designed by Sasaki, Walker and Associates. World-class artworks were created by Marino Marini, Henry Moore, Charles Perry and Jan Peter Stern; the hypnotic bubble fountain was designed by Robert Woodward. Unfortunately, like most Modernist monuments, the building presents a blank concrete facade at street level, left over from the fortress mentality of the 1960s. Be sure to walk up the stairs to the wonderful raised plazas, where past dreams of a cleaner, more bucolic city-above-the-city temporarily come true. ●

San Francisco **Architect** Skidmore, Owings & Merrill **Year** 1967
Address 300 Clay Street, San Francisco, CA 94111

Open to Public No **Free Entrance** No **Café/Restaurant** Yes
Overnight Accommodation No **Gift/Bookshop** No

Crown Zellerbach Building

San Francisco **Architect** Skidmore, Owings & Merrill **Year** 1959
Address One Bush Plaza, 1 Bush Street, San Francisco, CA 94104

Open to Public No **Free Entrance** No **Café/Restaurant** No
Overnight Accommodation No **Gift/Bookshop** No

Crown Zellerbach, also known as One Bush Plaza, was the first International Style glass curtain wall tower to be built in San Francisco. And it's still by far the best. Built as the headquarters of the Crown Zellerbach Corporation (it's now owned by Tishman Speyer and contains several companies), this twenty-story structure floats on dark steel columns above a tall, glass-clad lobby and a sunken Japanese-inspired plaza. It shows off an aluminum-framed curtain wall, with light-green tinted windows alternating with darker-green spandrel glass. A separate service core, to the west, is clad with a subtle mosaic of dark tiles. The lobby, illuminated by a series of small lights, is accessible via a concrete bridge. The plaza, which is well worth a visit, contains a glass-enclosed circular pavilion with an amazing accordion roof, now home to E-Trade Financial. Crown Zellerbach, known to architecture aficionados as the Lever House of the West Coast, typifies the refined elegance – or some might say detached coolness – of corporate Modernism. Inside, horizontal steel girders allow each level to be uninterrupted by columns. This technique is widely credited (or blamed) with introducing the age of cubicles, a new approach to office privacy. ●

There is perhaps only one example in the world of a closed store that is still worth a visit just to peer inside. That's Frank Lloyd Wright's V.C. Morris Shop, located on Maiden Lane, around the corner from Union Square in San Francisco. Its most recent iteration, Xanadu Gallery, closed in August 2015, after a multi-million-dollar restoration. The space began as an upscale boutique, its flat brick facade pierced with a multi-layered Romanesque entrance arch, whose glazed doors lead to a short glass tunnel. Peering through a metal grille you can clearly spy the interior's highlight: a precast concrete spiral ramp, leading to a circular mezzanine. This was Wright's prototype for the Guggenheim Museum in New York. The space maintains a constant glow thanks to the cast white plastic bubble ceiling. Built-in wood and glass furnishings are also composed of circle segments, while circular merchandise display portholes pierce the curved walls of the ramp. According to the Frank Lloyd Wright Foundation, the shop has been bought by (once again) a 'high-end designer fashion boutique', so it appears it will have a new lease of life sometime soon. ●

San Francisco **Architect** Frank Lloyd Wright **Year** 1948
Address 140 Maiden Lane, San Francisco, CA 94108

Open to Public No **Free Entrance** No **Café/Restaurant** No
Overnight Accommodation No **Gift/Bookshop** No

Embarcadero Center & Hyatt Regency

49

San Francisco **Architect** John Portman **Year** 1973
Address 5 Embarcadero Center, San Francisco, CA 94111

Open to Public Yes **Free Entrance** No **Café/Restaurant** Yes
Overnight Accommodation Yes **Gift/Bookshop** No

John Portman's architecture is frozen science fiction and one of the best examples is his Hyatt Regency at the Embarcadero Center, a giant complex located on the eastern edge of San Francisco's financial district. The Embarcadero Center is famous as the largest downtown development in America since Rockefeller Center in New York and its interconnected raised walkways and thin precast concrete facades could be taken as a Modernist interpretation of that famous urban landmark. Outside, the Hyatt's staggered and stepped masses roughly resemble typewriter keys or an accordion file. Walk inside a relatively tiny entry and you're treated to a cavernous interior, carved out like a quarry with balconies cantilevering shockingly as they rise. It's all a bit vertiginous and resembles a set for *Buck Rogers*, particularly with the zooming glass elevators piercing the floors and ceilings. The central sculpture, a spherical aluminum piece called *Eclipse*, by Charles O. Perry, serves as the foreground to views that include wedges of light jutting into the seventeen-story atrium. The whole thing conjures up visions of the exhilarating but sanitized world that '60s-era planners were dreaming of, but never quite pulled off. ●

49

Embarcadero Center & Hyatt Regency

Darling House

Richard Neutra's Darling House is aptly named, although not on purpose. The residence, built for a doctor named Darling (his first name is not listed) and clad in horizontal redwood siding, really is a darling little house, located on a quiet street in the hills above Cole Valley, around the corner from the University of California, San Francisco. The Darling House – the architect's first wood-clad home – represents a fascinating combination of Europe's International Style and woodsy Bay Area Modernism. In front its boxy, L-shaped form – subtly offset with narrow painted casement windows and an overhanging canopy entryway – meshes with its shingled, historic neighbors. At the back the structure shows off more daring moves, like cantilevered deep eaves and a longer set of ribbon windows, all overlooking the hilly neighborhood. The Bay Area contains Neutra's largest concentration of 1930s houses outside of Southern California and this one marks the architect's first embrace of the local vernacular. He built a similarly-clad house, the Ford-Aquino Duplex, at 2430 Leavenworth Street on Russian Hill the same year and went on to design the redwood-clad Davey House in Monterey and the 'Three Small Houses in an Orchard' in Los Altos, all in 1939. He collaborated with the German architect Otto Winkler, with whom he worked on about a dozen houses in the Bay Area. ●

San Francisco **Architect** Richard Neutra **Year** 1937
Address 90 Woodland Avenue, San Francisco, CA 94117

Open to Public No **Free Entrance** No **Café/Restaurant** No
Overnight Accommodation No **Gift/Bookshop** No

San Francisco **Architect** Anshen & Allen **Year** 1955
Address 2 Clarendon Avenue, San Francisco, CA 94114

51

2 Clarendon Avenue Residence

Open to Public No **Free Entrance** No **Café/Restaurant** No
Overnight Accommodation No **Gift/Bookshop** No

Sitting on a lofty perch in San Francisco's Twin Peaks is one of Anshen & Allen's few single family residential commissions. It doesn't disappoint. The simple white rectangle is quite deceptive, presenting a uniform white front facade, marked only by slit windows shielded by protruding boxes. But thanks to a somewhat miraculous curved pathway next door through a vacant lot, you can shuffle down and see the main event: a rear elevation filled with a syncopated wall of windows, culminating with a single glazed tower fronting a narrow stair. Somehow it resembles a residential cathedral. There's a subtle grandness that still feels human-scale and residential. Anshen & Allen, which was swallowed by corporate architecture and engineering giant Stantec in 2010, was one of those firms that everyone should know, but they don't. Among its triumphs: the Chapel of the Holy Cross, built into a red sandstone outcropping in Sedona, Arizona; the International Building in downtown San Francisco; Eichler homes throughout the West and excellent university and hospital buildings throughout the country. ●

St. Mary's Cathedral

52

San Francisco **Architect** Pietro Belluschi and Pier Luigi Nervi **Year** 1971
Address 1111 Gough Street, San Francisco, CA 94109

Open to Public Yes **Free Entrance** Yes **Café/Restaurant** No
Overnight Accommodation No **Gift/Bookshop** Yes

The depth of Modernist invention in ecclesiastical architecture is, to put it simply, a revelation. One of the most transporting examples is Pietro Belluschi and Pier Luigi Nervi's St. Mary's Cathedral, situated in San Francisco's Western Addition. Everything about this wondrous (albeit intimidating) building is grandiose. Its concrete saddle roof, clad in travertine tiles, rises to become four interlinked parabolic hyperboloids, forming a cross from above. A raised plaza, paved with geometric patterns of red and white brick, creates a dramatic entry. Inside, the sweeping, triangular-patterned concrete cupola seems to float above you, supported only by four corner pylons. Narrow strips of colored glass by Gyory Kepes illuminate the spaces between the roof's quadrants, ushering beams of light inside and culminating in a thin cross-shaped skylight. A glimmering, delicate metallic *baldacchino* by Richard Lippold hangs from above, reinforcing the general sense of awe. More art, from intricate bronzes to colorful glass, surrounds you. It should be noted that Belluschi and Nervi, both Italian, collaborated with local architects John Michael Lee, Paul A. Ryan and Angus McSweeney. While in the area, walk across the street to observe Yoshiro Taniguchi's Japantown Peace Pagoda, a concrete interpretation of a Buddhist *stupa*. ●

52

St. Mary's Cathedral

San Francisco State University Student Union

Back when Brutalism ruled the Modernist world, the movement's once light, simple structures had transformed into heavy, acrobatic concrete buildings that were as much sculpture as habitable space. One of the Bay Area's leading practitioners of the style was Paffard Keatinge-Clay, who designed San Francisco State University's Student Union, which wraps its two cement wings around a paved plaza and then meanders in varying directions along its site. It consists of, among other bold elements, stepped pyramids, thrusting rooflines, exposed columns and bleacher-like roof lookouts. Keatinge-Clay actually lost a competition to Moshe Safdie for the project, but Safdie's equally ambitious plans fell through. From above, the M-shaped, angular structure resembles a sinister spaceship from a 1980s video game. Its most memorable component is the oversized trapezoidal form that rises from its roofline like an off-center hat. Inside, a rough-hewn, multi-level atrium allows access to all corners of the building. A recent renovation has covered some of the center's raw glory, but the majority remains intact. Keatinge-Clay's other famous campus design is that of the Brutalist Zellerbach Quadrangle for San Francisco Art Institute on Russian Hill (800 Chestnut Street), whose angled concrete roof deck and slanted cone-shaped skylights could have been set pieces on *Battlestar Galactica*. ●

San Francisco **Architect** Paffard Keatinge-Clay **Year** 1973
Address 1756 Holloway Avenue, San Francisco, CA 94132

Open to Public Yes **Free Entrance** No **Café/Restaurant** No
Overnight Accommodation No **Gift/Bookshop** No

San Francisco **Architect** Mario Ciampi **Year** 1959
Address 725 Southgate Avenue, Daly City, CA 94015

Open to Public No **Free Entrance** No **Café/Restaurant** No
Overnight Accommodation No **Gift/Bookshop** No

54 Vista Mar Elementary School

Mario Ciampi's Vista Mar Elementary School, now known as Marjorie H. Tobias Elementary, is one of the most unusual learning spaces you'll ever visit. The circular structure – could this have been an inspiration for Norman Foster's new Apple Headquarters in Silicon Valley? – protecting a grassy inner courtyard wonderfully knits together its community. The building's groovy zigzag roofline serves more formal purposes: it allows for peaked clerestory windows to bring light into classrooms. Inside, these spaces open via glass walls (protected by deep eaves) to the inner garden, a picturesque hill with a single tree in its middle and planter boxes around its edges. Ciampi added other animated details inside the courtyard, like umbrella-shaped shades and outside, like colorful tiles to enliven the building's beige masonry blocks. It's a great example of Ciampi's unpredictability as an architect: 'I was kind of a middle-of-the-roader, always looking for directions that would lead to successful solutions and not trying to put my own personal Frank Lloyd Wright stamp on it, or Mies van der Rohe,' he once said. The architect designed several schools in the area, but this is by far the best preserved. The second on this list, Westmoor High, is sadly crumbling and the glorious glass walls of its gymnasium have been covered over. ●

Ascension Chapel, Holy Cross Catholic Cemetery

55

San Francisco **Architect** Unknown **Year** Unknown
Address 1500 Mission Road, Colma, CA 94014

Open to Public Yes **Free Entrance** Yes **Café/Restaurant** No
Overnight Accommodation No **Gift/Bookshop** No

It's unlikely that you would be traveling to Colma, a working-class city south of San Francisco. But it's worth it to visit one of the most startling architectural juxtapositions you'll ever see, at the Holy Cross Catholic Cemetery. It's the city's oldest and largest – which is saying something, because Colma fashions itself as the 'city of cemeteries.' Right in the middle of a sea of tradition – classical gray stone tombs, Tudor buildings and an Egyptian mausoleum – sits a peach-colored circular building covered in a gridded band of concrete block and two levels of radiating curved thin shell canopies. Topped by a green, arrow-shaped spire, the structure contains several chapels, including Resurrection, Ascension and Coronation, each highlighted by curved ceilings and exposed wood beams extending from the building's center. After you get your fill of tropical Modernism, it's worth wandering around the cemetery, which contains the graves of baseball legend Joe DiMaggio, former California governor Pat Brown and founder of the *San Francisco Chronicle* Michael Henry de Young. Walk a few hundred feet and you can also check out another Modernist addition, the Our Lady of Peace Chapel, with its zigzag concrete canopy. ●

56

College of San Mateo Library

John Carl Warnecke was one of the Bay Area's workhorses, designing, often without acclaim, many of the region's notable buildings and monuments. One example of his hidden talents is a place you would never visit unless you were hunting for architecture: the College of San Mateo, a junior college located on a peaceful hilltop overlooking the San Francisco Bay. Warnecke, who originally designed twenty-seven buildings on the campus, drew inspiration from Frank Lloyd Wright's Florida Southern College, also designed under the hand of a single architect. But Warnecke's college is typically understated and classical, with simple but elegant Modernist buildings connected by long axes and, often, covered walkways. The centerpiece is the library, a glassy rectangular structure shaded by flat eaves, wavy canopies and diamond-patterned masonry vaults. The building, whose folds of structural concrete can be seen from the underside of the double-height space inside, is fronted by a large, deep reflecting pool, connecting it to the arts complex straight opposite. Make sure to take a slow stroll around the campus, which boasts fantastic views, serene pathways and a steady repetition of Warnecke's simple but effective language. ●

San Francisco **Architect** John Carl Warnecke **Year** 1963
Address 1700 W Hillsdale Boulevard, Building 9, San Mateo, CA 94402

Open to Public No **Free Entrance** No **Café/Restaurant** No
Overnight Accommodation No **Gift/Bookshop** No

Life House, The Highlands

57

To this day Eichler Homes remains the only commercial builder in the United States to create Modernist homes on a significant scale, constructing over eleven-thousand residences in twelve tracts throughout California. Eichler hired innovative architects like Jones & Emmons, Claude Oakland & Associates, Anshen & Allen and Raphael Soriano to design 'California Modern' post-and-beam homes that merged inside and outside and incorporated clean, geometric design. The vast majority of Eichler developments were created in Northern California and the largest is The Highlands, in the hills above San Mateo, containing almost seven-hundred homes. The symbol for this development became Pietro Belluschi's Life House, which the architect designed for both the Eichlers and *Life Magazine*, as a model for its series of stories on American housing. *Life* asked him for a house that could be built for less than $4,000 (£2,700). The result was a lofty, pitched-roof building with deep overhanging eaves. The open-plan interior contained combined living, dining and kitchen spaces, all lit by double-height windows. The home was a huge success, as was the whole development. The Highlands remains a popular destination for young families and many of its homes have been spectacularly renovated, many showing off new colors and amenities. ●

San Francisco **Architect** Pietro Belluschi **Year** 1955
Address 1651 Yorktown Road, San Mateo, CA 94402

Open to Public No **Free Entrance** No **Café/Restaurant** No
Overnight Accommodation Yes **Gift/Bookshop** No

San Francisco **Architect** Bill Patrick **Year** 1952
Address 831 Midglen Way, Woodside, CA 94062

Open to Public No **Free Entrance** No **Café/Restaurant** No
Overnight Accommodation No **Gift/Bookshop** No

58

Midglen Way House

It's astonishing to explore Frank Lloyd Wright's outsized influence throughout the West Coast. Yet another Wright apprentice, Bill Patrick, built one of the few 'textile block' houses you'll see outside of Los Angeles in the hilly hamlet of Woodside. Patrick, who apprenticed at Taliesen West from 1943 to 1945, was a Wright die-hard: he edited the Taliesen newsletter and stayed true to his organic ideals throughout his career. He worked with two other apprentices on the residence, tucked into a landscape of coast live oaks and redwoods, that combines the austerity of thick textile block walls (pressed on site) with the warmth of wood, extensive clerestories and red concrete cantilevered balconies. The three were cocky, or inspired, or both. According to Patrick's son Akio, the architects asked a realtor to find them the most difficult site possible. The composition, which has since been enlarged by Patrick's sons with a sympathetically designed office for their firm, Midglen Studio, is entered through an open central stair and focuses around an Asian-inspired, light-infused double-height office space that carries out Wright's compression-and-release spatial strategy expertly. Other rooms are equally infused with illumination and nature. The building's original cantilevered balcony is steel; the additions were achieved with post-tensioned concrete. ●

Nail House

59

San Francisco **Architect** Beverley David Thorne **Year** 1954
Address 78 Deodora Drive, Atherton, CA 94027

Open to Public No **Free Entrance** No **Café/Restaurant** No
Overnight Accommodation No **Gift/Bookshop** No

Built for art dealer Harry C. Nail, Beverley David Thorne's Nail House is imbedded into a site of thick, gnarled oak trees on a quiet street in Atherton. It's notable for its long sharply sloping roof, which – supported by a steel frame – projects from the first floor at the residence's rear to cover both the ground floor and the tree-house-like, glass-enclosed second-floor living room. The glassy, 'free-form' home, shaped by its site and the spatial needs of the clients, is protected by an entry wall, behind which living spaces open onto a back pool and courtyard. A pool house and more bedrooms were added in subsequent years. Thorne, known for heroic floating forms, deliberately ran from publicity in fear of getting distracted and overwhelmed, which is why you've probably not heard of him. He changed his name to David from Beverley mid-way through his career, further confusing things. If you're in the neighborhood, you should visit Frank Lloyd Wright's little-known Arthur Mathews House (83 Wisteria Way), just a few blocks from the Nail House. It's hard to see from the street but worth a peek. You'll notice the low-lying red brick, Usonian-style structure, with a prairie roof and small windows behind a thick array of ancient oaks. ●

60 Sunset Magazine Headquarters

Few buildings represent the merger of landscape and architecture that was a feature of the Mid-Century Modern style as effectively as Cliff May's Sunset Magazine Headquarters. *Sunset* played a major role in promoting the post-war California Ranch House, so it made sense to hire May to build a head-quarters that emulated the company's ideals. The low-lying wood-clad structure, with its gabled roof and deep eaves, bridges indoor and outdoor working spaces and is filled with interior courtyards and patios opening to the exterior. The building wraps around a series of gardens by Thomas Church that represent the plants and landscapes of California's different regions, like the Northwest, Northern California, central California, the southwest desert and Southern California. Unfortunately, the building and gardens are temporarily closed to the public, as *Sunset* moved its offices to Oakland's Jack London Square in fall 2015. Time Inc., the magazine's owner, sold the seven-acre (three hectare) property to San Francisco-based real estate group Embarcadero Capital Partners. There is hope that at least the gardens will be bought by nearby Menlo College, but for now their future remains in flux. ●

San Francisco **Architect** Cliff May **Year** 1951
Address 80 Willow Road, Menlo Park, CA 94025

Open to Public No **Free Entrance** No **Café/Restaurant** No
Overnight Accommodation No **Gift/Bookshop** No

First United Methodist Church of Palo Alto

61

San Francisco **Architect** Carlton Arthur Steiner **Year** 1963
Address 625 Hamilton Avenue, Palo Alto, CA 94301

Open to Public Yes **Free Entrance** Yes **Café/Restaurant** No
Overnight Accommodation No **Gift/Bookshop** No

This remarkable church near downtown Palo Alto was built in what was described as a 'Contemporary Gothic' style, melding medieval and Mid-Century Modern languages. The A-frame concrete building consists of nineteen poured-in-place concrete piers that extend from beneath the basement to meet seventy-three feet (twenty-two meters) above the main aisle. Precast roof panels, raised by crane, were tied together at the ridge and 1,500 brightly hued small glass inserts were installed. The unique circular lighting fixtures, made of spun steel with a brass finish, weigh six-hundred pounds (272 kilograms) each and were bolted to the roof. That circular theme can be seen throughout: on the screen framing the cross, in the chancel railing, and in the pew ends. Sitting inside the dark sanctuary is like experiencing a light show, as bright colors emanating from the thousands of stained-glass pieces bombard your senses. The texture and shape of the walls add to the feeling of movement and activity. Be sure to take it all in from the undulating balcony above. Steiner, a Berkeley-based architect, built a number of commercial and residential projects in the Bay Area, but this was by far his most ambitious. The *Palo Alto Times* in 1964 remarked that the church was 'often called the most spectacular church on the mid-peninsula.' ●

61 First United Methodist Church of Palo Alto

Don't turn down a chance to visit Frank Lloyd Wright's Hanna House. Perched atop a small hill in Palo Alto, just above the Stanford University campus, the residence was commissioned by Jean and Paul Hanna, two Midwest-born educators who moved here to teach at Stanford. Wright's first home in the Bay Area, the residence was donated to Stanford in 1975 and opened to the public in 1999. The L-shaped structure (now U-shaped after an addition in 1961 by Wright's successor firm, Taliesen Associated Architects) was built – as per Wright's philosophy of organic architecture – to harmonize with its surroundings, particularly the site's plentiful oak trees. The home is sited around an internal courtyard, whose stepped fountain has been turned off due to the state's drought. Its horizontal focus, another Wright staple, is reinforced by large overhanging eaves, board-and-batten timber walls and horizontal bricks. If you look closely, you'll even see that every nail-head faces sideways. Wright used this home to 'break open the box.' It's the first that he built on a hexagonal grid, rather than an orthogonal one and there are no right angles in the plan. Hexagons are everywhere, from floor tiles to floor plans, to sofa cushions, to a six-sided shower and fireplace. A flowing combination of living, kitchen and dining spaces all open to large banks of windows overlooking the hillside, while bedrooms line up along the courtyard. ●

San Francisco **Architect** Frank Lloyd Wright **Year** 1936
Address 737 Frenchmans Road, Stanford, CA 94305

Open to Public Yes **Free Entrance** No **Café/Restaurant** No
Overnight Accommodation No **Gift/Bookshop** No

San Francisco **Architect** Ernest Kump **Year** 1961
Address 12345 El Monte Road, Los Altos Hills, CA 94022

Open to Public Yes **Free Entrance** Yes **Café/Restaurant** Yes
Overnight Accommodation No **Gift/Bookshop** No

63

Foothill College

Ernest Kump and Masten & Hurd's Foothill College is one of the most unusual university campuses you'll ever visit. It's essentially the culmination of the Pavilion Style of Modernism, marked by shingled, truncated hip roofs topped with square parapets, made famous by commercial establishments such as Denny's and Howard Johnson. I like to call the campus 'Denny's U,' for its unending examples of this typology, organized around a vaguely axial plan. The campus' founders believed that it should 'have a quiet dignity,' and it really does, with the redwood-clad buildings loosely organized by function and curriculum. It's too bad this style got watered down in strip malls, office parks and roadways around the country. You may gain an appreciation for it here that you never thought you could have. The centerpiece of the main campus is the lofty library, one of two buildings on campus standing two stories high, its long beams protruding well beyond its deep eaves. It's fronted by a lovely brick plaza filled with modern sculptures. The athletic complex is accessed via a long bridge over Perimeter Road, and a few octagon-shaped buildings balance out all the pavilion structures. The wonderfully calming landscape, designed by famed firm Sasaki, Walker and Associates, links the buildings via outdoor spaces that feature rolling lawns and winding paths. ●

Sunnyvale Bank of the West

64

San Francisco **Architect** Melvin Rojko **Year** 1962
Address 380 S Mathilda Avenue, Sunnyvale, CA 94086

Open to Public Yes **Free Entrance** Yes **Café/Restaurant** No
Overnight Accommodation No **Gift/Bookshop** No

With its protruding circular roof, continuous glass walls, wrap-around railing, finger-like split columns and a curved row of circular lights under its soffit, the Sunnyvale Bank of the West is often compared to a flying saucer. Branch employees have nicknamed it 'The Starship Enterprise.' It also resembles an oyster tray or a cheese platter. The beige building (the color is its least appealing part), set in a parking lot near downtown Sunnyvale, opened as a branch of First National Bank of San Jose at a time when space-age banks were all the rage. It once contained four drive-through tellers on all sides, like a drive-in restaurant. Rojko, known for his space-age aesthetic, designed several banks in the area, including the glassy, butterfly-roofed Salinas Valley Savings & Loan (now a Chase Bank, at 1725 Saratoga Avenue, San Jose) just down the street. Inside, the open-planned building, which contains a spiral stair and a ringed mezzanine, is in remarkably good condition; in contrast to most Mid-Century Modern banks, which have been worked over by corporate formulas. Look up and you'll see a small geodesic dome wedged into the ceiling. ●

Located on Santa Clara's strip mall-filled El Camino Real, next to an establishment called Adult World sits a Googie gem: Tan's Touchless Car Wash. Supported by steel boomerang columns jutting through the blue building's V-shaped roof, the establishment is all hot rod. Diagonal lines suggest movement and energy and swiss cheese holes in the columns suggest lightness and rocket ships. The original 1960s structure was taken over by entrepreneur Hlatin Tan in 1982 and has been run by his family ever since. There's another Tan's about a mile away in San Jose, opened in 1992. It's a fun place to get your car washed, if you're willing to wait in line for a little while. Googie designs are much less prevalent in this region (which is more interested in Google than Googie) than in Southern California, but there are still a few gems like the Capitol 6 drive-in theater in San Jose and Pleasant Plaza in Pleasanton. The prognosis is poor for most: local legend Jimmy's Restaurant in San Jose closed in 2015 after a fire, Lyon's Coffee Shop in San Bruno (which became Melaka Restaurant) was recently demolished, and Biff's Coffee shop in Oakland is facing demolition. ●

San Francisco **Architect** Unknown **Year** Unknown
Address 3455 El Camino Real, Santa Clara, CA 95051

Open to Public Yes **Free Entrance** Yes **Café/Restaurant** No
Overnight Accommodation No **Gift/Bookshop** No

Tan's Touchless Car Wash

Center for the Performing Arts

After Frank Lloyd Wright passed away, his ideas and projects were carried on until 2013 by his office, Taliesen Associated Architects, based at Taliesen West in Scottsdale, Arizona. A prime example is the Center for the Performing Arts in San Jose, a strange folly on the edge of downtown, next to the city's civic center. Its design was led by Wright's unheralded right-hand man, William Wesley Peters and by talented local architect Aaron Green. The brown, drum-shaped hall, home to both Ballet San Jose and Broadway San Jose, resembles a Burger King crown or a birthday cake, depending on your mood. It's fronted by a glass wall and repeating arches of curved stucco, inset with interlocking brass circles and arches and the globe lights that were prevalent in Wright's later work. Like the architect's Guggenheim Museum in New York, the building focuses on a spiral ramp. Actually two: interior and exterior, leading first to the entry and then spinning around the plush lobby, with its enormous chandelier, custom couches and rounded walls. Inside the space evokes – and was a precursor to – the polished, brassy modern hotel designs of the '70s and '80s. The 2,677-seat main auditorium has no center aisle, so, much to the chagrin of its patrons, getting in and out of the seats is a small nightmare. ●

San Francisco **Architect** Taliesin Associated Architects **Year** 1972
Address 255 S Almaden Boulevard, San Jose, CA 95113

Open to Public Yes **Free Entrance** No **Café/Restaurant** No
Overnight Accommodation No **Gift/Bookshop** No

San Francisco **Architect** Ralph Rapson **Year** 1965 **Address** Theater Arts Department, J-106 Theater Arts Center, University of California, Santa Cruz, CA 95064

Open to Public Yes **Free Entrance** No **Café/Restaurant** No **Overnight Accommodation** No **Gift/Bookshop** No

Perhaps the most stirring campus in the University of California system is University of California, Santa Cruz, a hilltop village winding through redwood forests, sited atop vast meadows overlooking the Pacific. The school's progressive vision for a campus of small residential colleges and eclectic Modernist buildings was led by landscape architect Thomas Church and carried out by architects John Carl Warnecke; Ernest Kump; Wurster, Bernardi & Emmons; Joseph Esherick; Anshen & Allen; Hugh Stubbins; MLTW; and others. The team focused their plans on the trees and the summits, rather than on the open lands beneath them. 'Instead of remaking the land, the land must remake our standard conceptions of building and place', said Church. Ralph Rapson's Theater Arts Center is made up of a series of blocky, angular structures arranged under a giant floating canopy. Elsewhere on the campus, Esherick's Stevenson College sits down a long pathway, with its shed roofs and saddlebag-style rooms, not far from MLTWs Kresge's College and Wurster, Bernardi & Emmons' Cowell College. UCSC has grown considerably over the decades, adding an uneven mix of new buildings and complexes of all styles. But the core is still here and still remarkable. ●

67

UC Santa Cruz Theater Arts Center

Community Hospital of the Monterey Peninsula

89

San Francisco **Architect** Edward Durell Stone **Year** 1962
Address 23625 Holman Highway, Monterey, CA 93942

Open to Public No **Free Entrance** No **Café/Restaurant** No
Overnight Accommodation No **Gift/Bookshop** No

It may come as a surprise that one of the most remarkable buildings in Monterey is a hospital. But Edward Durell Stone's Community Hospital of the Monterey Peninsula, known by its strange acronym, CHOMP, is a case study for how medical architecture can create natural, healing environments rather than sterile places to be feared. The facility was the dream of Tom Tonkin, the hospital's first CEO, who in the 1950s spearheaded an ambitious campaign to fund the Stone-designed facility so that 'people coming to it would perhaps be free of some of the fears and anxieties usually attendant on hospitalization.' The building, imbedded in a grove of Monterey pines overlooking Monterey Bay, takes advantage of the site, with low, deep rooflines allowing spaces to open up via large sheets of glass lining private rooms (these were the first private hospital rooms in the country) and hallways and numerous skylights. Inside, Stone's embrace of the natural world continues, with large fountains and copious indoor plantings acting as the focal points for many public spaces. Stone, one of the leading practitioners of highly ornate, classically inspired New Formalist style, integrated geometric tiles and various other ornaments into the design. In 2008 HOK Architects designed an addition, doubling the hospital's size and adopting much of its architectural language. ●

Community Hospital of the Monterey Peninsula

Sadly, Richard Neutra's Connell House, located a pitching wedge away from the Pebble Beach Golf Links, was at the time of publication, set for demolition; dark-green fences obscuring its cantilevered walls and enclosed courtyard. But just around the corner, at the edge of the curving coast, you can still discover Mark Mills' The Shell, a fan-shaped house with a barrel-vaulted roofline that from above indeed looks just like a sea shell. The shape, made of concrete vaults supported by thin exposed wooden beams, creates giant arched windows that frame unbelievable views of the idyllic oceanfront from every room. At the back is an eye-shaped pool, accessible via the common spaces. The raw materials give it the protected feeling of a cave, albeit a cave with one of the best views in the world. The owner, Janice O'Brien, has been living here since the residence's construction in 1972. Her husband, James, passed away years ago, but she never left, hosting her sizable family whenever possible. 'I love this place. It feels like an igloo', she says, sitting on the built-in couch, looking out at the ridiculously beautiful coast. ●

San Francisco **Architect** Mark Mills **Year** 1972
Address 3137, 17 Mile Drive, Carmel, CA 93953

Open to Public No **Free Entrance** No **Café/Restaurant** No
Overnight Accommodation No **Gift/Bookshop** No

San Francisco **Architect** Frank Lloyd Wright **Year** 1951
Address 26336 Scenic Road, Carmel, CA 93923

Open to Public No **Free Entrance** No **Café/Restaurant** No
Overnight Accommodation No **Gift/Bookshop** No

70 Walker House

Few of Frank Lloyd Wright's commissions embody his embrace of nature quite like the Walker House, a single-story, five-room residence perched on a blond stone outcropping in Carmel, just a few feet from the Pacific Ocean. Depending on the tide it sometimes even touches the ocean. The home's original owner, Della Walker, affectionately called it the 'Cabin on the Rocks.' You can see the home's entry clearly from Scenic Road, taking in its field-stone cladding and slightly angled, deeply overhanging patinated copper roof. But the best view is via the beach, reached via a small path just south of the property. From here you can peer right through the house, taking in its open-plan living spaces, built-in wood furniture and stone cladding through continuous bands of glass. The flatness of the roof, as well as the horizontality of the structure as a whole, evokes Wright's Prairie School architecture, adapted seamlessly into the ultimate California setting. From here the house looks more like a boat and you wonder how it hasn't floated away, considering the legendary crashing waves here. Sitting on the beach, staring at the house, is the perfect way to meditate, taking in one of the most beautiful sites of the natural world, as well as a masterpiece of the man-made one. ●

Hass House

71

San Francisco **Architect** Mark Mills **Year** 1950
Address 62 Yankee Point Drive, Carmel, CA 93923

Open to Public No **Free Entrance** No **Café/Restaurant** No
Overnight Accommodation No **Gift/Bookshop** No

Mark Mills, a student of Frank Lloyd Wright and a close compatriot of Paolo Soleri, is relatively unknown outside of Carmel. His imaginative, free-spirited work emerged from Wright's organic philosophy, but progressed into a more unrestrained, even bizarre realm. He built more than thirty houses in the area. The Hass House, located on an ocean-gazing cliff between central Carmel and Big Sur, has a tube-shaped exterior finished with an elastic neoprene coating mixed with crushed walnut shells to give it a rough texture. Visible from over a rickety wooden fence, from the street it looks like a submarine, or a phallus (Mills nicknamed it the Limp Penis House), or a home in Santorini in the Greek Islands. Its portholes protrude from its north side, with a large bubble skylight at the intersection of its T-shaped plan. A small shingled guest cabin sits across from the house's small yard to the north. Other strange details include a statue of a bird above the chimney flue, a bonsai tree and a dark wood door with colorful circular windows. Beyond this is just the blue of the ocean and to the right you can see a wonderful little patio for its owners to take it all in. ●

Drive along the winding road from Carmel about fifteen miles (twenty-four kilometers) east to Carmel Valley and you enter a different world: a place that's hilly, green and dominated by farms, not beach houses. Hiding among the ranch-style and Spanish houses and traditional rural architecture is a steel gem by Pierre Koenig, the Johnson Riebe House, commissioned by Cyrus and Elizabeth Johnson and Koenig's only home in Northern California. You can see the battleship gray residence clearly from the road above, starting with its corrugated-steel-sided walls and a long span canopy extending into a carport outside the entrance. Inside, the steel-framed home showcases Koenig's typical open plan, with the living room, dining area and kitchen flowing into one another, as well as one of Koenig's signature see-through central fireplaces. Rhythmic exposed steel soffits lend a touch of drama to the minimal palette. The unique raised viewpoint allows you to see the house's cruciform design, built around large snaking trees and opening up at the rear through glass walls and sliding doors to a wondrously lush backyard and simple patio. ●

San Francisco **Architect** Pierre Koenig **Year** 1962
Address 54 La Ranchería, Carmel Valley, CA 93924

Open to Public No **Free Entrance** No **Café/Restaurant** No
Overnight Accommodation No **Gift/Bookshop** No

72

Johnson Riebe House

Nepenthe Restaurant

Resting on a bluff far above the Pacific Ocean, Rowan Maiden's Nepenthe serves as the perfect exclamation point to a day exploring one of the most beautiful places on earth: Big Sur, California. Local pioneers Lolly and Bill Fassett hired Maiden, a Frank Lloyd Wright apprentice, to build the structure using native redwood, along with steel and glass. Its projecting, triangular form, exposed wood beams and awnings and long, view-framing glass walls give it the bucolic charm of a ski chalet, but in a sun-drenched California setting. Large covered and open patios embrace the splendid view, which you can't stop staring at. Just be sure to protect your cheese plate from the birds, who won't hesitate to dive-bomb. The restaurant was an addition to an existing three-room wood and adobe cabin, which still exists, just above the main terrace. Orson Welles and Rita Hayworth had bought this unique residence before the Fassetts took ownership. The name Nepenthe means 'isle of no care' in Greek and the place has long served as a destination for artists and bohemians. Now it's especially popular with wealthy tourists, but no matter, it still maintains a free-spirited vibe. And how couldn't it? ●

San Francisco **Architect** Rowan Maiden **Year** 1948
Address 48510 Highway One, Big Sur, CA 93920

Open to Public Yes **Free Entrance** Yes **Café/Restaurant** Yes
Overnight Accommodation No **Gift/Bookshop** No

San Francisco **Architect** Nathaniel Owings and Mark Mills **Year** 1957
Address 49620 Grimes Canyon Road, Big Sur, CA 92920

Open to Public No **Free Entrance** No **Café/Restaurant** No
Overnight Accommodation Yes **Gift/Bookshop** No

Wild Bird

Visiting Mark Mills' and Nathaniel Owings' Wild Bird is an architectural pilgrimage. Every bend in the road (and there are many) brings you closer to this architectural legend, an A-frame concrete house for Owings that hugs a small rocky outcrop above the six-hundred-foot-tall (183-meter) cliffs, as if it were about to take off and fly. Much of the structure cantilevers over the cliff and it seems a miracle that the house doesn't slide down the side. The mix of the two architects was an odd one: Mills was known for strange, one-off organic forms and Owings for corporate architecture at one of the largest firms in the world, Skidmore, Owings & Merrill. But the combination worked, each adding his own elements to an incredible composition. Linear skylights allow sun into a wide, open living and kitchen space, filled with local woods and stones, with views down the coast framed by a huge triangular wall of glass. Bedrooms below look out at the coast through tall square windows. Owings, who played an active role in limiting commercial development in Big Sur, is remembered here with the Nathaniel Owings Memorial Redwood Grove at Big Sur. Visitors can rent Wild Bird, which was altered inside after a 2012 fire. Otherwise, your best bet is to pull onto one of several nearby lookouts to enjoy the view from down the street or across a ravine. ●

Kundert Medical Clinic

75

San Francisco **Architect** Frank Lloyd Wright **Year** 1955
Address San Luis Obispo, 1106 Pacific Street, San Luis Obispo, CA 93401

Open to Public No **Free Entrance** No **Café/Restaurant** No
Overnight Accommodation No **Gift/Bookshop** No

Frank Lloyd Wright's work spans the whole West Coast, from Los Angeles to Washington State, often appearing where you'd never expect. A good illustration is the Kundert Medical Clinic, a small doctor's office on a small residential street in San Luis Obispo, north of Santa Barbara. Wright designed the building for Karl Kundert, an ophthamologist who had been impressed with the Wright houses he had seen in Madison, Wisconsin and had pleaded with Wright over the course of half a dozen meetings to take the commission. Wright originally wanted to build the low, L-shaped building with Usonian concrete block, but local building codes forbade this, so he chose red brick instead, the mortar in its vertical joints matching the bricks to emphasize their horizontality. The remainder of the facade contains a projecting, flat roof, and a band of translucent horizontal glazing, superimposed with a thin layer of wood cut with curved shapes vaguely resembling an upside-down mountain range. The exterior is carried inside, the pierced wood panels bringing glowing light into a tall, wood-and-brick-clad waiting room, whose high glass doors open to a deck and then to the San Luis Obispo Creek. The office now belongs to a cardiologist, but it's been well preserved, remaining as beautiful as ever. ●

Kundert Medical Clinic

Los Angeles

76 Oyler House **77** Storke Tower, UCSB **78** Kem Weber House **79** Slavin House **80** California Lutheran University **81** Wave House **82** Hunt House **83** Stevens House **84** Congregational Church of Northridge **85** Balboa Highlands Eichler Homes **86** Sepulveda Unitarian Universalist Society **87** Sunkist Headquarters **88** Casa de Cadillac **89** St. Michael and All Angels Episcopal Church **90** Walstrom House **91** Case Study House #16 **92** Sheats Goldstein House **93** Gould Residence **94** Crestwood Hills **95** Sturges House **96** Tischler House **97** Charles E. Young Research Library, UCLA **98** Sheats Apartments **99** Strathmore Apartments **100** Twenty-Eighth Church of Christ, Scientist **101** Strick House **102** Rustic Canyon Kappe Colony **103** Freedman Residence **104** Case Study House #20 **105** Eames House **106** Santa Monica Civic Auditorium **107** Century Plaza Hotel **108** Century Plaza Towers **109** Perpetual Savings and Loan **110** Union 76 Gas Station **111** Norms **112** Schindler House **113** Lloyd Wright Studio & Residence **114** Trousdale Estates **115** Case Study House #21 **116** Chemosphere **117** Jacobsen and Polin Houses **118** Garcia House **119** The Boat Houses **120** Wolff House **121** Polito House **122** Kun House **123** Cinerama Dome **124** Case Study House #22 **125** Capitol Records **126** Samuel-Novarro House **127** Moore House **128** Ennis House **129** Lovell Health House **130** Avenel Housing **131** Hollyhock House **132** Bubeshko Apartments **133** Neutra Colony **134** Neutra VDL Research House **135** How House **136** First United Methodist Church of Glendale **137** Rodriguez House **138** Art Center College of Design **139** Millard House **140** Norton Simon Museum **141** Ambassador Auditorium **142** Poppy Peak **143** Norton House **144** Case Study House #10 **145** 1414 Fair Oaks **146** Airform Bubble House **147** Beckman Auditorium **148** Stuart Pharmaceutical Company **149** Covina Bowl **150** Mar Vista Tract **151** Robert Lee Frost Auditorium **152** Buck House **153** LACMA **154** Dunsmuir Flats **155** Mackey Apartments **156** Premier Car Wash **157** Home Savings of America **158** Ahmanson Center **159** St. Basil Church **160** Founder's Church of Religious Science **161** American Cement Building **162** Dodger Stadium **163** Los Angeles Department of Water and Power **164** Music Center **165** Holman United Methodist Church **166** Westin Bonaventure Hotel **167** University of Southern California **168** Pan American Bank **169** Iwata House **170** IBM Aerospace Headquarters **171** LAX Theme Building **172** University Christian Church **173** St. Jerome Roman Catholic Church **174** Pann's **175** The Forum **176** South Bay Bank **177** Chips **178** Compton City Hall and Civic Center **179** California State University, Dominguez Hills **180** Riviera Methodist Church **181** Bowler House **182** Wayfarers Chapel **183** Brady Residence **184** Killingsworth Brady Smith Offices **185** Cambridge Building **186** Gibbs & Gibbs Architects Office Building **187** Rancho Estates **188** Kimpson Nixon Residence **189** Opdahl Residence **190** Case Study House #25 **191** California State University, Fullerton **192** Hope International University **193** Anaheim Convention Center & Arena **194** Stuft Shirt Restaurant **195** The Arboretum (Drive-In Church) **196** Lovell Beach House **197** Horizon House **198** University of California, Irvine **199** University of California, Riverside **200** Crafton Hills College

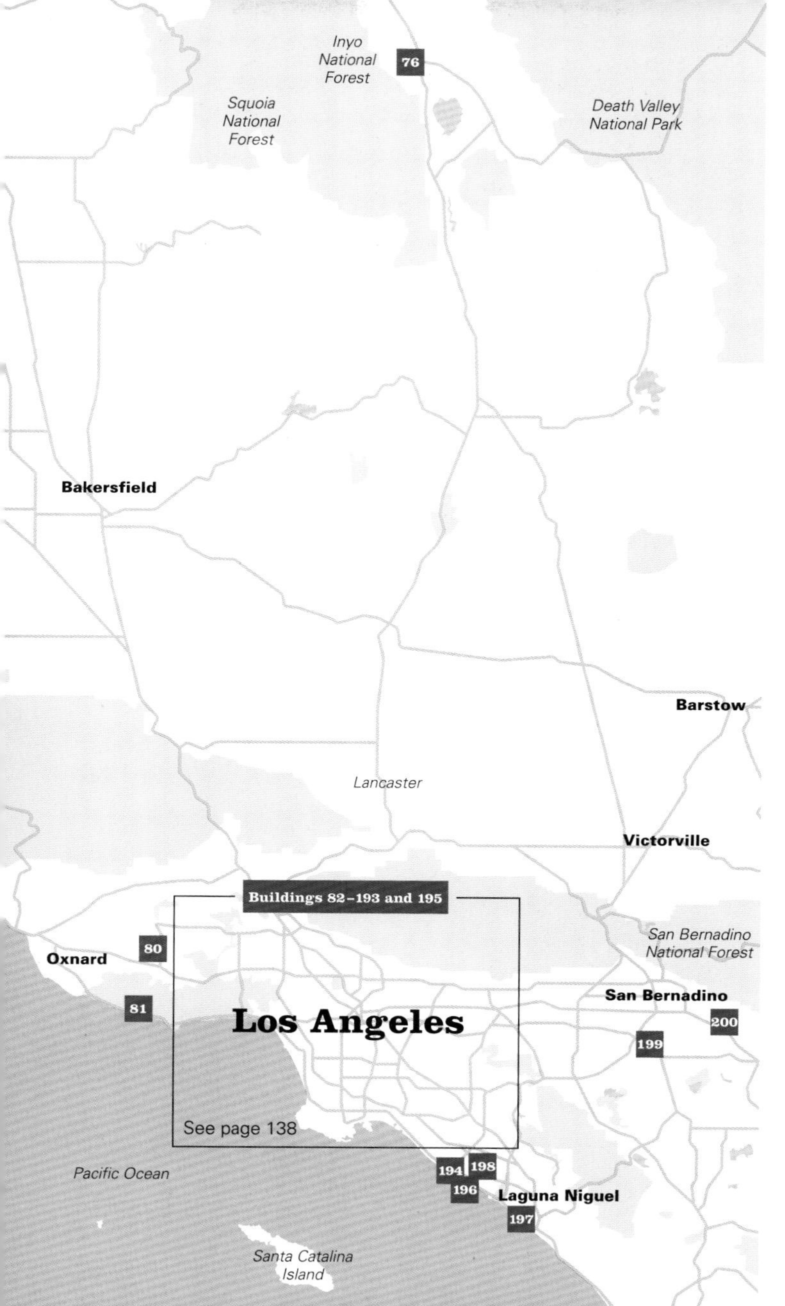
Inyo
National
Forest
76
Squoia
National
Forest
Death Valley
National Park
Bakersfield
Barstow
Lancaster
Victorville
Buildings 82–193 and 195
San Bernadino
National Forest
80
Oxnard
San Bernadino
81
Los Angeles
200
199
See page 138
194
198
Pacific Ocean
196
Laguna Niguel
197
Santa Catalina
Island

Los Angeles

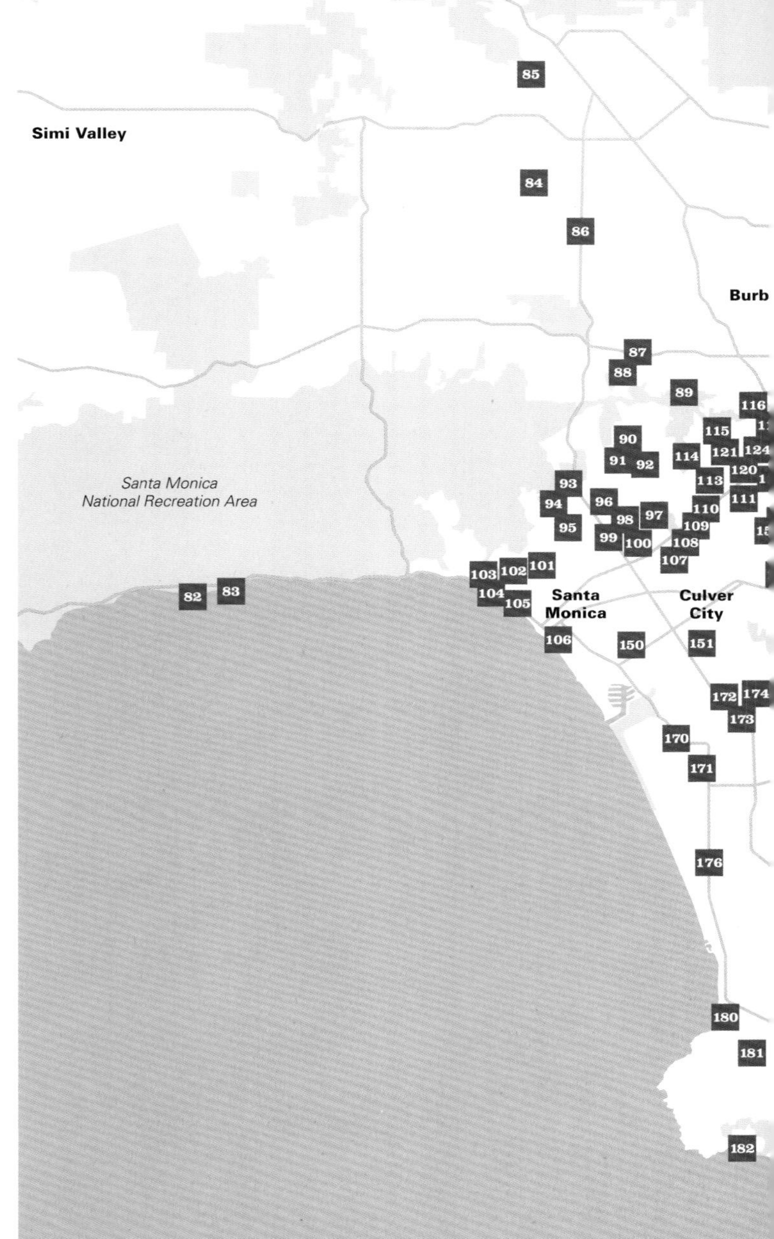
Simi Valley
Burb
Santa Monica
National Recreation Area
Santa Monica
Culver
City
82
83
84
85
86
87
88
89
90
91
92
93
94
95
96
97
98
99
100
101
102
103
104
105
106
107
108
109
110
111
113
114
115
116
120
121
124
150
151
170
171
172
173
174
176
180
181
182

Angeles
National Forest
Twin Peaks
East
137
138
139
Pasadena
136
140
141
148
142
144
147
Glendale
143
146
129
128
130
127
135
145
132
134
131
133
149
162
Los Angeles
158
160
163
West Covina
161
159
164
166
169
168
167
Whittier
178
191
192
179
183
184
185
186
187
193
195
Long
Beach
188
189
190
Santa
Ana
Pacific Ocean

Oyler House

76

Los Angeles **Architect** Richard Neutra **Year** 1959
Address 771 Thundercloud Lane, Lone Pine, CA 93545

Open to Public No **Free Entrance** No **Café/Restaurant** No
Overnight Accommodation No **Gift/Bookshop** No

Not all of Richard Neutra's desert houses are located in Palm Springs. One of the most fabulous is even further from civilization in Lone Pine, a tiny hamlet of about two-thousand people in the Eastern Sierras, about three hours due north of Los Angeles. It's surprising that Neutra accepted the commission from Richard Oyler, who was Inyo County Treasurer and had little budget for the famous architect's work. Oyler, who respected Neutra's views on architecture's connection with the environment, wrote him a letter out of the blue having seen his work in a book he'd checked out of the local library. Neutra accepted. The two developed a friendship that lasted the rest of Neutra's life. The home, facing gargantuan boulders (the two largest look like rabbit ears), with the Sierra Nevadas forming a snowy backdrop, consists of two staggered, single-story post-and-beam volumes, clad in glass, steel, stucco and wood. The open-plan home was built in a linear fashion, so every room would have a view through floor-to-ceiling windows, allowing the exterior to dominate every inch. 'I could be in the living room or wherever and I'm outdoors too', said Oyler. 'You can't imagine what it's like here on a dark night, when the stars are just busting themselves'. ■

Storke Tower, University of California, Santa Barbara

If you're tired of the idyllic Mission Style architecture in Santa Barbara, you can head to University of California, Santa Barbara (UCSB), the third campus to have opened in the state's university system after Berkeley and University of California, Los Angeles (UCLA). The school was master planned by formidable firm Pereira and Luckman and there are worthwhile buildings from the likes of Edward Durell Stone and other Mid-Century Modern masters. But the focal point is the ultra-spare, ultra-high Storke Tower. The 175-foot-high (53-meter) rectangular carillon is the tallest concrete and steel structure in the country. It contains sixty-one bells of wildly varying sizes and was named for Thomas M. Storke, a Pulitzer Prize-winning journalist and US senator who helped found UCSB. Designed by Bay Area firm Clark & Morgan, the rough concrete-clad pylon, with its arched base and finger-shaped crowning windows, rises high above Communications Plaza, a Modernist variation on a Mission plaza, with its sunken hardscape and Brutalist perimeter loggia. While you're at UCSB visit Moore and Turnbull's iconic Faculty Club, an angular, village-like composition just around the corner, situated on the school's gorgeous lagoon. But at the time of this writing the structure was undergoing extensive renovations, rendering it unviewable. ■

Los Angeles **Architect** Clark & Morgan **Year** 1969
Address Isla Vista, CA 93117

Open to Public No **Free Entrance** No **Café/Restaurant** No
Overnight Accommodation No **Gift/Bookshop** No

German-born Kem Weber was famed for his streamlined industrial designs, often mentioned in the same breath as legends such as Raymond Loewy and Edward G. Budd. But he was also an accomplished architect, creating uniquely modern, carefully crafted designs that were far ahead of their time. His most famed commissions include the Bixby House in Kansas City and Walt Disney's original animation studios in Burbank. If you're in Santa Barbara you can visit his own home, a complex redwood-paneled, pitched structure at the bottom of a sloping site shaded by thick, gnarled trees. Weber built much of the property with his own hands and after he died his widow remained there for more than two decades. The view from the end of its driveway is blocked by a carport, so head further up the street to get a better vantage. The skewed rectangle is clad with floor-to-ceiling saw-tooth windows that open onto a stone patio, flooding the interior with soft light and ensuring privacy. Interior spaces, filled with built-in furniture, flow from the central living space, a central beam above touching every room. Weber's floating, rustic studio is located further down the hill. ■

Los Angeles **Architect** Kem Weber **Year** 1952
Address 1000 Tunnel Road, Santa Barbara, CA 93105

Open to Public No **Free Entrance** No **Café/Restaurant** No
Overnight Accommodation No **Gift/Bookshop** No

Los Angeles **Architect** Richard Neutra **Year** 1956
Address 1322 Dover Road, Santa Barbara, CA 93103

Open to Public No **Free Entrance** No **Café/Restaurant** No
Overnight Accommodation No **Gift/Bookshop** No

Slavin House

79

Another exception to Santa Barbara's single-minded commitment to the Spanish Mission style is Richard Neutra's Slavin House, a low-lying home projecting off the side of a hilltop in the winding hills of northern Santa Barbara. The single-story residence shows a striking similarity to Beverley David Thorne's Case Study House #26, otherwise known as the Bethlehem Steel House, in San Rafael. Like that home, the flat, exposed timber chassis, hovering on steel stilts, cantilevers out over the canyon. In this case it contains a row of continuous glazing on one side and a projecting deck on the other. Inside, open spaces, an exposed wood ceiling and lovely plywood built-in furniture give the home a raw but refined essence, opening to ocean views to the south and to a patio and pool area to the east. Neutra was one of the few Modernists to work in Santa Barbara, also completing the Tremaine House (1642 Moore Road, still beautiful, but difficult to see from the street), the Chase House (4254 Cresta Avenue, since destroyed and replaced with a regrettable 'McMansion'), the Bell House (222 East Constance Avenue, altered with an insensitive red tile roof) and the Shinoda House (1124 Camino Del Rio, destroyed) in and around the city. ■

California Lutheran University

Los Angeles **Architect** Jefferson A. Elmendorf **Year** 1962
Address 60 West Olsen Road, Thousand Oaks, CA 91360

Open to Public Yes **Free Entrance** Yes **Café/Restaurant** Yes
Overnight Accommodation No **Gift/Bookshop** Yes

Do you or anyone you know love Modernist barrel vaults? If so, head directly to California Lutheran University. It's about as deep into the San Fernando Valley as you can get, but you'll thank us. Incorporated in 1959 on the undulating 225-acre (91-hectare) site of a former ranch in Thousand Oaks, the campus is organized into four quadrants, the south side containing most of the academic buildings. Many were designed by architect Jefferson A. Elmendorf, who masterminded eight white concrete barrel-roofed buildings here. Most were clad in brick, stucco and glass, while the centerpiece was a large round structure fronted in floor-to-ceiling glazing. Elmendorf chose the buildings' scalloped forms – with deep overhangs to shield from the valley's sun – because they required no structural support, thus creating open, uncluttered spaces inside. They also reflected the school's vision of itself as an optimistic, futuristic place. The cluster was going to be a shopping center to employ students while raising revenue for the campus, but that vision was never realized and most became academic facilities. The central building is now the Centrum Café. The charming campus (save for all the surface parking) has grown considerably since then, but this unique core is still in remarkably good shape. ■

80

California Lutheran University

Building unforgettable, organic-shaped homes 'in total compatibility with the environment' was Harry Gesner's specialty. Arguably the most dramatic is his Wave House, jutting over the sandy beach in Watkins Cove, Malibu. The glass-clad residence, with its bulky curving balcony, floats on stilts over a concrete base. It's topped with (of course) a wave-shaped, green copper-tiled, deeply overhanging roof, its beams extending in sharp points, recalling oceanic forms and Polynesian design. Inside, the roof's dual curves – opening up large living spaces – are supported by thin laminated beams that branch out like trees. Bedrooms are located in the home's two-story recti-linear portion, clad with white vertical siding. Gesner reportedly sketched his first designs for the home while bobbing in the ocean on his surfboard. It is said that its design inspired Jørn Utzon, who designed the Sydney Opera House (1973). Gesner designed a trio of houses on the beach here, including the so-called High Tech House and the Lighthouse House. None are accessible via the road, so, like John Lautner's nearby Stevens House (page 134), you have to amble onto the beach to get a look. His nearby Eagle's Watch House (21363 Rambla Vista), visible from the Pacific Coast Highway, is known in town for being the cliff-side residence that looks like a giant Viking longship. ■

Los Angeles **Architect** Harry Gesner **Year** 1957
Address 33602 Pacific Coast Highway, Malibu, CA 90265

Open to Public No **Free Entrance** No **Café/Restaurant** No
Overnight Accommodation No **Gift/Bookshop** No

Los Angeles **Architect** Craig Ellwood **Year** 1957
Address 24514 Malibu Road, Los Angeles, CA 90265

Open to Public No **Free Entrance** No **Café/Restaurant** No
Overnight Accommodation No **Gift/Bookshop** No

82

Hunt House

After moving to Los Angeles from Washington DC, Victor and Elizabeth Hunt were determined to have a modern home on the beach in Malibu. According to author Neil Jackson, after seeing Craig Ellwood's Pierson house down the street from their lot, Elizabeth exclaimed, 'Oh, this is what I've been looking for.' The single-story, H-shaped home, which Ellwood worked on with his talented associate Jerrold Lomax, consists of two rectangular volumes raised on steel stilts on a steep ocean-front site. From the road you can see twin garages, fronted by bluish-green panels, divided by a frosted-glass entryway. This piece is connected by a staircase to the residential unit, open to the ocean via floor-to-ceiling windows and built around an exposed central patio. You get slight hints at how this unfolds if you peer over the fence or look around the home's sides. The view was once much clearer before development popped up around the house. At the time of publication, the home was still standing, but like many Mid-Century Modern gems, it faces an existential threat. In 2013 the current homeowner filed for a permit to demolish the house and replace it with a twenty-eight-foot-tall (eight-meter) two-story residence. The City of Malibu has postponed a decision on the home's fate, but there is a sad chance that it could be gone by the time you get there. ■

Stevens House

83

Los Angeles **Architect** John Lautner **Year** 1968
Address 23524 Malibu Colony Road, Malibu, CA 90265

Open to Public No **Free Entrance** No **Café/Restaurant** No
Overnight Accommodation No **Gift/Bookshop** No

Don't even bother trying to visit John Lautner's Stevens House from the street. There's enough security in its celebrity-filled community, Malibu Bay Colony, to protect El Chapo. But you can easily reach it via the beach, a short stroll from the Malibu Lagoon. The house, which sits on a large platform right on the ocean, is made up of two overlapping concrete curves that not only mimic the waves and provide shade and shelter, but also bring light and views into most of the narrow lot through giant, ocean-facing panes of douglas fir-framed glass. This embrace of the elements stands in stark contrast to the home's generic neighbors. The home, sided with concrete and timber, contains five rooms, although you'd never be able to tell from the beach side. The curve of the walls allows them to act as both dividers and ceilings. A mezzanine connects the double-height first floor with the second. Apparently the original owner, Dan Stevens, interviewed several architects for the job and they all told him it would be impossible. For Lautner there was no such thing as impossible. ■

84

Congregational Church of Northridge

The tile-covered, pyramidal roof of A. Quincy Jones' Congregational Church of Northridge is easy to miss when you drive by. But once you spot it, your brain starts to churn, trying to figure out exactly what it is: A teepee? A spaceship? But it's the interior that truly sticks in your head; it feels like being inside a cave, a cabin and a sacred space at the same time. That pyramid is supported by gridded timber rafters and a frame of large laminated timber columns, which meet near the top in a crucifix formation. Above this, light flows in through a pyramidal skylight, which mimics the sun and via hanging lights that recall the stars. The laminated beams extend down beyond the roof's eaves, touching the ground outside. Lower bands of windows bring the surrounding landscape inside. Originally there was no glazing here, nor entry doors; it was a semi-covered shed with a soil threshold. But the congregation balked at the noise and the intrusion of outside elements. Nonetheless, when you're here you're still far removed from the suburban context, focused on the spiritual and natural worlds. ■

Los Angeles **Architect** A. Quincy Jones **Year** 1962
Address 9659 Balboa Boulevard, Northridge, CA 91325

Open to Public Yes **Free Entrance** Yes **Café/Restaurant** No
Overnight Accommodation No **Gift/Bookshop** No

Balboa Highlands Eichler Homes

85

Los Angeles **Architect** Various **Year** 1964
Address Darla Avenue, Los Angeles, CA 91344 and surrounding streets

Open to Public No **Free Entrance** No **Café/Restaurant** No
Overnight Accommodation No **Gift/Bookshop** No

Joseph Eichler, legend has it, fell in love with Modernism after living for a short time in Frank Lloyd Wright's Bazett Residence in Northern California and he went on to build most of his empire in that region. But the Eichler Homes company was also active in Southern California, developing five tracts in newly developing areas of Los Angeles – two north of the city at Balboa Highlands and and Grenada Hills and three south of the city, all in Orange County. An elegant case study for the SoCal version is Balboa Highlands, located on an elevated site in Granada Hills, on the northern edge of the valley just south of Santa Clarita. The Eichlers recruited some of the same talented architects involved up north, including Jones & Emmons and Claude Oakland. Like most Eichler buildings, the simple homes were largely closed to the street, but opened up dramatically inside with clerestory windows, skylights and floor-to-ceiling glass walls opening to central atria and back yards. Succulents and other semi-arid landscaping merge with the area's rolling landscape, dotted with cyprus and eucalyptus trees. With their smart, determinedly Modernist forms, the Highlands have become one of the most popular destinations in the city for film shoots, TV shows and commercials, despite their considerable distance from Hollywood. ■

85

Balboa Highlands Eichler Homes

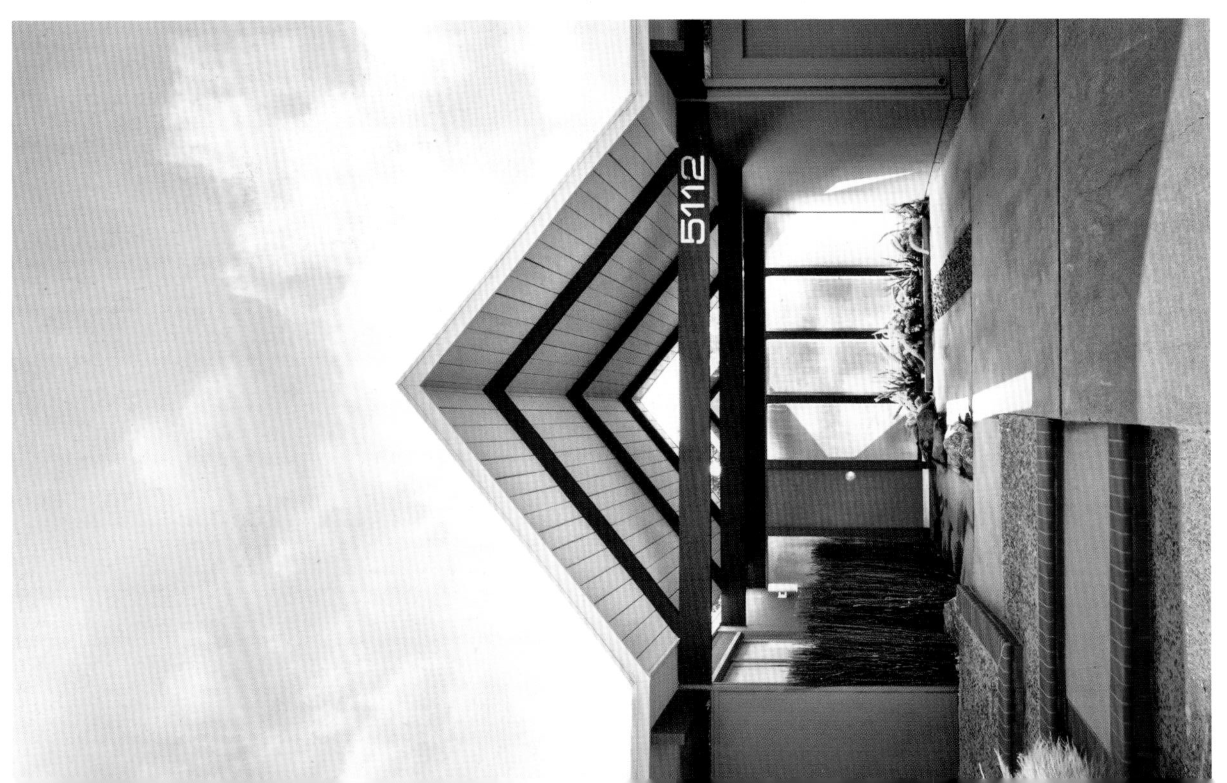

Sepulveda Unitarian Universalist Society

98

Los Angeles **Architect** Frank Ehrenthal **Year** 1964
Address 9550 Haskell Avenue, North Hills, CA 91343

Open to Public No **Free Entrance** No **Café/Restaurant** No
Overnight Accommodation No **Gift/Bookshop** No

One of the strangest of Los Angeles' very strange structures is the Sepulveda Unitarian Universalist Society, also known as 'The Onion', in the San Fernando Valley neighborhood of North Hills. It's nicknamed this for good reason: the bulbous, red-shingled building, sited on the woodsy five-acre (two-hectare) site of a former horse ranch, looks exactly like an onion. Or a piece of garlic. It could be either, really. The architect, Frank Ehrenthal, a Universalist himself and a student of Richard Neutra, designed the church in the round so every congregant could face each other, with no hierarchy. (One of the church's fundamental principles is inclusiveness.) Inside, the building is lined with a beautiful array of slatted wood, blond laminated beams and copper ribs, each still in exquisite condition after all these years. The floor steps down as you walk to the center, where the sound bounces back down, making loud speeches a challenge. Another acoustical oddity: if you whisper along the edges of the sanctuary, you can be heard by someone on the other side. A wood-shingled building adjacent contains the church's offices and beyond that is a lovely playground for nursery school children. ■

87

Sunkist Headquarters

Leave it to the San Fernando Valley to produce a Modernist ziggurat erected to the glory of Sunkist. Especially when the area had recently been paved over to replace orange groves with tract housing and offices. But all ironies aside, AC Martin's Sunkist Headquarters, a glass box floating on sloping concrete columns, covered with a progressively widening gridded concrete shell, is a remarkable example of late Modern sculpturalism. Some say the edifice – dramatically visible from the nearby 101 Freeway – resembles an orange crate. AC Martin, who built many of downtown Los Angeles' most notable skyscrapers, including Bank of America Plaza, City National Plaza and Union Bank, was just as busy building offices in the suburbs. At sunset the waning light contrasts light and dark frontages and accentuates the long shadows created by all the deep angles. You enter via tall stairs, which all seems vaguely Mayan. The large surface parking lot makes the building feel lonely, but it's softened with remarkable rows of, naturally, orange trees. Sunkist recently left its headquarters for (slightly) greener pastures in Santa Clarita. But this inverted pyramid remains a monument to creative corporate architecture in unlikely places. ■

Los Angeles **Architect** AC Martin **Year** 1969
Address 14130 Riverside Drive, Los Angeles, CA 91423

Open to Public No **Free Entrance** No **Café/Restaurant** No
Overnight Accommodation No **Gift/Bookshop** No

Casa de Cadillac

88

How better to celebrate Los Angeles' car culture than to visit its most famous Modernist car dealership? Originally named for its owner, Don Lee Cadillac, the Casa was designed by Randall Duell, who was not just an architect but a Hollywood set designer. His background shows in the building's dramatic presence on Ventura Boulevard. The building, topped with elegant cursive neon letters, is fronted by huge sheets of glass – to show off the sizable merchandise, of course – with a blocky stucco tower rising above. Inside, the cars are the focus but now that Cadillacs look like all other cars, the building – with its terrazzo floors and large tropical plants – is more interesting than the vehicles. Walk beyond the showroom and you'll come upon an outdoor courtyard with more landscaping and slatted screens giving a vaguely tropical vibe. The building recently underwent an extensive renovation, bringing it back to its original glitzy glory. Also take a look at the garage, with its zigzag trusses, a fun throwback to a time when even raw industrial spaces had architectural character. ■

Los Angeles **Architect** Randall Duell and Philip Conklin **Year** 1949
Address 14401 Ventura Boulevard, Los Angeles, CA 91423

Open to Public Yes **Free Entrance** Yes **Café/Restaurant** No
Overnight Accommodation No **Gift/Bookshop** No

68

St. Michael and All Angels Episcopal Church

Los Angeles **Architect** Jones & Emmons **Year** 1962
Address 3646 Coldwater Canyon Avenue, Los Angeles, CA 91604

Open to Public Yes **Free Entrance** Yes **Café/Restaurant** No
Overnight Accommodation No **Gift/Bookshop** No

As you wind through Coldwater Canyon Avenue from the San Fernando Valley to the Hollywood Hills, one of the first things you'll see is Jones & Emmons' triangular-shaped St. Michael and All Angels Episcopal Church, one of four churches that the firm built and one of two in the valley. The four-hundred-seat structure, tucked up against a steep, ivy-covered hillside, smartly merges engineering and spirituality. Its defining element, the tapering shingled roof, is fronted by a glass panel facade and supported by steel trusses, whose triangular red anchors rest just outside the building. Inside, the space is shaped by repeating laminated timber beams, which extend from the low eaves and come together at the tip of the ceiling, where a strip of narrow skylights bring in light from above. They then bend and shoot upward toward the sky, like palms held together in prayer. A rear window wall gives congregants a view of the dense foliage behind the church. Combined with gardens on both sides, the landscaping envelopes the complex in idyllic calm. The firm designed several more ambitious buildings for the church that were never built. ■

Walstrom House

Rising impossibly high on a secluded street in once-bohemian Laurel Canyon, John Lautner's Walstrom House is less renowned than the architect's iconic homes like Chemosphere and Garcia (pages 170 and 172), but it is no less breathtaking. Seen from the road, the home, built into the rise of a steep canyon and surrounded by large, gnarled trees, is an exercise in neck craning. Facing you is a giant wall of glass, save for a couple of blond timber diamond patterns. The triangular composition, which recalls a Swiss chalet, a log cabin and a James Bond villain's lair, hovers over a lonely first floor and carport. Its roofline angles steeply, suggesting an even greater loft than it has and emphatically opening interior spaces, which include an open living area, a wooden loft, a library, floating stairs and varied spaces and hidden gardens that blur inside and out. Inside the home, with its exposed rafters, large laminated beams and constant views outside, you feel like a bird that might fly into a glass wall at any moment. The home's flanks are less transparent than the front, but still largely open to the thick foliage around them. ■

Los Angeles **Architect** John Lautner **Year** 1969
Address 10500 Selkirk Lane, Los Angeles, CA 90077

Open to Public No **Free Entrance** No **Café/Restaurant** No
Overnight Accommodation No **Gift/Bookshop** No

Los Angeles **Architect** Craig Ellwood **Year** 1953
Address 1811 Bel Air Road, Los Angeles, CA 90077

Open to Public No **Free Entrance** No **Café/Restaurant** No
Overnight Accommodation No **Gift/Bookshop** No

There are few instances in which I would recommend driving miles to see not much more than a carport. This house is one of those instances. First of all, the long drive is through the curving hills of Bel Air, so you'll get to see some of the biggest, wackiest, most ridiculous celebrity mansions along the way to this Modernist mecca. Once you arrive you'll see the first of Craig Ellwood's three homes for *Art & Architecture* magazine's Case Study House Program. The other two were Case Study House #18, in Beverly Hills and Case Study House #4, also in Bel Air. From the street, the glass, steel and wooden box is screened by translucent glass panels, while the carport is open to views. The frosted wall also faces an interior courtyard, which fronts the bedrooms. The home's interior walls are floating panels set between steel posts, extending out onto an exterior hillside terrace. The home is full of built-in furniture and a huge natural rock fireplace extends through the floor-to-ceiling glass walls to the patio. ■

Sheats Goldstein House

Few residences in the world tap into our desire to be both sheltered and elevated like John Lautner's Sheats Goldstein House. Sited at the height of a south-facing canyon-side lot in Bel Air, the structure, built for Paul and Helen Sheats, is organized as a series of unforgettable experiences. You enter through a narrow concrete hall, which opens to a wildly tropical garden with a glass walkway bridging a koi pond. From here the main space unwraps until you reach the living room, with its spectacular gridded, angular roof (Lautner pierced its star-like holes with drinking glasses) opening via a tall glass wall to a large canyon-side balcony and infinity pool. Spaces weave in and out of the jungle-like forest, exposing you to views of greenery and of the expanding city through frameless windows. All the while thick interior walls and compressed spaces provide a sense of enclosure. An adjacent cliff-side tennis court is now being redeveloped by the home's second owner, eccentric real estate mogul James Goldstein, into an office-nightclub-private resort. He's also built a James Turrell *Skyspace* in the canyon, accessible via steep, blade-like stairs. The house is not visible from the street, however it's worth checking with local architecture organizations such as the American Institute of Architects, Los Angeles, and the MAK Center for tours. ■

Los Angeles **Architect** John Lautner **Year** 1963
Address 10104 Angelo View Drive, Los Angeles, CA 90210

Open to Public No **Free Entrance** No **Café/Restaurant** No
Overnight Accommodation No **Gift/Bookshop** No

Los Angeles **Architect** Ray Kappe **Year** 1968
Address 12256 Canna Road, Los Angeles, CA 90049

Open to Public No **Free Entrance** No **Café/Restaurant** No
Overnight Accommodation No **Gift/Bookshop** No

Gould Residence

Just around the corner from Crestwood Hills (page 146), at the very top of the Brentwood slopes, lies Ray Kappe's Gould Residence, which takes the planning of a Greek mountainside village and inserts it into a Modernist context. The home, clad in dark wood siding, drops forty-two feet (thirteen meters) over a precipitous slope from the roof of the master bedroom to the terraced garden and infinity pool below. From the street you can begin to see the structure step down its canyon site. What you can't see, unfortunately, is a double-height living space clad in gigantic windows (framed by thick timber beams) that envelopes you in the canyon. In fact, just about every space inside feels as though you're wobbling on the edge of a precipice. Heading downhill, Canna Road turns into Tigertail, which is a super place to see more architecture, from Mid-Century Modern to contemporary. For instance take time to look at Raul Garduno's Franks House (1249 N Tigertail), with its Asian influences and giant glass walls and Patrick Tighe's 'Tigertail', a contemporary residence that looks like origami, with its folded planes and soaring roofline. Architect William Krisel's own home (568 Tigertail) was once located here, but was torn down in 2014. ■

In 1946 a group of four musicians formed a cooperative housing group called the Mutual Housing Association (MHA). Its lofty goal was to build 'innovative structures that could be erected simply and cheaply and that reflected the politically progressive visions of the founding members.' Purchasing eight-hundred acres (324 hectares) in the Santa Monica Mountains, they put together a team of designers that included architects A. Quincy Jones and Whitney R. Smith and engineer Edgardo Contini and the plans grew beyond houses to include a nursery school, tennis courts, swimming pool and a market. Homes ranged from 1,100 to 3,000 square feet (100 to 280 square meters), costing $10,000 to $30,000. Other well-respected architects became involved, like Craig Ellwood, Rodney Walker, Ray Kappe, William S. Beckett and Richard Neutra. MHA grew to upward of five-hundred members and the community, Crestwood Hills, became legendary around the design world. For good reason. This collection of rustic modern homes built of redwood, plywood, concrete and glass and tucked into the hillsides is a revelation. There are now over three-hundred, all built under strict guidelines. The original twenty-nine are bold yet modest, experimental yet practical. Perhaps the most famous is 990 Hanley Avenue, which was once the MHA offices: a glass and wood residence that bridges the canyon and the road beneath it. But walk and drive around to take in the stunning variety of forms and ideas and the notion that middle-class housing can be sublime. ■

Los Angeles **Architect** A. Quincy Jones and others **Year** 1950s
Address 1016 Hanley Avenue, Los Angeles, CA 90049

Open to Public No **Free Entrance** No **Café/Restaurant** No
Overnight Accommodation No **Gift/Bookshop** No

Los Angeles **Architect** Frank Lloyd Wright **Year** 1939
Address 449 N Skyewiay Road, Brentwood Heights, CA 90049

Open to Public No **Free Entrance** No **Café/Restaurant** No
Overnight Accommodation No **Gift/Bookshop** No

Of Frank Lloyd Wright's many California homes, only one is considered a Usonian – his single-story residences built as affordable alternatives for the middle class. That would be the Sturges House, perched atop a steep hill in Brentwood, which is ironically now one of the least affordable areas of Los Angeles. Built for George D. Sturges under the supervision of Wright's protégé John Lautner (yes, that John Lautner), the home consists of a complex interlocking combination of a concrete base, staggered brick walls and a large redwood banded balcony. Much of the home's east end juts over the hillside, bringing to mind Wright's Fallingwater in Pennsylvania or the prow of a large boat. While the open-planned home appears gigantic from the street below, it only contains 900 square feet (84 square meters) of interior living space. But the wraparound deck adds another 380 square feet (35 square meters), a perfect combination in Southern California. Inside, Wright's artful built-in furniture, exposed beams and bricks and masterful succession of spaces makes the most of every inch. At sunset the light makes the red bricks glow, giving it a profound presence that stands in stark contrast to many of the neighborhood's tacky faux-Mediterranean-style buildings. ■

Los Angeles **Architect** Rudolph Schindler **Year** 1949
Address 175 Greenfield Avenue, Los Angeles, CA 90049

Open to Public No **Free Entrance** No **Café/Restaurant** No
Overnight Accommodation No **Gift/Bookshop** No

This narrow, multi-level residence in Westwood, accessible via a steep stair along its edge, is one of the architect's greatest surprises – the closest thing to a treehouse you'll find in his extraordinary repertoire. The stucco, wood and concrete block composition steps up a sharply sloping, ivy-covered lot. Its light beige cruciform shape is marked with dramatically protruding dark wood balconies and trellises. Its dramatically pitched roof, which appears ready to launch into the street, is clad in blue corrugated fiberglass, now partially covered in wood to reduce heat gain. Adolph Tischler, an artist and silversmith, discovered Schindler through *Arts and Architecture* magazine and appropriately designed much of its furnishings and silverware. Taking advantage of views and light, the top level of the home contains the living room, with guest rooms below, separated by a large gap in the house. Below that is a carport that was once used as Tischler's studio. Looking at the home from the side you can see it float over its woodsy surroundings; from here the home resembles a series of bridges as much as anything. The home was at first considered an eyesore in the neighborhood and Tischler told the *L.A. Times* that some tried to sign a petition to stop it. Now it's a landmarked treasure. ■

97

Charles E. Young Research Library, UCLA

While its Westwood campus opened in 1929, University of California, Los Angeles' (UCLA) significant legacy of Modernist buildings didn't take off until Wurdeman and Becket (later Welton Becket & Associates) became the school's supervising architects in 1948. From this point on, the campus was blessed with structures by many of the region's Modernist stalwarts. Of the many fine buildings here, standouts include Maynard Lyndon's Bunche Hall, a twelve-story social sciences building that hovers on two-story-high concrete columns, opening up to a large, heavily planted internal courtyard. The rectangular slab building is accentuated by projecting square windows designed to filter sunlight and allow for natural ventilation. Not far from here is A. Quincy Jones' Charles E. Young Research Library (pictured), a simple, gridded white building floating over an outdoor lobby and, beyond that, a lovely paved plaza. Other must-sees include Austin, Field & Fry's post-and-beam Faculty Center, Smith & Williams' Sunset Canyon Recreation Center and Ralph Cornell's gently undulating Franklin Murphy Sculpture Garden, featuring works by Henry Moore, Jacques Lipschitz and several more. On the edge of campus is Richard Neutra's University Elementary School – a series of brick bars and small classroom pavilions populating a beautiful wooded ravine. ■

Los Angeles **Architect** A. Quincy Jones, Maynard Lyndon and others
Year 1959 **Address** 405 Hilgard Avenue, Los Angeles, CA 90095

Open to Public Yes **Free Entrance** Yes **Café/Restaurant** Yes
Overnight Accommodation No **Gift/Bookshop** Yes

Down the block from Richard Neutra's Strathmore Apartments (page 151, opposite) is another remarkable multi-family housing experiment, John Lautner's yellow-colored Sheats Apartments. Once known as 'L'Horizon' or 'The Treehouse', the building features curving, mushroom-like forms and squared canopies and balconies jutting toward the street. The eight-unit building, built for well-known artists Helen Taylor Sheats and her husband, professor Paul Sheats (the same couple that later commissioned the Sheats Goldstein House – page 144), is a Lautner-like departure from the typical: a series of drum-shaped volumes, with generous curved windows shaded by thin overhangs, which step up the landscaped hillside – including trees, plants and even a waterfall – connected by bowed pathways and shaded by a 35-foot-wide (11-meter) platform. Each of the building's self-contained units have their own views and their own walls, as well as personal balconies, decks and outdoor gardens. Yet they still maintain what Lautner called 'the infinite variety of individual life within some kind of total world.' Unfortunately they're also in poor condition, brought on by hard-partying UCLA students (this block is a center for student Greek life). It's strangely fitting that such a great work by Lautner, who by the end of his life felt bitter from his lack of recognition, would suffer the same fate. ■

Los Angeles **Architect** John Lautner **Year** 1949
Address 10919 Strathmore Drive, Los Angeles, CA 90024

Open to Public No **Free Entrance** No **Café/Restaurant** No
Overnight Accommodation No **Gift/Bookshop** No

Los Angeles **Architect** Richard Neutra **Year** 1937
Address 11005 Strathmore Drive, Los Angeles, CA 90024

Open to Public No **Free Entrance** No **Café/Restaurant** No
Overnight Accommodation No **Gift/Bookshop** No

Strathmore Apartments

99

Many of the architectural icons in Westwood get overlooked, especially those near UCLA, where students are more interested in flirting or rushing to class than examining buildings. A good example is Strathmore Drive, which contains two of the most remarkable multi-family apartments in the region. Richard Neutra's Strathmore Apartments reveal one of his overlooked talents: planning. Like Gregory Ain and Rudolph Schindler, Neutra had a rare gift for seamlessly merging single- and multi-family typologies. From the street the gray stucco apartments, with their International Style ribbon windows and silver metallic overhangs, look like houses. But walk up their flanking stairs and you'll discover eight units in four buildings, stepping up the hillside in smartly varied configurations. All are enveloped in a rich composition of Southern California landscaping. Units are modestly sized, but all borrow space and light in a way that makes them feel spacious, gracious and Californian. A few blocks down the street is John Lautner's off-yellow Sheats Apartments, its curving forms and square canopies jutting toward the street (page 150, opposite). ■

Twenty-Eighth Church of Christ, Scientist

This one-of-a-kind edifice, located on the eastern edge of the University of California, Los Angeles (UCLA) campus in Westwood, doesn't look like much when you approach. But it's a worthy illustration of the subtle mastery of Maynard Lyndon, who disdained ostentation and was an expert with space and light. The sacred space's facade is fronted by a curved concrete screen punctured with small holes. It looks fortress-like, but when seen from the glassy lobby behind, it allows soft light to filter through in an enchanting way. The interior resumes this language of hidden beauty. Proceeding past a wall of blank doors you enter the sloped, mesmerizing auditorium. Concrete walls extending from either side of the stage are glazed to about a third of their height, revealing lush landscaping in the garden courtyard behind, but still maintaining focus on the solemn interior, whose scattered dots of light above recall the night sky. Walk through a covered arcade along Hilgard to enter this hidden courtyard, which includes sunken gardens, grassy islands and a variety of trees. The formally obsessed younger generation of architects could learn a lot from Lyndon, who was able to create architectural power not through Instagram-worthy stage sets, but through light, movement and spatial transition. ■

Los Angeles **Architect** Maynard Lyndon **Year** 1955
Address 1018 Hilgard Avenue, Los Angeles, CA 90024

Open to Public Yes **Free Entrance** Yes **Café/Restaurant** No
Overnight Accommodation No **Gift/Bookshop** Yes

Los Angeles **Architect** Oscar Niemeyer **Year** 1964
Address 1911 La Mesa Drive, Santa Monica, CA 90402

Open to Public No **Free Entrance** No **Café/Restaurant** No
Overnight Accommodation No **Gift/Bookshop** No

Brazilian master Oscar Niemeyer designed the entire Brazilian capital, Brasilía, as well as astonishing, sculptural buildings around the world. But he only built one residence in the United States: the Strick House, on quiet La Mesa Drive in Santa Monica. There's a white brick fence in front, but the building is clearly visible over this barrier, particularly from the walkway entrance. The T-shaped, single-story home is sited in a jungle of sensuous landscaping, with tropical curving palm trees, reddish rocks, lush succulents and meandering paths. These lead your eye toward a dramatic International Style composition of white brick, glass walls and exposed posts and beams, radiating toward you and creating a rhythmic syncopation of form, light and shadow. Note the painterly sky-blue door. Yes, it's all very Brazilian. The back of the house, which isn't visible from the street, features a luxurious pool area and a clear view of the Santa Monica Mountains. Niemeyer designed the house for Hollywood writers and producers Anne and Joseph Strick, who moved here from their home at Gregory Ain's Mar Vista Tract. It was subsequently renovated by house collectors Michael and Gabrielle Boyd. La Mesa Drive also features homes by Lloyd Wright (2323), J. R. Davidson (2501) and Paul Williams (2209). ■

Rustic Canyon Kappe Colony

102

Los Angeles **Architect** Ray Kappe **Year** 1960s (various)
Address 715 Brooktree Road, Los Angeles, CA 90272

Open to Public No **Free Entrance** No **Café/Restaurant** No
Overnight Accommodation No **Gift/Bookshop** No

One of Southern California's greatest treasures is Ray Kappe, who not only created one of the richest bodies of architectural work in the area's history, but also helped found the architecture programs at SCI-Arc (Southern California Institute of Architecture) and Cal Poly Pomona. The most extensive collection of Kappe buildings is located on Brooktree Road in Los Angeles' Rustic Canyon, including his own home. That building, perched steeply uphill from the street, bridges over not just the canyonesque hillside, but also a spring-fed creek. Its laminated-fir support beams span six concrete towers and inside lofty spaces are staggered around a double-height living room, with view corridors connecting virtually the entire space. Massive windows all around make you feel like you're in a tree house in the woods, creating an unforgettable sensorial experience. In both directions from the residence are similarly impressive Kappe homes at numbers 680, 681, 717 (pictured above), 727, 739 (pictured right) and 755 Brooktree Road. Ranging from post-and-beam cedar cabins to multi-story timber and glass compounds, they all tap into a primal sensation of uplift, excitement and raw architectural power, as well as providing a sensual combination of building and nature, maximizing both in a way that few architects have been able to do. ■

102

Rustic Canyon Kappe Colony

Freedman Residence

103

Once a haven for artists and free spirits, Pacific Palisades is largely off limits to the creative classes these days. But that doesn't mean you can't visit the glorious remnants of a more egalitarian age, in a windswept, inspiring setting with killer views of the ocean. A house with one of the best settings of all is Richard Neutra's Freedman Residence, located at the very end of Via De La Paz, edging a jogging trail that looks down on the Pacific, hundreds of feet below. The original home consists of an open-planned, L-shaped volume, its oceanfront edge clad entirely in a band of large panes of clear glass. A recent addition by Santa Monica-based Peter Grueneisen added a stepped second story that provides unimpeded views and is, miraculously, almost impossible to differentiate from the first from the outside. The pre-existing home flows right into the new space, both fitted with minimal adornments and lots of white. On closer inspection the new segment is full of modern amenities, larger rooms and contemporary touches like hardwood paneling that buildings in Neutra's time seldom had. The new composition opens to a pool in back, but for the visitor, the highlight is taking in the original form straight on, then going for a walk along the cliffs. ■

Los Angeles **Architect** Richard Neutra **Year** 1949
Address 315 Via De La Paz, Los Angeles, CA 90272

Open to Public No **Free Entrance** No **Café/Restaurant** No
Overnight Accommodation No **Gift/Bookshop** No

Los Angeles **Architect** Richard Neutra **Year** 1948
Address 219 Chautauqua Boulevard, Los Angeles, CA 90272

Open to Public No **Free Entrance** No **Café/Restaurant** No
Overnight Accommodation No **Gift/Bookshop** No

Case Study House #20

Just down the curving drive from the Eames House (page 158) is a residence that's often overlooked in the pantheon of the Case Study House Program: Case Study House #20. Not to be confused with Case Study House #21, which was built in the Hollywood Hills for a different Bailey family, this gorgeous, L-shaped home typifies Neutra's ability to connect architecture with nature. The post-and-beam building's continuous long, low walls of glass are topped by deep overhanging wood eaves. A particularly large sliding door opens the south wall of the living area to the garden, while bedrooms open up to this green space as well. The edifice has seen significant change. Two early additions added new bedrooms, a new playroom and a pool. A seven-thousand-square-foot (650 square-meter), four-bedroom home was built alongside Case Study House #20 in 2010 which is now used as the main residence, with the Case Study House serving as guest accommodation. Neutra, who designed over three-hundred houses, appeared on the cover of Time Magazine in 1949, shortly after Case Study House #20 was completed. 'I feel that his house does not just sit here passively… it draws me to it', Dr. Bailey wrote to Neutra in 1958. 'After ten years, students still come from all over the world and stand there in postures of reverence.' ■

Los Angeles **Architect** Charles and Ray Eames **Year** 1949
Address 203 Chautauqua Boulevard, Los Angeles, CA 90272

Open to Public Yes **Free Entrance** No **Café/Restaurant** No
Overnight Accommodation No **Gift/Bookshop** No

The Eames House, also known as Case Study House #8, is as delightfully quirky, magical and transformative as its creators, Charles and Ray Eames. Sited on a pastoral bluff, dappled with light through copious eucalyptus, acacia and pepper trees, the colorful, gridded steel home is a perfect combination of the 'less is more' ethos of the Bauhaus and the 'more is more' ethos of the Eames'. As per the dictates of the Case Study House Program, the design features pre-fabricated off-the-shelf materials, promoting the ideals of mass production. Large glass expanses overlap with gridded windows and solid white walls, like a Mondrian painting. Inside, double-height spaces flow from one to the next, showing off, of course, famous Eames furniture and other designs. Walking the dirt and stone path around the house feels like a Los Angeles rite of passage and it's the best way to take in the home's energy. The meadow around it is, to this author, a healing spot, particularly if you choose to sit in the grass, on a stump overlooking the Pacific, or on the swing hanging from one of the trees. While here you need to explore the colony of Case Study homes around the Eames House, including Eero Saarinen's Entenza House, Richard Neutra's Case Study House #20 (page 157) and Rodney Walker's Case Study House #18. ■

Eames House

Santa Monica Civic Auditorium

106

Los Angeles **Architect** Welton Becket & Associates **Year** 1958
Address 1855 Main Street, Santa Monica, CA 90401

Open to Public No **Free Entrance** No **Café/Restaurant** No
Overnight Accommodation No **Gift/Bookshop** No

Located just a few blocks from the beach, on the south end of the Santa Monica Civic Center, Welton Becket's Santa Monica Civic Auditorium has a peculiar retro flair that suggests Latin America, circa 1960. Highlighted by its six seventy-two-foot-tall (twenty-two-meter) masts – arguably suggestive of a classic Cadillac's fins – which support a long white canopy, the building is fronted by a glass curtain wall shielded by a large patterned cast concrete block wall. The building's hydraulically-operated tilting floor allows for it to be adjusted for various configurations, from trade shows to theater to concerts. It's hard to overestimate how cutting-edge that technology was when the complex opened. The building, looking lonely next to its large parking lot, is now mostly dormant, save for private events and filming rentals. A planned renovation was cancelled in 2012 when the city's redevelopment agency went under. This tenuous situation belies a rich past that includes hosting the Academy Awards from 1961 to 1968, not to mention concerts by Frank Sinatra, the Eagles and the Rolling Stones. One only hopes that someone with vision and lots of money chooses to restore this local fixture to its former glory. ■

Life isn't as elegant as it used to be. But you can get a taste of the sophisticated excitement of a bygone era at Minoru Yamasaki's Century Plaza Hotel, a curved monolith made up of an endless, hypnotic grid of glassy bays and concrete balconies. And it's glammed up with accents of anodized aluminum, courtesy of developer Alcoa (Aluminum Company of America). The sizable motor court is classic sixties-era carphilia, indicative of a place where walking was considered passé. A sunken court in front is strangely barren, but somehow still impressive. Inside, the long, thin lobby focuses on a curved marble bar and two large bars occupy either end of the hotel. To keep the lobby open, shops, restaurants and a ballroom were all buried below ground. Rooms have glass sliding doors that open onto the sizable balconies. It's all been renovated but the Mid-Century Modern essentials, like terrazzo floors and majestic chandeliers, harken to a classier time. In 2009 the building was threatened with demolition, but was saved by a coalition led by the Los Angeles Conservancy and architecture activist, actress Diane Keaton. ■

Los Angeles **Architect** Minoru Yamasaki **Year** 1966
Address 2025 Avenue of the Stars, Los Angeles, CA 90067

Open to Public No **Free Entrance** No **Café/Restaurant** Yes
Overnight Accommodation Yes **Gift/Bookshop** No

107 Century Plaza Hotel

The Twin Towers still exist to some extent in Los Angeles. You need to head to Century City, that most modern (and least walkable) of neighborhoods, master planned by Welton Becket and the Alcoa Aluminum Company of America on the former site of 20th Century Fox Studios. Here Minoru Yamasaki, designer of the World Trade Center in New York, dreamed up the Century Plaza Towers, two forty-four-story triangular-planned glass high-rises, their verticality accentuated by vertical stripes of concrete and shiny aluminum. The pair, which are the tallest buildings in Los Angeles outside of downtown, rise above glassy bases. The towers are unique sculptures carving out their place in the skyline and providing tenants with floor-to-ceiling windows inside. It's their dialogue with each other, especially as they face inward, that makes them most effective. Like the Twin Towers, the buildings are framed largely with perimeter steel trusses, allowing for clear-span spaces inside. Between the structures a hardscape of stone and concrete has been replaced with lawns and flowering plants and trees. Glassy lower floors have also been updated and are no longer recognizable. While underappreciated, like much of Yamasaki's work, they've appeared as the backdrop to countless television shows, films and commercials and are as symbolic of corporate Los Angeles as any buildings in the city. ■

Los Angeles **Architect** Minoru Yamasaki **Year** 1975
Address 2049 Century Park East, Los Angeles, CA 90067

Open to Public Yes **Free Entrance** Yes **Café/Restaurant** Yes
Overnight Accommodation No **Gift/Bookshop** No

Perpetual Savings and Loan

109

Los Angeles **Architect** Edward Durell Stone **Year** 1961
Address 9720 Wilshire Boulevard, Los Angeles, CA 90212

Open to Public No **Free Entrance** No **Café/Restaurant** No
Overnight Accommodation No **Gift/Bookshop** No

Wilshire Boulevard in Beverly Hills contains a world-class mix of Modernist office and bank buildings, from cool glass boxes raised above heavy pedestals to concrete skyscrapers with tapered columns to ornamental New Formalist concoctions. Probably the best example of the last category is Edward Durell Stone's Perpetual Savings and Loan, rising behind a gray and white polka-dotted terrazzo plaza and circular fountain in the heart of the city's business district. The eight-story edifice, originally designed as an office for the Perpetual Savings and Loan Association, is actually quite simple: it's a boxy, glass-skinned tower. But it's covered in a bold concrete screen of continuous parabolic arches. 'This man from Arkansas has a way with boxes!' wrote one reporter for the *Kansas City Star* in 1964. The arches are tallest at the bottom, where you can visit the minimal lobby. Stone famously designed the Museum of Modern Art in New York in 1939. His later work, containing solid forms, ostentatious materials and gaudy ornament, was looked down on by his purist colleagues and predecessors from the Modernist movement. But for a while at least, he was one of the most influential architects in the world. ■

Located on the corner of Crescent Drive and Little Santa Monica Boulevard in Beverly Hills, this is the best remaining Modernist gas station in Los Angeles. It was designed by Gin Wong, a longtime employee of William Pereira's, who eventually became president of Pereira & Associates and went on to form Gin Wong Associates. Among many other projects, Wong helped design CBS Television Studios, the Transamerica Pyramid, Union Oil, the AT&T Building, Arco Towers and Geisel Library at University of California, San Diego (UCSD) (page 304). He's especially known for his work on the Theme Building at Los Angeles Airport (page 231) and he originally intended this gas station to be a complement to that space-age building. The station's swooping canopy floats on thin columns next to the gas pumps. Its white underside – lined with neon tubes that make it more impressive at night – resembles the hull of a massive ship. The roof is decorated on its side edges with a repeating pattern of simple red squares, creating a sense of movement and, now, nostalgia. The only station that comes close to this in the city is Steven Kanner's much more recent curved design for United Oil in Ladera Heights. While you're checking out Union 76, visit Beverly Hills' Spanish Revival City Hall and the new Wallis Annenberg Center for the Performing Arts, both located across the street. ■

Union 76 Gas Station

110

Los Angeles **Architect** William Pereira & Associates **Year** 1965
Address 427 N Crescent Drive, Beverly Hills, CA 90210

Open to Public Yes **Free Entrance** Yes **Café/Restaurant** No
Overnight Accommodation No **Gift/Bookshop** No

Los Angeles **Architect** Armet & Davis **Year** 1957
Address 470 – 478 N La Cienega Boulevard, Los Angeles, CA 90048

Open to Public Yes **Free Entrance** No **Café/Restaurant** Yes
Overnight Accommodation No **Gift/Bookshop** No

It took several decades, but 'Googie', the space-age, car-dominated style made famous in Mid-Century Modern Southern California diners, motels, car washes and other establishments is finally being recognized as a vital part of the region's architectural legacy. Perhaps the most famous example of Googie is the tan and bright-orange Norms on La Cienega, in West Hollywood, the flagship location of a chain of restaurants across the Southland. The design is by Armet & Davis, the most prolific practitioners of the form. You should explore more of the firm's Googie designs, including Pann's (page 234) and Mel's (14846 Ventura Boulevard). But start at Norms with a greasy plate of eggs, sausage and hash browns. If you're feeling really hungry, the pancakes are good too. But be prepared to wait. After all these years it's still exceedingly popular and you'll need to wait in line if you want breakfast. The building itself is textbook Googie style: a deeply overhanging, sharply angled roof, large glass walls and an open interior covered with blond flagstone. It's a wonderful time capsule that feels simultaneously futuristic and retro. ■

Los Angeles **Architect** Rudolph Schindler **Year** 1922
Address 835 N Kings Road, West Hollywood, CA 90069

Open to Public Yes **Free Entrance** No **Café/Restaurant** No
Overnight Accommodation No **Gift/Bookshop** Yes

How often do you get a chance to step inside one of the most famous houses in the world? The Schindler House, otherwise known as Rudolph Schindler's Kings Road House, is widely considered the architect's masterpiece. Decades ahead of its time, it personified the architect's progressive commitment to construction innovation, communal living and an indoor-outdoor lifestyle. He designed the house over a two-month period, in November and December 1921. Laid out on a pinwheel plan, which opened as much surface as possible to grassy gardens on all sides, the home was constructed using tilt up, precast concrete modules. He warmed the concrete with a Japanese-influenced system of floor-to-ceiling redwood-framed windows as well as clerestories. Sleeping porches pop up from the top level. The home also became a laboratory for invention. Schindler here devised famous homes like the Lovell Health House (page 184), the Lovell Beach House (page 258), Pueblo Ribera Court (page 310) and the Wolfe house and he hosted architectural and intellectual legends like Frank Lloyd Wright and his son Lloyd, Edward Weston, John Cage, the progressive dancer John Bovingdon, the poet Sadakichi Hartmann and Galka Scheyer. ■

Frank Lloyd Wright's son Lloyd started his own practice in 1916 and in 1927 built a studio and residence on North Doheny Drive in West Hollywood. Like many structures by Lloyd Wright and his father, its early completion date makes categorization misleading. The two were so far ahead of their time that their work fit the Mid-Century Modern mold even though the time period didn't. The heavy beige stucco residence, clad largely in patterned concrete blocks reminiscent of the elder Wright's textile block homes, looks like a ruin in the South American jungle; it's almost completely enveloped in thick ivy and messy vines, its interlocking volumes forming a dark, temple-like entry. A narrow band of windows, almost completely devoid of mullions, extends from a corner of the otherwise solid second story. Patterned block continues inside, where a shallow living room opens via a wall of sliding doors to a thin patio, surrounded by tall, ivy-covered walls and shaded by the home's large trees. Just up the street is Frank Lloyd Wright's Storer Residence (8161 Hollywood Boulevard), yet another patterned-block masterpiece at the foot of the Hollywood Hills. ■

Los Angeles **Architect** Lloyd Wright **Year** 1927
Address 858 N Doheny Drive, West Hollywood, CA 90069

Open to Public No **Free Entrance** No **Café/Restaurant** No
Overnight Accommodation No **Gift/Bookshop** No

Lloyd Wright Studio & Residence

Trousdale Estates

114

Just as Crestwood Hills has become the gold standard for middle-class Modernist housing tracts, its upscale sister is Trousdale Estates, located nearby at the tippy top of Beverly Hills. Indeed, Modernist architects did cater to luxury tastes, if you want to look at it that way. Developer Paul Trousdale, who built structures around the country, lured some of the best talent in Los Angeles – including A. Quincy Jones, Cliff May, Paul R. Williams, Richard Dorman, Harold Levitt, Allen Siple and even Wallace Neff and Lloyd Wright. They built in an eclectic range of styles, including modern interpretations of California Ranch, Hollywood Regency and Organic, Latin American, International Style and even Rustic Modern. Because of the area's concentration of wealth and fame, homes are often hidden behind one of the widest varieties of concrete and steel screens you'll ever see. But while much larger than those at Crestwood Hills, the homes are still mostly single story. The fantastic designs, views and cachet of the development drew stars like Elvis Presley, Frank Sinatra, Dean Martin, Ray Charles and even Groucho Marx and continues to draw celebs like Jennifer Aniston, Vera Wang, Jane Fonda and Ellen DeGeneres. It's worth a trip, to see how the other half (well, now, the 1 per cent) live. ■

Los Angeles **Architect** A. Quincy Jones, Cliff May among others **Year** 1960s
Address 1510 Loma Vista Drive, Beverly Hills, CA 90210 among others

Open to Public No **Free Entrance** No **Café/Restaurant** No
Overnight Accommodation No **Gift/Bookshop** No

Los Angeles **Architect** Pierre Koenig **Year** 1959
Address 9038 Wonderland Park Avenue, Los Angeles, CA 90046

Open to Public No **Free Entrance** No **Café/Restaurant** No
Overnight Accommodation No **Gift/Bookshop** No

Case Study House #21

115

Often overshadowed by Pierre Koenig's Case Study House #22 (page 178), located just a few minutes away, the Bailey House, also known as Case Study House #21, is remarkable in its own right. Koenig designed the home – set to become a prototype for modern, mass-produced, steel-framed living – for psychologist Walter Bailey and his wife, Mary. Located in a canyon site, the home doesn't have #22's sweeping views, so instead Koenig focused the drama on water; specifically, shallow pools that surround the entire building. The moats reflect the house vis ally, cool it, calm it and add psychological space. The square-shaped residence, clad in corrugated steel and edged by an open carport, is defined inside by open, continuous spaces that connect not just with each other but also with the outside environment, through front and back glass walls and sliding glass doors. Simple prefabricated components delineate uses and an open bathing courtyard in the home's center creates a further connection with the elements. The home had fallen victim to neglect and alteration until film producer Dan Cracchiolo bought the house and hired Koenig himself to undertake an ambitious and very successful renovation. The building is now owned by Korean gallery Seomi International.

■

Chemosphere

116

Los Angeles **Architect** John Lautner **Year** 1960
Address 7776 Torreyson Drive, Los Angeles, CA 90046

Open to Public No **Free Entrance** No **Café/Restaurant** No
Overnight Accommodation No **Gift/Bookshop** No

It's hard not to think that John Lautner's Chemosphere is the most spectacular house in Los Angeles and one of the most sublime in the world. Lautner designed the residence for aerospace engineer Leonard Malin, who offered the architect a small budget and an 'impossible' steep lot in the Hollywood Hills, on the edge of the San Fernando Valley. Instead of building into this slope, Lautner levitated the house above it on a single concrete column, imbedded into a buried concrete pedestal. Atop this stick, Lautner designed an eight-sided home, banded on all sides by horizontal glazing, attached to the pole via a series of protruding steel struts that work like an umbrella. The residence got its name from sealing manufacturer Chem Seal Corporation, which sponsored the home and it embodies California's brave (some might say reckless) mid-century embrace of technology – a sense that progress could conquer all. You can see it from the street, but better to keep heading up Torreyson to view it from a higher perspective. The home, now owned by art book publisher Benedikt Taschen, was meticulously renovated at the turn of the millennium by Silver Lake firm Escher Gunewardena. Inside, the combination of wondrous framed views of the valley below and the sense that you're somehow in a primal cave is hard to believe. Lautner's noteworthy Harpel House is just around the corner, but not visible from the street. ■

Jacobsen and Polin Houses

Prime examples of John Lautner's passion (and genius) for rethinking living patterns through spatial and technical experiment are the Jacobsen and Polin Houses, twin ledge-top residences on adjacent sites in the Cahuenga Pass. Topped with floating, prefabricated hexagonal steel roofs, the unusually shaped concrete and rosewood structures are supported by protruding trios of spider-leg steel trusses that minimize the need for load-bearing walls, allowing for open plans and uninterrupted glass surfaces. Lautner worked on the system with structural engineer Edgardo Contini, one of the masterminds behind Crestwood Hills (page 146), employing it in other projects like his nearby Carling House. Enveloped in thick trees and lush ivy, the homes' relatively small footprints stretch beyond their hexagonal cores, featuring large decks and compressed living and sleeping spaces. The Jacobsen House was featured in the film *Twilight*, with Paul Newman and Gene Hackman, making it just one of many Lautner abodes to star on the big screen. Others include the Sheats Goldstein House in *The Big Lebowski* (page 144), Chemosphere in *Body Double* (page 170, opposite), Garcia House in *Lethal Weapon 2* (page 172), the Elrod House in *Diamonds are Forever*, Silvertop in *Less Than Zero* and the Schaffer Residence in *A Single Man*. ■

Los Angeles **Architect** John Lautner **Year** 1947
Address 3540 Multiview Drive, Hollywood, CA 90068

Open to Public No **Free Entrance** No **Café/Restaurant** No
Overnight Accommodation No **Gift/Bookshop** No

Garcia House

118

Los Angeles **Architect** John Lautner **Year** 1962
Address 7436 Mulholland Drive, Los Angeles, CA 90046

Open to Public No **Free Entrance** No **Café/Restaurant** No
Overnight Accommodation No **Gift/Bookshop** No

Another floating Lautner wonder is the Garcia House, an eye-shaped, thoroughly glassy construction levitating on two V-shaped supports in the Hollywood Hills. Built for jazz composer Russ Garcia, the house, topped by a thin clear-span steel roof, is split in two by a central entry stair, which carves out two living zones and allows the home to unfold from there, combining cavernous living spaces and compressed private ones. Lautner's use of steel construction allowed him to open the floor plan and the views, completely. Thanks to the massive glass walls, you can see into much of the home – and through the open stair – from Mulholland Drive. But the best view of the 'Rainbow House', as it's sometimes known, with its gridded glazed facade and projecting central balcony, is from down the hill, from a split in La Castana Drive. In 2002 it received an extensive renovation by a local practice, experts in Mid-Century Modern architecture, Marmol Radziner. The Garcia House received its Hollywood close-up in *Lethal Weapon 2*, when Mel Gibson tore the whole house down the hill by tying his pickup truck to one of those V-shaped supports. The filmmakers built a replica Garcia House on their lot to make this stunt possible. ■

When you drive by Harry Gesner's Boat Houses, twelve single-family residences spaced around the tight curves of Woodrow Wilson Drive and Pacific View Drive in the Cahuenga Pass, you wonder if you really just saw what you just saw. Each measuring 800 to 1,200 square feet (74 to 111 square meters), the properties, projecting off the hillside via stilts, really do look like boats: they're long, wood-clad and angular (they're shaped a little like the tops of tiki torches) and contain large balconies, like nautical decks. It's for good reason: Gesner, who was a longtime surfer, famous for building large water and longboat-inspired residences in Malibu including his most famous, the Wave House (page 132), hired Norwegian ship builders to help create the properties. They used hand axes to sculpt redwood and create a handcrafted look. Inside, the abodes are tightly-spaced, have angled walls and windows and are full of exposed timber beams and built-ins. So yes, they feel like boats here too. Gesner is famed for turning down Frank Lloyd Wright's invitation to come to Taliesen West and study with him. 'I didn't want to be another little Frank Lloyd Wright, so that's when I made my decision to self-educate', he told *Vanity Fair*. It's clear that this self-direction fostered some of the most original designs ever created in Southern California. ■

Los Angeles **Architect** Harry Gesner **Year** 1959
Address 7041 Woodrow Wilson Drive, Los Angeles, CA 90068

Open to Public No **Free Entrance** No **Café/Restaurant** No
Overnight Accommodation No **Gift/Bookshop** No

The Boat Houses

Wolff House

Just above the Sunset Strip, not far from Pierre Koenig's Case Study House #22 (page 178), is another superlative residence seemingly floating above the metropolis: John Lautner's Wolff House. Interior designer Marco Wolff asked Lautner to design a 'Fallingwater in the Hollywood Hills' and indeed this four-bedroom home shows more similarities to Lautner's mentor Frank Lloyd Wright's work than almost any other, including a jagged stone facade, hipped copper roof and stepped, cantilevered masses, hovering over the hillside street like Wright's masterpiece in Bear Run, Pennsylvania, floats over a waterfall. The tower-like three-story home – whose deep floor plates and floor-to-ceiling windows help shape views of the Los Angeles Basin – is best seen from below, where you can watch it unfold, its projecting planes defying gravity and imagination. 'It isn't architecture unless it's alive', Lautner once said. From above you can look straight through much of the home, thanks to a wide gap through the middle, similar to that of the architect's Garcia House (page 172). All this exposure is moderated by thick landscaping, ivy growing up some of the walls and several eucalyptus trees on the property, which grow around and seemingly through, the house. ■

Los Angeles **Architect** John Lautner **Year** 1961
Address 8530 Hedges Place, Los Angeles, CA 90069

Open to Public No **Free Entrance** No **Café/Restaurant** No
Overnight Accommodation No **Gift/Bookshop** No

Los Angeles **Architect** Raphael Soriano **Year** 1938
Address 1650 Queens Road, Los Angeles, CA 90069

Open to Public No **Free Entrance** No **Café/Restaurant** No
Overnight Accommodation No **Gift/Bookshop** No

121

Polito House

As early Modern residences go, Raphael Soriano's Polito House is a tower, rising three stories on a tight hillside lot above the Sunset Strip. From the street the white stucco home maintains a solid profile. But from the back it unfolds to the yard, the pool and the views of the city below, stepping back progressively as it rises. The home's first two floors – containing kitchen, living and dining spaces below and bedrooms above – are wrapped with bands of horizontal steel casement windows. The second floor contains cantilevered balconies, which also serve to shade the spaces below. The third level contains an elevated, L-shaped roof garden. All three stories are connected on their north facade by a multi-story opaque window, which parallels the internal staircase. While you can't see the home unfold in this manner from the street, its white surface serves as a canvas for the shifting shadows of the site's heavy vegetation. If you enjoy visiting this home, you should travel to more Soriano gems in Los Angeles, including the Lipetz House in Silver Lake (1843 N Dillon Street), the Glen Lukens House in West Adams (3425 West 27th Street) and, while hard to see from the street, the outdoor-oriented Julius Shulman House in the Hollywood Hills (7875 Woodrow Wilson Drive). ■

Kun House

Built for Joseph Kun, publisher of the *Los Angeles Examiner*, this International Style home, resting high in the hills above Laurel Canyon, is now most famous for launching the career of legendary architectural photographer Julius Shulman. One of Richard Neutra's draftsmen took Shulman to see the house and after the architect saw the young photographer's prints he bought them and subsequently hired him to capture most of his work from then on. Shulman then went on to shoot the architecture of most of his colleagues. From the street, the Kun House looks like a small guest home, popping up from the top of a steep hill. But from the base of that slope, the three-story structure unfolds like a large villa, its repeating rows of ribbon windows; long, wraparound balconies; rooftop patio; and thin overhanging eaves taking advantage of splendid views and its L-shaped walls protecting it from the sun and giving it a distinctive profile. A second Neutra house, inspired by the first, was built fifteen years later on the slope above the Kun House and the two now make up one of the city's great architectural compounds. ■

Los Angeles **Architect** Richard Neutra **Year** 1936
Address 7960 Fareholm Drive, Los Angeles, CA 90046

Open to Public No **Free Entrance** No **Café/Restaurant** No
Overnight Accommodation No **Gift/Bookshop** No

Los Angeles **Architect** Welton Becket & Associates **Year** 1963
Address 6360 Sunset Boulevard, Los Angeles, CA 90028

Open to Public Yes **Free Entrance** No **Café/Restaurant** Yes
Overnight Accommodation No **Gift/Bookshop** Yes

123

Cinerama Dome

When looking for famous theaters in Los Angeles, most tourists make a beeline to Grauman's Chinese, on Hollywood Boulevard, only to be hassled by aggressive hawkers wearing Superman costumes. What they don't know is that the coolest movie theater in Los Angeles is Welton Becket's Cinerama Dome, also located in Hollywood on Sunset Boulevard. The seventy-foot-tall (21-meter), bright white structure was the first concrete geodesic dome in the world, put together with more than three-hundred textured pentagonal and hexagonal panels. As usual, Becket, whom I like to call the Rodney Dangerfield of Los Angeles architecture, gets no credit for this masterpiece of LA vernacular. The theater was built as a prototype, showcasing the new Cinerama process, combining three movies stitched together and projected side by side for an extra-wide picture. But the Cinerama's cost meant that it was never widely adopted and only a few other Cinerama theaters were ever built, such as Raymond Peck's Cinerama Seattle. Still the Cinerama Dome, now owned by the popular Arclight movie chain (there's a complex of contemporary buildings around the Cinerama, partially obscuring it) remains a fixture of Hollywood. Get a ticket to see a movie there, put on some 3-D glasses and thank us later. ■

Case Study House #22

124

Los Angeles **Architect** Pierre Koenig **Year** 1960
Address 1635 Woods Drive, Los Angeles, CA 90069

Open to Public Yes **Free Entrance** No **Café/Restaurant** No
Overnight Accommodation No **Gift/Bookshop** No

No home on the West Coast is more emblematic of the simple, elegant, forward-looking ethos of Mid-Century Modern architecture than Pierre Koenig's Case Study House #22. There's one chief reason: Julius Shulman's black-and-white shot of two women staring down at the lights of Los Angeles (literally looking ahead to the future) from this steel house jutting over the side of a cliff is one of the most famous architectural photographs of all time. The L-shaped home – built on a tiny lot that owner Buck Stahl and his wife, Carlotta, shored up with discarded concrete – perches over the city like a hawk. Clad almost entirely in huge sheets of floor-to-ceiling glass and enclosed and shaded by sturdy planks of corrugated steel, it provides uninterrupted views of the city from the Griffith Observatory to the Pacific Ocean. Being inside makes you feel as if you're floating, even flying over the city. The house also provides you with the chance to re-create Shulman's famous shot, taken outside the glassy living space from the pool. It will soon become a popular part of your Facebook and Instagram feeds. ■

Case Study House #22

Capitol Records

125

Los Angeles **Architect** Welton Becket & Associates **Year** 1955
Address 1750 Vine Street, Los Angeles, CA 90028

Open to Public No **Free Entrance** No **Café/Restaurant** No
Overnight Accommodation No **Gift/Bookshop** No

Among Welton Becket's unheralded collection of iconic, Mid-Century Modern vernacular Los Angeles buildings, none has the immediate impact of Capitol Records, which has become as synonymous with Hollywood as the Hollywood sign perched in the hills behind it. The thirteen-story, reinforced-concrete building, known as the first circular high-rise office, has a simple design concept, executed perfectly. It's alleged by some to resemble a stacked turntable, with bands of glass on each floor representing records. (Lined up side by side, the small windows look like record grooves.) Giant white sunshades add three-dimensionality to the conceit and on top is a giant spire, which of course represents the needle to stack the records. Legendary acts who recorded at Capitol Studios, in the building's basement, included Frank Sinatra, Nat King Cole and Judy Garland. Becket's company, Welton Becket & Associates, became one of the largest architecture firms in the world, not only designing Los Angeles icons like the Cinerama Dome (page 177), the Music Center (page 222) and the Beverly Hilton, but also creating huge office towers, civic centers and large master plans. ■

126 Samuel-Novarro House

You can't see Lloyd Wright's Samuel-Novarro House from its street address in the foothills of Beachwood Canyon. But if you bend around to the road below, you'll watch a structure unfold above you that's unlike almost any other. The four-story residence, built for manager Louis Samuel and his wife, is clad in white concrete and green oxidized copper, stamped with abstract, leaf-like patterns. The copper forms a stepped, vertical axis, following the house as it stacks down its steep slope. At the top, a square pavilion containing bedrooms sits over a row of living spaces (living room, dining room, dining terrace and lounge) fronted by a row of horizontal windows. Below this is the music room, designed for small concerts; a cocktail bar; and support spaces for laundry, storage, garage and so on. Built at such an early date, this home doesn't fit the timeline for a Mid-Century Modern house. But it is resolutely modern: an important and often overlooked precursor to rethinking architectural design and function and a resolutely simple and linear construction despite its exceptional embellishments. ■

Los Angeles **Architect** Lloyd Wright **Year** 1928
Address 2255 Verde Oak Drive, Los Angeles, CA 90068

Open to Public No **Free Entrance** No **Café/Restaurant** No
Overnight Accommodation No **Gift/Bookshop** No

Just around the corner from Frank Lloyd Wright's Ennis House (page 183, opposite) and down the hill from the Griffith Observatory, is a hidden home that's just as remarkable: Craig Ellwood's Moore House, built for Intel co-founder Gordon Moore. It's a raised rectangular glass and wood pavilion (a change from Ellwood's common use of steel) enveloped in vegetation and divided into three open sections: a living room and two bedrooms; a galley kitchen; which acts as a spatial divider; and a master bedroom. Storage is hidden behind hinged doors built into the walls and a large fireplace highlights the public areas. The landscape is spectacular, including gardens, water features, mature trees, seating areas, winding paths and a spa tucked into the building's uphill side. It makes seeing the house a challenge, but persevere. If you like the Moore House you should visit the fraternal twin of this house: Ellwood's Kubly House in Pasadena (215 La Vereda Road). It's also a challenge to see from the end of the driveway, but if you peek around the corner, you get another sense of Ellwood's deftness at creating magic with glass, structure and landscape. ■

Los Angeles **Architect** Craig Ellwood **Year** 1965
Address 4791 Bonvue Avenue, Los Angeles, CA 90027

Open to Public No **Free Entrance** No **Café/Restaurant** No
Overnight Accommodation No **Gift/Bookshop** No

Los Angeles **Architect** Frank Lloyd Wright **Year** 1924
Address 2607 Glendower Avenue, Los Angeles, CA 90027

Open to Public No **Free Entrance** No **Café/Restaurant** No
Overnight Accommodation No **Gift/Bookshop** No

Ennis House

The last and most famous of Wright's textile block houses, this structure, perched high in the hills near Griffith Observatory, is a dead ringer for a Mezo-American temple, except it's in Los Feliz. It's been in more movies than almost any home in the world – from *House on Haunted Hill* to *Day of the Locust* to *Blade Runner* – and for good reason. Designed by Wright and his son Lloyd for retailer Charles Ennis and his wife, Mabel, the structure, with its interlocking planes staggering and stepping in unfathomably dramatic fashion, was constructed of more than twenty-seven-thousand exotically patterned concrete blocks, rising up out of a massive base, which doubles as a retaining wall. The home and an adjacent chauffeur's residence, wrap around a paved courtyard, with unimpeded views of the city below. Lush gardens make their way around the home's exterior, while the interior consists of narrow hall-ways, colorful mosaics, dramatic double-height spaces and other cinematic spatial gestures. The residence was bought in 2011 by billionaire Ron Burkle, who is financing a thorough restoration. ■

Yet another iconic Richard Neutra residence is the Lovell Health House, tucked at the top of a steep slope, accessed via a secluded road that curves through the Los Feliz Hills. Built for Philip Lovell, a self-described health food and natural remedy fanatic (and a prolific writer on the subject) and the same client who commissioned Rudolph Schindler's Lovell Beach House (page 258), the three-level, bright white stucco home is supported by an extensive, prefabricated steel frame, which allowed the architect to open up interior spaces to a degree that few homes ever had at the time. The two-and-a-half-level home unfolds to the hillside with large balconies, terraces and a giant wall of casement windows, wrapping around the residence, both defining it and providing spectacular views down the hillside. Guests access the home at its cantilevered top level, which contains the sitting room, bedrooms and sleeping porches. From there they progress down the open, view-enveloped stairway to the spacious living and dining areas, stunningly projecting over the hillside, as well as guest rooms, kitchen and service areas. Below that a verdant garden contains trees, shrubs and colorful flowering plants. The best view is slightly down the hill, looking at that great glass facade and a composition that Lovell described as providing 'the maximum degree of health and beauty.' ■

Los Angeles **Architect** Richard Neutra **Year** 1929
Address 4616 Dundee Drive, Los Angeles, CA 90027

Open to Public No **Free Entrance** No **Café/Restaurant** No
Overnight Accommodation No **Gift/Bookshop** No

Los Angeles **Architect** Gregory Ain **Year** 1947
Address 2839–2849 Avenel Street, Los Angeles, CA 90039

Open to Public No **Free Entrance** No **Café/Restaurant** No
Overnight Accommodation No **Gift/Bookshop** No

Avenel Housing

Perhaps the best-known of Gregory Ain's groundbreaking multi-family apartment buildings, Avenel Housing, located on a sloping residential street in Los Angeles' Silver Lake neighborhood, is intricate and simple at the same time. The scheme, which was originally cooperatively owned, consists of two rows of five duplex apartments, angled in a sawtooth pattern to create privacy within and views out from private back patios and balconies. From the roadway you only see the first unit of each row, staggering down the hillside and fronted with stucco and a grid of translucent glass. You enter from the building's flanks, progressing down landscaped pathways full of colorful succulents, vines and trees, all designed by Garrett Eckbo. Three-bedroom units are only 960 square feet (89 square meters), but are well proportioned, open and intimately connected to the outdoors through glass sliding doors and clerestories. Such bold experiments in communal living were not embraced at the time. Of the ten members of the original Avenel Cooperative, at least four were questioned by the House Un-American Activities Committee, leading some to call the project 'a cooperative living experiment for a group of communists.' ■

Hollyhock House

131

Los Angeles **Architect** Frank Lloyd Wright **Year** 1921
Address 4800 Hollywood Boulevard, Los Angeles, CA 90027

Open to Public Yes **Free Entrance** No **Café/Restaurant** No
Overnight Accommodation No **Gift/Bookshop** No

Frank Lloyd Wright's Hollyhock House in Los Feliz – built with the help of apprentices Rudolph Schindler, Richard Neutra and Wright's son Lloyd – is yet another example of the architect's obsession with Mayan and Aztec design. Located atop Barnsdall Park (a hidden treasure itself) the temple-esque beige concrete residence was built for eccentric oil heiress Aline Barnsdall, whose favorite flower, the hollyhock, appears in abstracted form throughout. When you enter through a diminutive, low-ceilinged hallway, you wonder what all the fuss is about. But go further and the ceiling explodes upward as you enter the home's highlight: its breathtaking living room. Centered around a huge stone fireplace, etched with a geometric frieze and fronted by what was once a moat, the room is filled with ornate woodwork, sleek Wright-designed furniture, striking stained-glass windows and wonderful views of the park and the city. The rest of the structure contains room after room, showcasing tilted concrete walls, narrow, leaded art glass windows, expansive clear glazing and bas-relief sculptures. The house is planned around a gorgeous central courtyard and amphitheater and the light-dappled rooms open out to the park. In 2015 the home underwent a $4.35 million renovation, finally bringing it back to its original glory after years of deterioration. ■

Hollyhock House

Bubeshko Apartments

132

Rudolph Schindler built only a few multi-family dwellings and the best known is the wonderfully exotic Bubeshko Apartments, above Griffith Park Boulevard in Los Angeles' Silver Lake neighborhood. Designed for Anastasia Bubeshko and her daughter Luby, the wood and stucco apartments were built on a model of a 'Greek hillside', stepping up their sloping, triangular lot. Six units (four on one side, two on the other), accessed via outdoor stairs, range from studios to duplexes. Each is closely connected to lovely patios and balconies and shaded by deep, heavy eaves. And while their sizes (and some of their amenities) would not meet most current standards, they feel as livable and hip as ever. Sculptor Gordon Newell's patterned decorative caps on the building's garage walls strongly allude to the Mezo-American-influenced textile block homes of Shindler's mentor, Frank Lloyd Wright. The woodsy paths and open spaces on the hilltop above the apartments are an example of the informal, communal atmosphere that Schindler loved to instill. Neighbors instinctually gather outside and it's no wonder that artists and architects still flock to get on the waiting list. The apartments were recently restored by local firm DSH, bringing back Schindler's original detailing, colors and sophisticated bohemian spirit. ■

Los Angeles **Architect** Rudolph Schindler **Year** 1941
Address 2044 Griffith Park Boulevard, Los Angeles, CA 90039

Open to Public No **Free Entrance** No **Café/Restaurant** No
Overnight Accommodation No **Gift/Bookshop** No

Los Angeles **Architect** Richard Neutra **Year** 1962
Address 2232 Silver Lake Boulevard, Los Angeles, CA 90039 among others

Open to Public No **Free Entrance** No **Café/Restaurant** No
Overnight Accommodation No **Gift/Bookshop** No

Neutra Colony

The VDL Research House (page 190) is the tip of the iceberg when it comes to Silver Lake Neutras. In the streets around the residence there is a group of ten homes designed by Richard Neutra and his son Dion, known informally as the Neutra Colony. All were built with the architect's simple International Style language of large windows, horizontal planes, deep and flat eaves and projecting walls and ceilings. Just around the corner from VDL is a cluster of Neutras on a street that has been named, appropriately, Neutra Place. The Neutra Reunion House (2440 Neutra Place), remodeled by Dion Neutra, features a first-floor sliding glass wall that opens completely to its verdant garden. It's surrounded by a community of smaller units, clad in dark wood, stacking up the hill, around a central pool, which Dion calls 'Treetops.' Nearby is the Akai House (2200 Neutra Place), a two-story glass box resting at the top of a hill. Another bunch of homes line the reservoir on Silver Lake Boulevard, including the Inadomi House (2238 Silver Lake Boulevard) and the Kambara House (2232 Silver Lake Boulevard), virtual twins whose stepped glass walls seem to cover their entire facades. All the homes are impressive, but what's most inspiring is sitting inside one, looking out at the splendid vistas and feeling the preternatural calm that all this openness creates. ■

Neutra VDL Research House

134

Los Angeles **Architect** Richard Neutra **Year** 1932 / 1966
Address 2300 Silver Lake Boulevard, Los Angeles, CA 90039

Open to Public Yes **Free Entrance** Yes **Café/Restaurant** No
Overnight Accommodation No **Gift/Bookshop** No

The Neutra VDL Research House, named for Dutch philanthropist C.H. Van Der Leeuw, who provided Richard Neutra the loan to build it, is arguably the architect's most famous work, although there is obviously stiff competition. Edging the idyllic Silver Lake Reservoir (aside from traffic on Silver Lake Boulevard), the glass house is filled with interlocking and projecting planes, large glazed walls, mirrors and clerestories. Strikingly ahead of its time, it showcases innovations that allow it to open to the elements, a stark contrast to the solid homes around it. These include glass-aluminum sandwich panels, foil insulation and other variations on the standard balloon frame house. While the street facade opens to the reservoir, the rear unfolds onto a luxuriant garden, with a small garden house beyond that. A 1963 fire destroyed most of the residence (except the garden house) and Neutra and his son Dion redesigned it, better accounting for the sun, including huge solar louvers, water roofs and adjusted orientation. They also formed it using a more complex version of the International Style, although some critics find that the home uses too many colors and materials. But visiting is still a must, particularly a climb up to the top-floor terrace, from where you can take in the reservoir and, even better, the kaleidoscopic collection of mid-century homes perched precariously in the hills above it. ■

134

Neutra VDL Research House

Take a winding Silver Lake road past several great post-and-beam houses with views onto the San Gabriel Valley and you approach the best of them all: Schindler's How House, built for James Eads How, a wealthy champion of the unemployed nicknamed the 'Millionaire Hobo.' It was built in 1925, but looks so modern that it could have been completed half a century later. From the street you can appreciate its placement in a lush bed of green succulents and scan the articulated horizontal board-and-batten bands of redwood and gray concrete under flat, overhanging eaves. The similarly banded windows edge out ever so slightly and allow you a peek into a remarkable, light-filled double-height living room, with its glazed corner outlooks. This top floor also contains dining, kitchen and study areas, sitting atop bedrooms, contained in the maze-like, concrete-clad basement, which opens to an outdoor space in back. How himself barely got to enjoy his exquisite house; he died of pneumonia in 1930, recently divorced from his wife, who claimed he preferred the company of hobos to her. ■

Los Angeles **Architect** Rudolph Schindler **Year** 1925
Address 2422 Silver Ridge Avenue, Los Angeles, CA 90039

Open to Public No **Free Entrance** No **Café/Restaurant** No
Overnight Accommodation No **Gift/Bookshop** No

136

First United Methodist Church of Glendale

Los Angeles **Architect** Flewelling & Moody **Year** 1961
Address 401 E Broadway, Glendale, CA 91205

Open to Public Yes **Free Entrance** Yes **Café/Restaurant** No
Overnight Accommodation No **Gift/Bookshop** No

Pasadena-based Ralph Carlin Flewelling and Walter Leland Moody were two of the gutsiest architects in Southern California, taking formal and structural risks that few are aware of today. To get a good idea of their style, head to Glendale to see the First United Methodist Church. The building, heralded outside by its one-hunred-and-twelve-foot-tall (thirty-four-meter) concrete trilon (triangular prism) topped by an aluminum cross, was planned by its congregation as the 'Cathedral of the West', a giant beacon with all the trappings (nave, transept and so on) of that building type. And it carries it out in a structurally expressive style, including an accordion thin shell concrete roof, protruding (and somewhat sinister) folded triangular canopies and angled columns, all built into a reddish, bunkerish masonry cladding. The entry is fronted by a fifteen-foot-tall (four-meter) aluminum Christ sculpture, affixed to a metal grille above the doorway. Inside forty-foot-tall (twelve-meter) stained glass windows flood the cavernous, travertine-floored space with multi-colored light. Look up at the exposed concrete of the zigzagging roof and take in the fish motif, anodized-aluminum acoustic screens and thorn sculpture sun-screens. It's a dazzling combination for a church that nobody outside of Glendale has ever heard of. ■

Rodriguez House

137

Los Angeles **Architect** Rudolph Schindler **Year** 1942
Address 1845 Niodrara Drive, Glendale, CA 91208

Open to Public No **Free Entrance** No **Café/Restaurant** No
Overnight Accommodation No **Gift/Bookshop** No

You don't need high-tech mechanical systems and endless architectural gizmos to produce a house that's sustainable and memorable. Rudolph Schindler's Rodriguez House in Glendale is a perfect case in point. Built for composer Jose Rodriguez in a distant corner of the city, it's sited to maximize direct sun in winter and minimize it in summer. Its L-shaped form carves out a beautiful back-yard, to which most rooms have direct access. Sited in thick foliage, the residence – which is viewable from the end of a short driveway – brings your pulse level down immediately. A long stucco and stone-clad bar fronts the structure, from which projects a large second-floor balcony, facing outsized windows and exposed structural members. You feel the civilized and simple spirit of Modernism here. Inside, typical Schindler built-in furniture and flowing open spaces make this a wonderful place to live. Out back, the building bridges over a pathway, connecting one end of the lush garden to the next. A pond near the road adds to the Zen-like atmosphere. ■

Art Center College of Design

Located in the highest reaches of Pasadena's foothills, Art Center College of Design was both Craig Ellwood's largest building and his last. It's essentially a giant black steel truss bridge spanning the site's undulating topography; – an infinitely preferable solution to the common (and more expensive) technique of leveling an area to build on flat land. Containing classrooms, studios, computer labs, galleries, offices, a library and a cafeteria, the building's exposed structure makes it feel light, elegant and extremely modern. Inside, you progress easily from one department to another, always oriented by the views nearby. 'In architecture, structure is the only clear principle', Ellwood once said. Because of the rising cost of steel (among other setbacks), the building took more than six years to complete and Ellwood associate architect Jim Tyler took on much of the design responsibility. Ellwood himself retired to Tuscany shortly after its completion. Several new structures have been added to the campus in subsequent years and in 2004 the school opened its new 'South Campus' in downtown Pasadena, housed in a former airplane wind tunnel, post office and office building. ■

Los Angeles **Architect** Craig Ellwood **Year** 1976
Address 1700 Lida Street, Pasadena, CA 91103

Open to Public Yes **Free Entrance** Yes **Café/Restaurant** No
Overnight Accommodation No **Gift/Bookshop** No

Millard House

Los Angeles **Architect** Frank Lloyd Wright **Year** 1923
Address 645 Prospect Crescent, Pasadena, CA 91103

Open to Public No **Free Entrance** No **Café/Restaurant** No
Overnight Accommodation No **Gift/Bookshop** No

The Millard House, also known as 'La Miniatura', was Frank Lloyd Wright's first textile-block home – the term he used for concrete block residences patterned like fabric – in Southern California. Visiting this three-story building, located just behind Greene and Greene's gorgeous Bentz House in Pasadena, feels like making an archaeological expedition. The cruciform-patterned beige blocks, formed with wooden molds, were created from sand and gravel found on the property. Its solid wood entry gates resemble ancient draw-bridges, reinforcing the sense that you've reached an Aztec fortress in the jungle. It wraps around a luxuriant courtyard thick with eucalyptus trees and meandering, lily pad-filled ponds. The home dramatically weaves indoors and outdoors, folding in and out of this natural scene, a concrete canopy connecting the main structure with a separate studio. Spaces open to the outdoors through large glass doors and expansive balconies. The exquisite blocks continue inside, blurring the distinction between what's considered an interior treatment. The verticality of the home is rare for Wright, but it makes sense on this tight lot in this setting and in the context of Latin American precedents. The living and dining rooms are stacked one atop the other to provide more space and of course there is plenty of Wright's built-in furniture, with many details containing beautiful geometric designs. ■

Ladd & Kelsey's Norton Simon Museum is not a traditionally beautiful structure. Because it was located in a domestic neighborhood, the museum asked the architects for a building that was 'residential in atmosphere' but not in scale. They lined its curved exterior walls with 115,000 hand-made deep-umber tiles, designed by artist Edith Heath, harkening to the darker tones of the area's nearby Craftsman masterpieces. Inside, they created spacious, curving galleries meant to show off large Modern pieces. In subsequent years both Craig Ellwood and Frank Gehry applied their own stamps on the original design. In 1977 Ellwood transformed the office space into additional exhibition galleries in the lower level. Gehry's alterations in 1999 included opening skylights, replacing parquet floors with sandstone and adding a spiral stair and new Asian galleries. Also part of that project was the museum's biggest highlight: the central garden by Nancy Goslee Power. The *Los Angeles Times* described this peaceful space as 'a romantic rhapsody of a fluid, Monet-like lily pond, groves of sycamores in flowing paths of decomposed granite and great plant combinations like brilliant pink canna lilies growing with orange lion's tail and gray euphorbias.' ■

Los Angeles **Architect** Ladd & Kelsey **Year** 1969
Address 411 W Colorado Boulevard, Pasadena, CA 91105

Open to Public Yes **Free Entrance** No **Café/Restaurant** Yes
Overnight Accommodation No **Gift/Bookshop** Yes

Norton Simon Museum

Another Pasadena secret is the campus of Ambassador College, which was master-planned by DMJM, designed by architect Peter J. Holdstock and landscaped by Garrett Eckbo. The astoundingly eclectic property, now mainly used by Marantha High School, contained a number of elegant mansions atop its hilly section. But Armstrong wanted to keep the campus modern, installing a number of Mid-Century Modern buildings below. Unfortunately, the campus has been severely compromised. Holdstock's honeycomb concrete block-clad fine arts, science and administrative buildings were all demolished in the last five years. But it still holds together very well. DMJM's Ambassador Auditorium is a soaring example of classical Modernism that rises above a large reflecting pool, fountain and curving concrete bridge by Eckbo. The building's waffle slab roof, floating on thin tapered concrete columns, projects over a glass facade, through which you can see a multi-level entryway with a grand crystal chandelier. It's as though the Music Center had been transplanted to Pasadena. And landscaping by Eckbo and others is second to none: including cascading streams, formal gardens, cypress allées and Modernist plazas. While you're here walk up the curving Ambassador Gardens to explore the mansions. Of course they're not Mid-Century in style, but they transport you to an older California and to the Mediterranean. ■

Los Angeles **Architect** Daniel, Mann, Johnson and Mendenhall (DMJM)
Year 1974 **Address** 131 S St. John Avenue, Pasadena, CA 91123

Open to Public No **Free Entrance** No **Café/Restaurant** No
Overnight Accommodation No **Gift/Bookshop** No

Los Angeles **Architect** Harwell Hamilton Harris, Richard Neutra and others
Year 1935–68 **Address** Poppy Peak Drive, Pasadena, CA 91105

Open to Public No **Free Entrance** No **Café/Restaurant** No
Overnight Accommodation No **Gift/Bookshop** No

142 Poppy Peak

When you think of Pasadena, Modernist architecture doesn't spring to mind but the city contains one of the richest collections of Mid-Century Modern buildings in Southern California. A great cluster is Poppy Peak, a twelve-acre (five-hectare), three-street plot located on the side of Poppy Peak, in the southwest corner of the city. Planned by developer William Carr, it features about thirty modernist homes (out of a total of forty-five in the neighborhood) designed by, among others, Richard Neutra; Harwell Hamilton Harris; Buff, Straub & Hensman; and local architects like Leland Evison and James Pulliam. As you wind up the area's curvy streets, you're greeted by these wonders one at a time. One of the first is Neutra's Perkins House (1540 Poppy Peak Drive), which steps up its site with an interlocking system of long walls, canopies and douglas fir posts and beams. The carport's roof serves as an outdoor deck. Around the corner is Harris' Laing House (1642 Pleasant Way – pictured), an International Style composition of interchanging, terraced forms that evokes both Frank Lloyd Wright and Japanese architecture. Buff, Straub & Hensman's 1595 Poppy Peak Drive is a long, Asian-inspired gable-roofed bar, floating above its carport. The other Mid-Century Modern homes in the district are almost all in exceptional shape and exhibit varied examples of low-slung Modernism and lush landscape integration. ■

Buff & Hensman (also known as Buff, Straub and Hensman and Buff, Smith and Hensman) created hundreds of homes in Southern California – from simple cabins to post-and-beam residences to elaborate mansions – helping as much as anyone to define the look of the area's Mid-Century Modern architecture. One of the team's hallmarks was creating spaces that were not just beautiful, but also exceptionally livable, through smart spatial arrangements and a keen sense of the natural world. The Norton House, a post-and-beam structure located in the hilly San Rafael Heights neighborhood, showcases their genius for this integration. Using Asian influences, the architects created a one-story, red-painted wood, steel and glass box, which is sited at the bottom of a lush site of terraced slopes, stepping stones, a small Japanese bridge and a stream. Bump-out volumes and decks cantilever from the main volume, adding space and animating the site. Inside, built-ins help maintain flowing spaces, serving as furniture and space dividers. You feel like you're equally in a Japanese temple, a luxury residence and the middle of the woods. The firm's breathtaking Bass House, otherwise known as Case Study House #20, is located in nearby Altadena (2275 North Santa Rosa Avenue), but unfortunately, all you can see from the street is its carport. ■

Los Angeles **Architect** Buff & Hensman **Year** 1954
Address 820 Burleigh Drive, Pasadena, CA 91105

Open to Public No **Free Entrance** No **Café/Restaurant** No
Overnight Accommodation No **Gift/Bookshop** No

Case Study House #10

144

Los Angeles **Architect** Kemper Nomland **Year** 1947
Address 711 S San Rafael Avenue, Pasadena, CA 91105

Open to Public No **Free Entrance** No **Café/Restaurant** No
Overnight Accommodation No **Gift/Bookshop** No

Not all Case Study houses wound up on magazine covers. One of the lesser-known versions is Case Study House #10, designed by Kemper Nomland, a relatively unknown designer who nonetheless possessed a profound gift for integrating innovative, low-cost architecture with its landscape. The home takes many of its design cues from its sloping corner lot on the west side of Pasadena. Its long shed roof, divided into two wings (they literally look like airplane wings) by a U-shaped entryway, follows the ground plane's downward angle, while its rear elevation is almost completely covered with floor-to-ceiling glass, opening to a back patio and yard. The rooms in the open-planned space flow easily from one to the next, unfolding on subtly shifting levels. The top level contains a studio; the middle contains bedrooms; and living spaces are beneath that. Nomland and his son built much of the home themselves and lived in the house for several years. Following in this DIY tradition, the current owners, Tim Morris and Diane Kawashima, led an extensive renovation, replacing the home's decaying surfaces with handsome blond plywood, removing years of ugly, claustrophobic remodeling and replacing aging, bulky mechanical systems (and hiding them within the walls). ■

1414 Fair Oaks

145

Visiting this office building in South Pasadena feels like stepping outside the banal corporate world, into a more imaginative and progressive time. Once containing the offices of Community Facilities Planners – an organization that included Smith and Williams, Garrett Eckbo and several planners and industrial designers responsible for parks, master plans and buildings throughout the region – 1414 Fair Oaks is now home to dentists, accountants and acupuncture specialists. Smith and Williams – another under-appreciated firm responsible for some of LA's best work – created an ingenious, region-appropriate office. A series of modular, cube-shaped work spaces, with large windows and exposed metal columns, beams and trusses, are set around an idyllic Eckbo-designed plaza, all shaded by a continuously vaulted, expanded metal mesh canopy and internal plants. The canopy is translucent from one angle and clear from another, creating a soft glow underneath. It picks up the blue of the sky and gold of the sun. You can enter the central plaza from the front or back entrances of the office. It's an ingeniously simple design accented by the trusses and structural members, as well as hanging globe lamps. ■

Los Angeles **Architect** Smith and Williams **Year** 1959
Address 1414 Fair Oaks Avenue, South Pasadena, CA 91030

Open to Public No **Free Entrance** No **Café/Restaurant** No
Overnight Accommodation No **Gift/Bookshop** No

146 Airform Bubble House

Los Angeles **Architect** Wallace Neff **Year** 1946
Address 1097 S Los Robles Avenue, Pasadena, CA 91106

Open to Public No **Free Entrance** No **Café/Restaurant** No
Overnight Accommodation No **Gift/Bookshop** No

Architect Wallace Neff was best known for designing Colonial Revival houses for Los Angeles' most rich and famous residents, including Judy Garland, Douglas Fairbanks and Mary Pickford and Groucho Marx. But Neff's proudest architectural achievements were his weird but modest Airform Bubble Houses. Anticipating the coming post-war housing shortage, Neff imagined the design one day when he saw a soap bubble forming on his bathroom sink. His idea of building with air – builders filled a giant balloon, sprayed it with Gunite (aerated concrete), then covered it in reinforcing bars and concrete – was born. He built, among other developments, a twelve-house bubble community in Virginia that became known as Igloo Village, a desert development in Arizona for the Litchfield Cotton Company and houses in Mexico, Africa and the Middle East. But the only surviving Neff Bubble Home is the architect's own. Set into a dirt yard planted with a few succulents off busy Los Robles Avenue, it looks like a domed native adobe house, or like a white, run-down Mickey Mouse hat, without the ears. But it's nonetheless wonderful to behold and a fun look at what's possible outside of our tried-and-true and often boring, construction methods. The home's Los Robles side is covered with hedges, but you can get a clear view from Wallis Street. ■

Beckman Auditorium

147

Los Angeles **Architect** Edward Durell Stone **Year** 1963
Address 332 S Michigan Avenue, Pasadena, CA 91106

Open to Public Yes **Free Entrance** Yes **Café/Restaurant** No
Overnight Accommodation No **Gift/Bookshop** No

Of the many Edward Durell Stone buildings in Southern California, this small event hall, named for Caltech professor and famed inventor Arnold Beckman, is this author's favorite. Located at the end of a grassy mall on one side and a long reflecting pool on another, in the center of the Caltech campus, the pristine circular pavilion appears to be a Modernist interpretation of the Temple of Hercules in Rome, from its rounded colonnade to its shallow, overhanging cone roof. What makes it distinctly Stone is its patterning, creating unique views and eclectic shadows everywhere you look. Your eye is always busy, scanning diamonds etched into the smooth white facade, semi-circular cutouts in the eaves and gridded black and white stone patterns on the ground of the colonnade. Globe lamps clustered like clover leaves hang from the eaves and if you take a long step back, you can see more atop the roof, which itself is patterned with perforated circles. There isn't too much great Modernism on this campus, originally master planned by the famed Bertram Goodhue, but if you're interested in Stone's university work, you can head to several schools in the area, from buildings at the University of Southern California (page 226), to Loyola Marymount's Edward T. Foley Center, with its thin Gothic-arched colonnades and long hexagonal facade patterning. ■

Stuart Pharmaceutical Company

Edward Durell Stone's classically-inspired New Formalist style is on fine display in the northeast corner of Pasadena, with offices and a factory for the Stuart Pharmaceutical Company. The glassy, graceful building – with its long, patterned concrete block screen, thin flat canopies, long reflecting pools and fountains, floating concrete bridges and manicured plazas – is a powerful example of Modernism's steady forays into the often-overlooked world of industrial architecture. It's also Stone's first use of the New Formalist style in California. The bold reinterpretation of Modernism made Stone plenty of enemies in the Modernism community; it also helped propel him to the cover of *Time Magazine* in 1958. In 2011 the western portion of the building, which had already been partially demolished, was transformed into the new home for local theater company A Noise Within, as well as an adjoining apartment complex. The interiors have been compromised, particularly the once-sublime two-story central atrium, which no longer contains its plaster coffered ceiling, ornate walls, marble floors, saucer-shaped planters and decorative globe lighting. But the exterior of the building, accessible only from the north and lit dramatically at night, is just as exceptional as when Julius Shulman immortalized it in its heyday. ■

Los Angeles **Architect** Edward Durell Stone **Year** 1958
Address 3360 E Foothill Boulevard, Pasadena, CA 91107

Open to Public No **Free Entrance** No **Café/Restaurant** No
Overnight Accommodation No **Gift/Bookshop** No

Covina Bowl

149

Los Angeles **Architect** Powers, Daly and DeRosa **Year** 1956
Address 1060 W San Bernardino Road, Covina, CA 91722

Open to Public Yes **Free Entrance** No **Café/Restaurant** Yes
Overnight Accommodation No **Gift/Bookshop** No

Because so many Modernist currents originated in Europe, Southern California's forever groovy 'Googie' architecture is the closest thing that the region has to its very own style. One of the (literally) largest temples to this type of energetic, bawdy design is Covina Bowl, with its Polynesian-inspired (or is it Egyptian?) steel and plywood A-frame roof; gargantuan, angular steel sign; floating canopies; textured stone walls; colorful interior details; and incredible spirit of fun. It's one of the few remaining Googie bowling alleys in the region, along with Mission Hills Bowl (originally Sepulveda Bowl) in Panorama City, Corbin Bowl in Tarzana and Friendly Hills Lanes in Whittier. Similar experiences can be had in the region's few remaining drive-in movie theaters and futuristic supermarkets. All fundamentally worship the city's car culture, not for what it's become – a traffic-clogged, antisocial nightmare – but for what it was supposed to be: the culmination of the American worship of freedom, speed, raw sexy power and self-sufficiency. ■

Mar Vista Tract

150

If ever there were an ideal template for middle-class housing in Southern California, it would be Mar Vista Tract, a collection of fifty-two residences designed by Gregory Ain – a longtime defender of social equity – with Joseph Johnson and Alfred Day. The development, originally marketed as the 'Modernique Homes', provided cost-efficient living for an area of the city whose population was exploding. It's notable for its combination of affordable, standardized building elements and simple variety. While the basic setup and square footage (1,060 square feet/98 square meters) of each house stayed the same, the designers shifted floor plans, moved garages, changed colors and inserted varying details, like canopies, clerestory windows, thin V-columns, steel-framed glazing and decorative screens. The other key to Mar Vista's magic was Ain's collaboration with landscape architect Garrett Eckbo, who used a massive variety of plants and configurations to create a park-like atmosphere. He also opened up flowing green spaces between houses to encourage social interaction, rather than creating strict boundaries like fences or hedges. At this point the trees and other plants have matured to a remarkable degree and walking through the development is like visiting a Modernist botanical garden, with the homes acting as sculptures. ■

Los Angeles **Architect** Gregory Ain **Year** 1948
Address 3533 Moore Street, Los Angeles, CA 90066

Open to Public No **Free Entrance** No **Café/Restaurant** No
Overnight Accommodation No **Gift/Bookshop** No

Robert Lee Frost Auditorium

It's amazing that a high school was able to construct one of the most impressive reinforced-concrete buildings in Los Angeles. Designed by local firm Flewelling and Moody, the Robert Lee Frost Auditorium conjures visions of the work of Eero Saarinen and Felix Candela. The structure consists of two conjoined components: a two-story brick-clad drum containing support spaces like classrooms, green rooms, storage and mechanical systems and an undulating concrete shell containing the auditorium itself. The two are connected by a large, arching wall of colored glass panels and the dome is anchored to the ground by a dinosaur-sized curved concrete leg. From the sky, the building looks like a massive white gingko leaf or a Chinese hand fan and from the ground it looks like almost no other building. The best view is inside, looking up at the underside of the giant folded roof. The facility is currently being renovated by local firm Hodgetts and Fung, which is unifying and structurally stabilizing a space that was getting claustrophobic and long-in-the-tooth. The high schoolers who use the facility have no idea how lucky they are. ■

Los Angeles **Architect** Flewelling and Moody **Year** 1964
Address 4601 Elenda Street, Culver City, CA 90230

Open to Public No **Free Entrance** No **Café/Restaurant** No
Overnight Accommodation No **Gift/Bookshop** No

Los Angeles **Architect** Rudolph Schindler **Year** 1934
Address 5958 W Eighth Street, Los Angeles, CA 90036

Open to Public No **Free Entrance** No **Café/Restaurant** No
Overnight Accommodation No **Gift/Bookshop** No

Rudolph Schindler's Buck House reflects the influence of Bauhaus, Streamline Moderne and International Style on his earlier work. Located on a tight triangular lot, the residence consists of two interlocking L-shaped volumes framing two courtyards. It was built for Los Angeles retail designer John J. Buck. From the front, the three-bedroom home, with its long, sleekly stepping roofline, is closed off, faced by pure-white stucco surfaces and thin bands of ribbon windows and clerestories. But at the back these open-plan volumes, full of natural light and elegant Schindler built-in furniture, unfold completely, via sliding walls of floor-to-ceiling glass, to their stepping, lush, bamboo-enclosed courtyards. The glassy interiors are protected by deeply cantilevered overhangs, embellished with dramatic returns. The immediate neighborhood, Miracle Mile, is a great location to explore Mid-Century Modern architecture. Besides Los Angeles County Museum of Art (LACMA) (page 210), Schindler's Mackey Apartments (page 213) and Gregory Ain's Dunsmuir Flats (page 212), also worth a visit are Welton Becket's Equitable Life (3435 Wilshire Boulevard) and Prudential Building, now known as Museum Square (5757 Wilshire Boulevard) and William Pereira's 5900 Wilshire Boulevard. ■

Los Angeles County Museum of Art (LACMA)

153

Los Angeles **Architect** William Pereira & Associates **Year** 1965
Address 5905 Wilshire Boulevard, Los Angeles, CA 90036

Open to Public Yes **Free Entrance** No **Café/Restaurant** Yes
Overnight Accommodation No **Gift/Bookshop** Yes

It doesn't get much love from those now hoping to replace it with an amoeba-shaped Peter Zumthor building, but William Pereira & Associates' Los Angeles County Museum of Art (LACMA) was once one of the grandest new cultural complexes in the world. The original facility, facing Wilshire Boulevard from a plaza raised above lovely reflecting pools and fountains, consisted of travertine-clad pavilions fronted with blond steel columns: the Ahmanson Gallery, for the permanent collection; the Lytton Gallery, featuring new exhibitions; and the Leo S. Bing auditorium. This original composition opened up to the street, but at the same time its watery base insulated it from the roar of traffic. It was also closely linked to the undulating, prehistoric landscapes of its setting, Hancock Park. But in the seventies the water features were removed and in the eighties a Hardy Holzman Pfeiffer addition plopped the new Robert O. Anderson building into the plaza, added a green atrium and walled the museum from Wilshire with a limestone and glass block wall. In the '80s Bruce Goff's eccentric Pavilion for Japanese Art emerged, with its leaf-shaped green forms, tusk toppings and extraordinary, open internal ramps and spaces. And from 2003 to 2010 Renzo Piano added the Broad Contemporary Art Museum, the Resnick Pavilion and the BP Grand Entrance, which has become the new heart of the complex. Where it all goes from here is an open question. ■

153

Los Angeles County Museum of Art (LACMA)

Dunsmuir Flats

The most famous of Gregory Ain's ingenious multi-family housing solutions is Dunsmuir Flats, four interconnected two-story buildings separated by narrow passageways in Wilshire Vista Heights. Following the site's sloping, irregular topography, the stepped and jagged cast concrete buildings, fronted by smooth white stucco walls and thin clerestory windows, use an elegant blend of Streamline Moderne and International Style languages. Something about the staggered, L-shaped composition – rising far above the street at its northern edge – suggests three-dimensional art, bringing dignity and elegance to living spaces meant for the middle class. (A rarity in today's diverging world.) Rising behind the entryway and a dark gray, rectangular garage, units contain continuous windows on their south elevations, creating light-filled first-floor spaces. Second-floor bedrooms open onto trellised balconies. All units have their own covered entries and their south sides contain patios and gardens. A bosque of trees and foliage infuses the entire composition with warmth and color. It's a typically smart solution from Ain, who worked with both Richard Neutra and Rudolph Schindler earlier in his career and was a master of Los Angeles's sorrowfully overlooked history of multi-family ingenuity. If you're intrigued by this tradition, visit Schindler's Mackey Apartments (page 213, opposite), just around the corner. ■

Los Angeles **Architect** Gregory Ain **Year** 1937
Address 1281 S Dunsmuir, Los Angeles, CA 90019

Open to Public No **Free Entrance** No **Café/Restaurant** No
Overnight Accommodation No **Gift/Bookshop** No

Los Angeles **Architect** Rudolph Schindler **Year** 1939
Address 1137 S Cochran Avenue, Los Angeles, CA 90019

Open to Public Yes **Free Entrance** No **Café/Restaurant** No
Overnight Accommodation No **Gift/Bookshop** Yes

Yet another example of early Modern Los Angeles' fine multi-family living experiments, Rudolph Schindler's Mackey Apartments consist of five units (there were originally four), each with its own personality and floor plan. Some are double height. What they do have in common are their compact layouts, incorporation of natural light (including clerestory windows and perforated interior walls), built-in furniture, variable ceiling heights and private outdoor gardens or mini balconies. From the outside the white stucco-clad building's facade seems to fracture, its interlocking L-shaped forms carving out space for copious glazing, while also protecting it from solar gain. It's a clear example of the Austrian architect's use of innovative materials and methods to control 'space, climate, light, mood', as he described it. The complex, owned by the MAK Center For Art and Architecture – which also owns and opens to visitors, Schindler's own house on Kings Road in West Hollywood (page 166) and the Fitzpatrick-Leland House, a beautiful, hovering example of Schindler's late work in the Hollywood Hills – now shelters MAK's artist-in-residence programs, after being thoroughly renovated between 1995 and 2004. ■

155 Mackey Apartments

Premier Car Wash

156

Los Angeles **Architect** Unknown **Year** Unknown
Address 17432 Ventura Boulevard, Encino, CA 91316

Open to Public Yes **Free Entrance** Yes **Café/Restaurant** No
Overnight Accommodation No **Gift/Bookshop** No

Not surprisingly for a city built around the automobile, Los Angeles has a collection of Mid-Century Modern car washes that is without parallel in the United States and probably anywhere in the world. They pop up in the most unexpected places, their fantastic structures and cladding part of the wonderfully strange vernacular of this modern city. One of the most iconic is the Premier Car Wash, designed by yet another anonymous architect on the endless stretch of Ventura Boulevard in Encino. It was recently featured in the opening shot for an episode of FX's miniseries *The People vs O.J. Simpson*, so its place in the cultural lexicon has been reinforced. Like so many Googie buildings, the flat-roofed structure's formal highlight is its signage, which is integrated into the design. Exploding from the base are modern interpretations of Greek columns, spare angled fins topped by inverted triangles, supporting sculptural atomic starbursts. Square signs under these columns spell out 'CARWASH', each representing a different letter. If you're ready for a Los Angeles Googie car wash tour, there are far too many to even begin a list. But you can't go wrong visiting the Expert Car Wash, with its repeating yellow steel A-frame roof at 900 S La Brea Avenue. ■

157 Home Savings of America

Pomona-based Millard Sheets is a (relatively) secret California treasure. The designer, who became a prominent painter and teacher before starting his architectural work, created over forty bank branch buildings across Southern California, imbedded with glass mosaic murals, for financier Howard Ahmanson and his Home Savings of America. The rectilinear structures, faced with stepped planes of travertine and rich stone, contain splendid narrative artwork, often indicative of their locations. Sheets collaborated with local architects and artists, commissioning sculptures, stained glass, fountains, landscapes and paintings. He began with the Beverly Hills Branch (9245 Wilshire Boulevard), a white, temple-like building adorned with louvered canopies, vertical gold ceramic tiles, stained-glass windows, bronze sculptures and a colorful mural depicting families throughout history. The Hollywood branch's mural showcases film stars in their most prominent roles and brilliant stained glass. His five banks in Claremont and Pomona became more exuberant over time, featuring the stories of Native Americans, railroad workers and cowboys, to name a few subjects. Chase has occupied most of the banks, largely maintaining the exteriors and, to a lesser extent, the interiors. While you're exploring, take a look at Sheets' mysterious Scottish Rites Masonic Temple (4357 Wilshire Boulevard), which is set to be turned into a gallery for the founders of the retail brand Guess, Maurice and Paul Marciano. ■

Los Angeles **Architect** Millard Sheets **Year** 1956
Address 2600 Wilshire Boulevard, Santa Monica, CA 90403 (among others)

Open to Public No **Free Entrance** No **Café/Restaurant** No
Overnight Accommodation No **Gift/Bookshop** No

Ahmanson Center

158

Cruising down the vertical spine of Wilshire Boulevard in your car is a predictable but difficult way to appreciate its eclectic, always-surprising architecture. A good example: you would never notice that Edward Durell Stone's Ahmanson Center (now called the Wilshire Colonnade), built for famed Los Angeles financier Howard Ahmanson, was a tribute to the curved colonnades of Bernini's Piazza San Pietro in Vatican City. So get out of your car and walk through this complex, a marble paved, elliptical plaza framed by two curved eleven-story buildings clad in vertical strips of glass and veined travertine that is centered around a tree-enclosed, circular fountain, which – depending on whether the California drought continues – may or may not be working. The arched colonnade along the perimeter of this broken horseshoe composition is dotted with hanging globe lights enclosed in hexagonal patterned lanterns. Such lanterns were a signature of Stone's, unique in pattern to each project. The compound was originally slated to have a forty-story tower at its rear, but that portion was scrapped. It's not a Mid-Century Modern building, but you still need to visit Morgan, Walls and Clements Wiltern Theater – an emerald green Art Deco marvel – just down the street at 3790 Wilshire Boulevard. ■

Los Angeles **Architect** Edward Durell Stone **Year** 1967
Address 3701 Wilshire Boulevard, Los Angeles, CA 90010

Open to Public No **Free Entrance** No **Café/Restaurant** No
Overnight Accommodation No **Gift/Bookshop** No

St. Basil Church

Los Angeles **Architect** AC Martin **Year** 1969
Address 3611 Wilshire Boulevard, Los Angeles, CA 90005

Open to Public Yes **Free Entrance** Yes **Café/Restaurant** No
Overnight Accommodation No **Gift/Bookshop** No

Sure, it's intimidating and a little ugly from the street, but visiting St. Basil Church on Wilshire is a must. From outside, the Brutalist building, sitting in a spare, raised courtyard just a block from the Moorish-style Wilshire Boulevard Temple, seems to be an exercise in how many rough, irregular concrete slab towers – separated by vertical shards of three-dimensional stained glass designed by mid-century master sculptor Claire Falkenstein – one can build. As Albert C. Martin, founder of AC Martin, put it, 'It is devoid of external embellishments as early churches were, but it is not a carbon copy of early churches.' But once inside, the atmosphere shifts to serene and awe-inspiring. That height, those undulating walls and the intricate, vertical shards draw your eye first upward toward the coffered concrete and timber ceiling, then toward the beams of colorful light and to the lofty, sinuous teak and metal altarpiece. The concrete that seemed off-putting in the harsh Los Angeles light now seems cool, smooth and poetic. The composition is warmed with more hardwood and with ornamental iron surfaces. Giant metal and stone sculptures by Herb Goldman and Rafe Afflick and intricate panels imbedded into the concrete walls by Franco Assetto lend a figural element to this sea of abstraction, capping off a moving experience that's one of the city's excellent surprises. ■

Founder's Church of Religious Science

160

Los Angeles **Architect** Paul R. Williams **Year** 1957
Address 3281 W Sixth Street, Los Angeles, CA 90020

Open to Public Yes **Free Entrance** Yes **Café/Restaurant** No
Overnight Accommodation No **Gift/Bookshop** No

The 'flying saucer' brand of Mid-Century Modern is alive and well at the Founder's Church of Religious Science, designed by architecture virtuoso Paul R. Williams, who worked in every style under the sun, from Hollywood Regency to the International Style. The church was founded by Ernest Holmes, whose long held dream was to 'have a great temple rise, representing all of the churches of Religious Science, but representing, too, all peoples and all faiths.' His other plan was to build a 'round church to symbolize that our arms embrace the whole world.' Williams' resulting structure is a smooth, reinforced-concrete dome, suspended four stories over the main auditorium, which stretches up to one-hundred feet (thirty meters) wide. It rests in a copious garden of thickly planted trees, hedges and winding pathways and is surrounded by a fourteen-foot-tall (four-meter), geometrically pierced concrete screen. The large church was one of the first to incorporate closed-circuit television, so congregants could watch the service in the chapel if the sanctuary filled up. Williams, a friend of Holmes (the religion was based on the teachings of Holmes' book, *The Science of the Mind*), began attending services himself, although not as a regular congregant. ■

What better way for the American Cement Company to showcase its product than through its headquarters? To do so it hired venerable Los Angeles firm Daniel, Mann, Johnson and Mendenhall (DMJM) to design the thirteen-story reinforced-concrete building, which was completed in 1964 on the west end of Los Angeles' MacArthur Park. The structure, which has a zigzag shell roof, is fronted with two screens of 225 precast concrete X's – each eleven feet (3.4 meters) tall, weighing about two tons (1.8 tonnes) – on its north and south facades. Ceramic artist Malcolm Leland consulted on this facade design. The decorative screens also help support loads, allowing for open, column-free spaces inside. The edifice sits atop a rectangular parking podium, which is fronted on its east side with more tightly packed abstractions. A protruding concrete canopy, cut with large holes to allow light (and views of the facade), welcomes visitors to the minimalist lobby. The building was converted to live-work lofts in 2002 and interiors were stripped back to their original bare glory. The new owners hired local artist Peter Lodato to paint a mural of geometric shapes on the east side. Units have either views of the hills framed by the concrete X's or open vistas of downtown. ■

Los Angeles **Architect** Daniel, Mann, Johnson and Mendenhall (DMJM)
Year 1964 **Address** 2404 Wilshire Boulevard, Los Angeles, CA 90057

Open to Public No **Free Entrance** No **Café/Restaurant** No
Overnight Accommodation No **Gift/Bookshop** No

American Cement Building

Dodger Stadium

162

Los Angeles **Architect** Emil Praeger **Year** 1962
Address 1000 Elysian Park Avenue, Los Angeles, CA 90012

Open to Public Yes **Free Entrance** No **Café/Restaurant** Yes
Overnight Accommodation No **Gift/Bookshop** Yes

Brooklyn Dodgers fans and the displaced former residents of Chavez Ravine, a Mexican-American village once clustered on the slopes of what is now Elysian Park, do not appreciate Dodger Stadium. But for everyone else, it's a delight. The last remaining Modernist stadium in the Major Leagues, it's still one of the world's best places to take in a baseball game. Dodgers owner Walter O'Malley asked his designer, architect and civil engineer Emil Praeger, to create an intimate place, open to the Southern California sun, without columns or other obstructions to block views. The overall look is simple, classic. But its flourishes – folded metal and concrete canopies, angular scoreboards, terraced entrances, spaceship-shaped planters and pastel-blue colors – stand out, perfectly evoking earnest Mid-Century futurism. Take a seat and enjoy not just the game, but also the swaying palm trees of the park in the distance. In 2013 the stadium underwent a $100 million renovation, spearheaded by local preservation virtuoso Brenda Levin. The one head-scratcher is that the Dodgers have kept a circle of surface parking around the stadium that's the size of a small city. Some Modernist inventions were not meant to stand the test of time. ■

Los Angeles Department of Water and Power

163

Where else but Los Angeles is a city's municipal utilities building one of its best structures? Built on Bunker Hill, the Department of Water and Power (LADWP), renamed the John Ferraro Building in 2000, is designed to glorify water and power through architecture. And does it ever. For water, the architects, A.C. Martin, devised a massive reflecting pool surrounding the place like a moat. Filled with fountains and public sculptures, it frames gorgeous uninterrupted views of the Bunker Hill towers to the south. For power, vertical steel columns support horizontal concrete floor slabs, cantilevered more than ten feet (three meters) beyond the building, shading offices and highlighting the structural system. At night, only these horizontal elements are visible; the rest of the glassy edifice becomes a glowing beacon. The lobby is graced with a huge spiral staircase, supported by steel columns and thin hanging steel wires, appearing to float. Architectural historian Reyner Banham described the LADWP as 'the only public building in the whole city that genuinely graces the scene and lifts the spirit.' A new sunken demonstration garden helps soften the impact of all this waste, reminding the public that the department is aware of succulents and gray water reuse, among other things. The building also contains water bottle filling stations. ■

Los Angeles **Architect** A.C. Martin **Year** 1965
Address 111 N Hope Street, Los Angeles, CA 90012

Open to Public No **Free Entrance** No **Café/Restaurant** No
Overnight Accommodation No **Gift/Bookshop** No

One of the great underrated architectural complexes in Los Angeles is the Music Center, which has been recently overshadowed by Frank Gehry's Disney Concert Hall and historically superceded by its cousins, the Lincoln Center in New York and the Kennedy Center in Washington DC. The complex consists of a raised super-block of classically proportioned and inspired Modern buildings – the Dorothy Chandler Pavilion (pictured), Ahmanson Theater and Mark Taper Forum – around a central plaza. The curved Chandler, with its weighty fluted colonnade and boat-like overhanging roof, is impressive inside, thanks to several gigantic chandeliers (any would be at home at the Met in New York) and a central series of zigzagging staircases. The Mark Taper, just across the plaza, rises from a reflecting pool, a floating drum embossed with continuous abstract relief. A freestanding Cubist colonnade surrounds the Mark Taper as well as the blockier Ahmanson Center to its north. In the center the plaza focuses around an organic 1969 Jacques Lipchitz sculpture, *Peace on Earth*, from where you can observe the LADWP Building (page 221) to the west and City Hall to the east. These grand axes are truly a spectacular architectural moment that few appreciate. ■

Los Angeles **Architect** Welton Becket & Associates **Year** 1964
Address 135 N Grand Avenue, Los Angeles, CA 90012

Open to Public Yes **Free Entrance** No **Café/Restaurant** Yes
Overnight Accommodation No **Gift/Bookshop** No

Los Angeles **Architect** Kenneth Lind **Year** 1958
Address 3320 W Adams Boulevard, Los Angekes, CA 90018

Open to Public Yes **Free Entrance** Yes **Café/Restaurant** No
Overnight Accommodation No **Gift/Bookshop** No

Holman United Methodist Church

West Adams, located just south of downtown Los Angeles, is a primarily African American neighborhood containing one of the greatest inventories of historic buildings in the city, from Victorian mansions to Craftsman bungalows. And Adams Boulevard, cutting right through this area and much of South Los Angeles, contains the highest concentration of churches in the city. Along this stretch you can visit Baptist, Methodist, Catholic, Episcopal and every other denomination under the California sun. One of the most unusual churches along this stretch is Holman United Methodist, a Modernist church designed by Kenneth Lind, a busy architect known for his multi-family apartments. You first notice the structure because of its space-age, white X-frame bell tower, offset by the building's dark front facade. But head down a paved pathway to the right and you approach a staggered white sanctuary lined with glass storefront windows and pierced by small colored glass windows in varying shapes. These create a light show effect inside an open space that, while not remarkable, has an exuberance that captures the Mid-Century Modern ethos of optimism. This is not an example of cool, travertine-clad Modernism. This is an example of how Modernism can uplift communities using simple materials and imaginative ideas. ■

Los Angeles **Architect** John Portman **Year** 1974
Address 404 S Figueroa Street, Los Angeles, CA 90071

Open to Public Yes **Free Entrance** No **Café/Restaurant** Yes
Overnight Accommodation Yes **Gift/Bookshop** No

Downtown Los Angeles features several notable glassy high-rises, like A.C. Martin's City National Plaza and Charles Luckman's Aeon Tower. But none are even close to as exceptional, or fun, as John Portman's Westin Bonaventure Hotel. Built during the late stages of Modernism, it exemplifies the adventurous structural experiment of its age, with four gridded glass cylinders surrounding a central tower, all floating above a six-story concrete base – which unfortunately deadens the streetscape around it, keeping the hotel relatively secret. Inside, its cavernous atrium, which explodes upward, is built like a mini city, with the cylinders intersecting to carve out roving walkways, hanging balconies, exposed concrete stairwells, indoor pools, an indoor running track and a host of other amazing oddities. You've stepped into the future, although it could use a little attention after nearly half a century. And then there's this: riding in one of the Bonaventure's glass elevators is one of the most thrilling and terrifying experiences in Los Angeles. Like the scene in *Charlie and the Chocolate Factory*, the pods seem to burst through the ceiling, continuing their way up the outside of the facade – all that's between you and the expanse of downtown is a thin shell of glazing. The destination: a rotating circular restaurant. What's not to love? ■

166

Westin Bonaventure Hotel

University of Southern California

167

Los Angeles **Architect** Various **Year** Various
Address University of Southern California, Los Angeles, CA 90089

Open to Public Yes **Free Entrance** Yes **Café/Restaurant** Yes
Overnight Accommodation No **Gift/Bookshop** Yes

Although the University of Southern California was founded in 1880, much of the school's physical development took place during the mid-century. Expanding on the classical outline set forth in USC's first significant plan by John Parkinson (1919), William Pereira & Associates, which also master-planned University of California, Irvine and Pepperdine University, put together a plan in 1961 that would almost double the school's size and bring in many of the region's top Modernist architects. Pereira himself designed about fifteen campus buildings between 1963 and 1979. While the architecture at USC is uneven, some of these additions are spectacular. The best include Edward Durell Stone's Von KleinSmid Center (pictured, above), a New Formalist centerpiece with a red brick facade, deep ornamental overhangs and tall arches forming a dramatic arcade around its internal courtyard. It's campanile-like tower is topped with a steel globe that's one of the campus's few recognizable icons. Pereira's Olin Hall belongs on this list, a muscular mass with a gridded concrete facade, floating over the entry to a grassy courtyard. There's also the A. Quincy Jones Annenberg School of Communications, with its concrete waffle slabs and projecting forms and Killingsworth, Brady, Smith's University Religious Center, which brings that firm's post-and-beam residential vernacular to an institutional scale. ■

167

University of Southern California

Los Angeles **Architect** Raymond Stockdale **Year** 1965
Address 3626 E First Street, Los Angeles, CA 90063

Open to Public Yes **Free Entrance** Yes **Café/Restaurant** No
Overnight Accommodation No **Gift/Bookshop** No

East Los Angeles is sorely under-represented on the Mid-Century Modern map of Los Angeles, but one wonderful exception is Raymond Stockdale's Pan American Bank in Boyle Heights. This institution was founded to provide financial services to a community that was badly underserved at the time. The New Formalist building, commissioned by bank treasurer Romana Acosta Bañuelos, is fronted with a row of storefront windows and dominated by an entryway of five narrow, pinkish archways (trimmed in blue), framing panels of famed Mexican artist José Reyes Meza's five-panel glass mosaic mural, *Our Past, Our Present and Our Future*. The colorful artwork tells the story of the Mexican American experience, combining contemporary characters with ancient myth and historical symbolism. Reyes Meza's work is part of the same school as legendary Mexican muralists like Diego Rivera, David Alfaro Siqueiros and José Clemente Orozco. Amazingly, LA's most evocative architectural storytelling takes place on the surfaces of its bank buildings, including this bank's murals, Millard Sheets' mosaic murals for Home Savings of America (page 215), the murals inside Paul R. Williams' Golden State Mutual Life Insurance Company Home Office in West Adams and Gilbert Leong and Eugene Kinn Choy's decorative Asian banks on Broadway in Los Angeles' Chinatown. ■

Only a fraction as famous as his Case Study House #22 (page 178), Pierre Koenig's Iwata House is a top-secret jewel that's worth the trip to Monterey Park, a remote part of the San Gabriel Valley that you've most likely not heard of either. Designed for Richard and Vicky Iwata and their large family, the three-story residence, perched at the edge of a sheer slope on (appropriately) Summit Place, is a series of stacked rectangular masses raised on columns to maintain the existing landscape, maximize views and open up the lower stories. Thanks to a rigorous series of structural steel beams, the top floor is the widest, its many bedrooms shielded from the valley's hot sun by projecting vertical concrete louvers. Concrete cladding throughout stands in contrast to Koenig's customary use of exposed steel, but it makes sense in this open context and hot climate. The home is fronted by a heavy gateway, but it's easy to see through the gate, past the pool, to the home itself. You can get a still better view from the empty lot next door. If only you could rent a helicopter, you could see how the home really unfolds from the other side of the impressive drop. ■

Los Angeles **Architect** Pierre Koenig **Year** 1963
Address 912 Summit Place, Monterey Park, CA 91754

Open to Public No **Free Entrance** No **Café/Restaurant** No
Overnight Accommodation No **Gift/Bookshop** No

169

Iwata House

IBM Aerospace Headquarters

170

Los Angeles **Architect** Eliot Noyes, A. Quincy Jones and Frederick Emmons
Year 1964 **Address** 9045 Lincoln Boulevard, Los Angeles, CA 90045

Open to Public Yes **Free Entrance** Yes **Café/Restaurant** No
Overnight Accommodation No **Gift/Bookshop** No

The Lincoln Boulevard campus of the Otis School of Art and Design, formerly IBM Aerospace Headquarters, is not a beautiful construction. But it's extremely interesting and the more you get to know it, the more you get to like it. The project was a collaboration between IBM design guru Eliot Noyes (who designed most of IBM's buildings, as well as many of its typewriters and computers) and Los Angeles architects A. Quincy Jones and Frederick Emmons. It couldn't be more different from the elite firm's usual projects in scale and style. Essentially this is a glass box floating on angled concrete piers, wrapped in a perforated concrete skin that recalls computer punch cards. Scientists here studied and built the earliest computers, so this literal design detail makes a lot of sense. The main building, the Kathleen Holser Ahmanson Hall, is viewable from a pleasant adjacent plaza. The highlight of the cramped, utilitarian interiors is the views outside from the small punch card windows. Unfortunately, many have been covered over by students and teachers. The Galef Center for Fine Arts, a 2001 addition by Frederick Fisher, is wrapped in corrugated aluminum and deftly provides the openness, light and views that its predecessor does not. ■

171 LAX Theme Building

Fittingly, no other building represents jet age Los Angeles better than the LAX Theme Building. Essentially, it is a disc-shaped, continuously glazed restaurant floating on spidery stucco-wrapped steel legs above the center of LA's once much-praised, now much-maligned international airport. If the building, with its amazing parabolic arches and flying saucer profile, were dropped into an episode of *The Jetsons*, nobody would blink an eye. It's wrapped with a circular geometric concrete block screen, which makes it difficult to find the entry. The warren of roads around it doesn't help either, which perhaps explains the recent closure of its restaurant, Encounter. After a half ton (454 kilogram) piece of stucco fell from the building in 2007, the structure underwent a $14.3 million renovation and seismic upgrade. But after all that work, there seems to be nothing ready to replace Encounter. This is a perfect example of maddening, inscrutable Los Angeles bureaucracy at its worst. ■

Los Angeles **Architect** Pereira and Luckman **Year** 1961
Address 209 World Way, Westchester, Los Angeles, CA 90045

Open to Public No **Free Entrance** No **Café/Restaurant** No
Overnight Accommodation No **Gift/Bookshop** No

University Christian Church

172

Los Angeles **Architect** Robert d'Arcy Bolling **Year** 1965
Address 5831 W Centinela Avenue, Los Angeles, CA 90045

Open to Public Yes **Free Entrance** Yes **Café/Restaurant** Yes
Overnight Accommodation No **Gift/Bookshop** No

For those with a taste for sculptural Modernism, head to University Christian Church in Ladera Heights. Its bulky, triangular folded plate roof, undulating above a red brick base, seems to lean forward, as if it were going to take a tumble. Inside, the structure creates a magical spatial experience, a rhythmic progression of angular surfaces accentuated by streams of light bouncing in from every direction. Color plays a role as well, streaming through a huge triangular stained-glass window in front and through smaller wedges along the building's sides. The bi-fold design opens up striated diamond-shaped skylights along the center of the pebble stucco ceiling, creating a distinct Wright-like feel. Born in 1923, Robert D'Arcy Bolling, who specialized in unglamorous institutional work, like naval bases, university halls, banks and administrative buildings – was one of the avalanche of talented architects to graduate from the University of Southern California (USC) in the middle of the century. The church, established in 1910 near USC, selected him to build its new facility in what was an emerging affluent community between Culver City and Baldwin Hills in 1965. ■

173 St. Jerome Roman Catholic Church

This eight-sided church, topped by a white, spaceship-like folded plate roof (with a spire that resembles a tall orange juicer) and clad in marble, stained glass and inlaid tile, the St. Jerome Roman Catholic Church is strikingly visible from the Tijera Boulevard off-ramp of the 405 Freeway. This makes it a true Los Angeles landmark, because everybody sees it, but no one knows what it is. There is some dispute as to who designed this structure. Some say it was created by Hugh Kinsler, a little-known architect who designed dramatic and remarkably similar sacred spaces in Glendale (Vallejo Seventh Day Adventist Church) and San Jose (Community of Christ Church). The church claims it was executed by Raymond Whalley, a St. Jerome parishioner hired by pastor Thomas McNicholas, who sadly died in a car crash just before its completion. Regardless of its authorship, it's a bold, curious sight, set back from a small landscaped plaza, fronting a large parking lot. The folds in the roof, the white starburst, exposed-beam ceiling and the stained glass and clear clerestories take on a heavenly quality, suggesting mountains, clouds, ocean waves and the stories of the Bible. ■

Los Angeles **Architect** Raymond Whalley **Year** 1966
Address 5550 Thornburn Street, Los Angeles, CA 90045

Open to Public Yes **Free Entrance** Yes **Café/Restaurant** No
Overnight Accommodation No **Gift/Bookshop** No

Pann's

174

There are so many great Mid-Century Modern Googie diners that it's hard to single one out. But Armet & Davis' Pann's is certainly worthy. Located at the edge of a corner lot in Ladera Heights, the building is fronted with thick tropical landscaping, which rests underneath a floating, textured, brown and white 'tortoise shell' roof. This covering, which extends so far down that you can almost walk onto it, shields huge plate-glass windows that open onto a textbook Googie interior of flagstone walls, terrazzo floors and indoor plantings. Pann's iconic, geometric yellow and red neon sign remains unchanged and its parking lot elevations are covered with murals of customers at the counter and of palm trees backed with California hills. The diner is still owned by the family of George and Rena Panagopoulos (their name is often shortened to Poulos), Greek immigrants who started Pann's in 1958. George has passed away, but Rena, at age 97, is still there most days, greeting patrons. ■

Los Angeles **Architect** Armet & Davis **Year** 1958
Address 6710 La Tijera Boulevard, Los Angeles, CA 90045

Open to Public Yes **Free Entrance** No **Café/Restaurant** Yes
Overnight Accommodation No **Gift/Bookshop** No

175

The Forum

Los Angeles **Architect** Charles Luckman **Year** 1967
Address 3900 W Manchester Boulevard, Inglewood, CA 90305

Open to Public Yes **Free Entrance** No **Café/Restaurant** Yes
Overnight Accommodation No **Gift/Bookshop** No

Los Angeles is certainly no ancient Rome. But the majority of its Mid-Century Modern civic buildings were inspired by classical architecture, like the 'Fabulous Forum' in Inglewood as it's known locally, which evokes the Roman Colosseum with its circular form and continuous ring of super-tall arches. Designed by Charles Luckman (famous, or infamous, for building Madison Square Garden in New York) and financed by Jack Kent Cook (who already owned the Washington Redskins and later bought the Los Angeles Lakers and founded the Los Angeles Kings), the building became most famous for hosting 'Showtime', the Lakers' remarkable string of championships in the 1980s. The arena's columns flare out at the top, creating a continuous colonnade, which in turn supports the roof via a concrete compression ring and suspension cables. This allows for an open, column-free space inside. After the Lakers and Kings moved to the Staples Center downtown in 1999, the building suffered from neglect until the Madison Square Garden company bought it in 2012, restoring it as an events venue. With the Los Angeles Rams moving in next door, Inglewood is about to become a major entertainment destination once again. ■

South Bay Bank

Before Craig Ellwood became world famous for his pristine cubes ensconced in idyllic gardens, he completed his first commercial project, the South Bay Bank (now Citizens Business Bank), a Mid-Century Modern treasure hiding in plain sight next to a series of strip malls along Manhattan Beach's busy Sepulveda Boulevard. The rectangular steel, concrete block and glass building is articulated in front with a long thin canopy and a gridded aluminum grille, carving out a small planted forecourt and shading the structure from the area's strong sunlight. Like so many Mid-Century Modern buildings, the impact of its floor-to-ceiling glass entry wall is minimized by the employees' liberal (but reasonable) use of sunshades. The lofty interior is in surprisingly good condition, showcasing original wood paneling, exposed thin steel columns and even Mid-Century Modern furniture, clocks and what appears to be a Calder mobile. Sure, the building doesn't look as magical as it did in the sexy photos taken when it was brand new that made it so famous, but its symmetry and lightness are still striking. Compared to the banal design of today's bank branches, it's an elegant revelation. ■

Los Angeles **Architect** Craig Ellwood **Year** 1957
Address 1800 N Sepulveda Boulevard, Manhattan Beach, CA 90266

Open to Public Yes **Free Entrance** Yes **Café/Restaurant** No
Overnight Accommodation No **Gift/Bookshop** No

Los Angeles **Architect** Harry Harrison **Year** 1957
Address 11908 Hawthorne Boulevard, Hawthorne, CA 90250

Open to Public Yes **Free Entrance** Yes **Café/Restaurant** Yes
Overnight Accommodation No **Gift/Bookshop** No

Chips

Not every Googie diner in Los Angeles was designed by omnipresent architecture firm Armet & Davis. Another talented designer was Harry Harrison, a Taliesen-trained architect who dreamed up Chips, a space-age building with references to his mentor, Frank Lloyd Wright. Harrison, who designed several retail and office buildings in the city, also worked with Harwell Hamilton Harris and Richard Neutra. Located in gritty Hawthorne, the white stucco building immediately induces rampant fifties nostalgia, with its large, folded plate-glass windows, angled and wavy overhanging roofline and amazing, stepped, slatted green steel sign and neon script lettering. (Natural colors, fieldstone walls and heavy eaves reference Wright's organic style.) Inside, the family-friendly restaurant, which has been in continuous operation since it opened, contains a classic dining counter; curving, no-frills pink vinyl banquettes; Formica tabletops; and an old-fashioned cash register. To be honest, the food here is not the reason to visit, but that's not the point, is it? A mediocre coffee in this ambiance is worth ten lattes in Silver Lake. The restaurant's longtime host, Filimon Lamas, was tragically murdered in 2012, but Chips is still as friendly as ever. ■

Compton City Hall and Civic Center

178

Los Angeles **Architect** Harold Williams **Year** 1977
Address 205 S Willowbrook Drive, Compton, CA 90220

Open to Public No **Free Entrance** No **Café/Restaurant** No
Overnight Accommodation No **Gift/Bookshop** No

It's a miracle that Harold Williams' Compton City Hall and Civic Center ever got built. After Williams (an apprentice to Paul R. Williams) was hired in 1968, the troubled city, according to the *Los Angeles Times*, churned through three mayors, eight city managers and ten council members. But Compton opened the complex – including the legislature, courthouse, police department and county library, arranged around a large paved central plaza highlighted by an angular, shard-like sculpture – in 1976. The two-story, glass-clad City Hall is shaded by massive vertical concrete fins, projecting far in front of the building. Its entry is marked with a concrete canopy that swoops up to greet visitors. The thirteen-story courthouse wraps a glass box in white concrete, exposing only narrow slit openings. The sculpture, which was a collaboration between Williams and artist Gerald Gladstone, consists of thin, angular white pieces connected by a metallic ring. Increasing in height around its circumference, it's meant to suggest the 'mountaintop' that Reverend Martin Luther King Jr. evoked in his 'I Have a Dream' speech. A mural on the street side of the complex (you enter through a break in the street wall) depicts all of these buildings and more local landmarks. It contains the Bible verse: 'You are the light of the world. A city that is set on a hill cannot be hidden'. ■

California State University, Dominguez Hills

Who would have guessed that California State University, Dominguez Hills, a state college in Carson, just outside of Compton, would be the brainchild of architectural hero A. Quincy Jones? The architect was hired to oversee its development in 1964 and he led its growth until he died in 1979. The 345-acre (140-hectare) campus (formerly South Bay State College) was once part of Rancho San Pedro, the first private land grant in California. It was originally planned for the cliffs of Palos Verdes, but after the Watts Riots in 1965, Governor Pat Brown decided to move it to this underserved area. Jones enlivened the site's flat topography by installing undulating hills and copious trees, above which Jones' off-yellow Modernist buildings (in Brutalist, International Style and New Formalist styles) are connected via raised concrete walkways. The buildings' most important features are their exposed concrete construction and planted, self-contained courtyard plans. Most feature large windows, vertical fins, geometric block screens and sizable roof overhangs marked with concrete waffle slabs. The most dramatic example is the Leo F. Cain Library (pictured), whose composition of floating boxes and an amazing cantilevered roof should be featured in architectural dictionary definitions for waffle slab. ■

Los Angeles **Architect** A. Quincy Jones **Year** 1964
Address 1000 E Victoria Street, Carson, CA 90747

Open to Public Yes **Free Entrance** Yes **Café/Restaurant** Yes
Overnight Accommodation No **Gift/Bookshop** No

With its tall glass facade, neo-classical proportions and tell-tale white post and lintel portico dramatically projecting toward the street, it's funny that most assume the Riviera Methodist Church in gritty Redondo Beach was built by Neutra and Alexander. That firm did indeed build the church's first structure, a small white stucco and staggered glass box with an upturned entry canopy along busy Palos Verdes Boulevard which now contains Riviera's offices. But it was Long Beach architects Killingsworth Brady Smith that designed the institution's monumental expansion ten years later. The lofty Killingsworth building's clear glass frontage floods the sanctuary with natural light. Its interior maintains the same post-and-lintel vocabulary, with vertical slat windows providing light and glimpses of the ocean beyond. A small courtyard to the right of the building, overlooking a parking lot, provides even clearer views to the majestic beachfront setting. While Richard Neutra only played a small role in this project, he was quite active in this area, designing Palos Verdes High School (600 Cloyden Road, Palos Verdes Estates), the Beckstrand House (1400 Via Montemar, Palos Verdes), the Dailey House (953 Granvia Altamira, Palos Verdes Estates), the Hafley House (5561 E La Pasada Street, Long Beach) and the Moore House (5551 La Pasada Street, Long Beach), among others. ■

Los Angeles **Architect** Richard Neutra and Killingsworth Brady Smith
Year 1957 **Address** 375 Palos Verdes Boulevard, Redondo Beach, CA 90277

Open to Public Yes **Free Entrance** Yes **Café/Restaurant** No
Overnight Accommodation No **Gift/Bookshop** No

Bowler House

181

Los Angeles **Architect** Lloyd Wright **Year** 1963
Address 3456 Via Campesina, Rancho Palos Verdes, CA 90275

Open to Public No **Free Entrance** No **Café/Restaurant** No
Overnight Accommodation No **Gift/Bookshop** No

After the stunning success of his Wayfarers Chapel (page 242), Frank Lloyd Wright's son, Lloyd Wright, was offered several more commissions in Palos Verdes, most of them residential. One of the most ambitious was the Bowler House, which has been nicknamed 'Bird of Paradise' for its exploding, triangular, bluish roofline. Commissioned by industrial building contractor John Bowler, the concrete-framed building has stucco, concrete and field-stone walls, with an angular roof jutting up from a fairly low height, composed of blue corrugated fiberglass, a material meant to blend with the sky above. Inside, angular rooms, crystal-shaped mirrors and triangular screens continue the exterior's geometric language, while the exterior is full of lush grass and pristine landscaping. Of Wright's remaining homes in the area, the Lombardi (804 Gatos Place), perched high in the hills, with a pyramidal red roof and long, bar-shaped body, is definitely worth an excursion, although you have to look up at it from the base of its long driveway. Sadly the glassy, X-shaped Moore House, the most adventurous of all Wright's homes in South Bay, was demolished by its owners in 2012, in favor of a Mediterranean McMansion. It was a shocking reminder of how vulnerable even the most exquisite Mid-Century Modern wonders remain. ■

Wayfarers Chapel

182

Los Angeles **Architect** Lloyd Wright **Year** 1951
Address 5755 Palos Verdes Drive S, Rancho Palos Verdes, CA 90275

Open to Public Yes **Free Entrance** Yes **Café/Restaurant** No
Overnight Accommodation No **Gift/Bookshop** Yes

Probably no architect in history has been more unfairly overlooked than Lloyd Wright. Such is the cost of being both the son and namesake of Frank Lloyd Wright. But Wright's portfolio of work, especially around Los Angeles, is almost unparalleled. His masterpiece is the Wayfarers Chapel, perched along the rocky cliffs of Rancho Palos Verdes, a well-to-do coastal city south of Los Angeles. The building was constructed for the Swedenborgian Church, a multi-denominational group that centers on the natural world as a source of spirituality. Inspired by the redwoods around it, the 'tree chapel' disappears into the forest, dominated by glass and local stone walls, internal plants, diamond and circle patterns (representing inclusiveness) and redwood beams. The beautiful compositions around it include rows of redwoods leading to the interior, a carefully landscaped rose garden, a peaceful reflecting pool and of course, views down the dramatic coast. Even if you're not religious, it's a spiritual experience. While in Rancho Palos Verdes be sure to check out a few more Mid-Century Modern churches, such as St. Paul's Lutheran Church (31290 Palos Verdes Drive South), with its boat-like form and cartoonishly large cross. ■

Wayfarers Chapel

Brady Residence

183

Los Angeles **Architect** Killingsworth Brady Smith **Year** 1970
Address 4204 Cedar Avenue, Long Beach, CA 90807

Open to Public No **Free Entrance** No **Café/Restaurant** No
Overnight Accommodation No **Gift/Bookshop** No

A short drive from the Opdahl and Case Study #25 houses (pages 250 and 251) is one more Kinllingsworth Brady Smith secret, the Brady Residence, home to one of the firms partners, Jules Brady. You can't see much behind the entryway, but the facade is weirdly special: a tall grid of solid walls, translucent glazing, exposed, projecting white columns and beams and another super-tall, extra-thin door. Its grandiose proportions and exaggerated sense of refinement suggest Hollywood Regency merged with Modernism, as does the manicured landscape framing the house and its location, known as Long Beach's Virginia Country Club neighborhood. Brady was born in Long Beach and, like Edward Killingsworth, studied architecture at University of Southern California. (Their third partner, Waugh Smith, graduated from UC Berkeley). Also like his partners, Brady began his career in the office of successful Long Beach architect Kenneth S. Wing, where the three met and eventually left to form their own partnership. Inside, the 3,100-square-foot (288-square-meter), two-bedroom home features a two-story, open-air entrance atrium, a double-height living room fronted with glass walls, a sculptural steel staircase and no fewer than nine skylights. It's utterly protected from the street and yet it still brings the outside in – a brilliant Brady specialty. ■

184 Killingsworth Brady Smith Offices

Arguably the best building on Long Beach Boulevard, the offices of Killingsworth Brady Smith remains in exquisite condition today. The glassy, one-story building consists of interconnected rectilinear pieces, framed with exposed wood posts and beams and fronted by large sheets of clear glass. All are focused around extensive landscaping, large (and productive) fruit trees and a peaceful reflecting pool. Thanks to all the glass, you can look clearly into the offices themselves, which are preserved as a monument to the Mid-Century Modern era, with their exquisite furniture, art, internal courtyards and interior design. Or you can see straight through them, enjoying views of the lush trees out back. It's all quite protected from the busy thoroughfare and from the sun, thanks to the thick landscaping and water features, in front. The temperature drops by about five degrees by the time you reach the door; it's like walking up to a floating pavilion in a botanical garden. The offices are now used by local firm Kelly Sutherlin McLeod Architecture, which painstakingly restored the building in 2012. If you drive down this stretch of Long Beach Boulevard, you'll get to see about half a dozen other pristine post-and-beam offices, many of them executed by Killingsworth Brady Smith. ■

Los Angeles **Architect** Killingsworth Brady Smith **Year** 1957
Address 3827 Long Beach Boulevard, Long Beach, CA 90807

Open to Public No **Free Entrance** No **Café/Restaurant** No
Overnight Accommodation No **Gift/Bookshop** No

Cambridge Building

The Cambridge Building, now home to Long Beach's Bayfront Youth and Family Services, was designed for local real estate investment company Cambridge Investment Corporation. It's one of several spectacular projects by Killingsworth Brady Smith in the immediate vicinity, which I've taken to naming Killingsworth Row. The complex's main structure is a Miesian white steel-framed glass box, neighbored on one side by a screened internal courtyard and on the other by an open external one, accessible via a series of stone tiles through a shallow reflecting pool. Exposed beams and slatted wood shades above create abstract shadows on the ground. A floating stair leads to a second-floor landing, from where you can get an excellent view of the composition coming together. Offices inside are quite open, but methodically spaced and shaded by large curtains. These elements were all common in Killingsworth Brady Smith's repertoire, but he combined them into a masterpiece here. The only disappointment is the olive-yellow wall color, which doesn't show in the historic photos. Besides that, Cambridge is in immaculate condition and a must-see if you're in the South Bay area. ■

Los Angeles **Architect** Killingsworth Brady Smith **Year** 1960
Address 324 E Bixby Road, Long Beach, CA 90807

Open to Public No **Free Entrance** No **Café/Restaurant** No
Overnight Accommodation No **Gift/Bookshop** No

Los Angeles **Architect** Donald Gibbs **Year** 1963
Address 3575 Long Beach Boulevard, Long Beach, CA 90807

Open to Public No **Free Entrance** No **Café/Restaurant** No
Overnight Accommodation No **Gift/Bookshop** No

Yet another example of Los Angeles' many hidden revelations, Long Beach Boulevard, in addition to containing a spectacular line-up of post-and-beam offices, comprises what appears from the street to be its own version of Mies van der Rohe's Barcelona Pavilion (1929). It is in fact the offices of Gibbs & Gibbs Architects, a firm that has existed in Long Beach since 1934 and still practices today under the name Gibbs Architects. The building's designer, Donald Gibbs, is a self-proclaimed Mies acolyte and he created a raised rectangle of continuous glass and fire-engine-red painted steel, softened and shielded by elegant jacaranda trees and gardens, with a wide open plan inside. He's also quite an artist and you can explore his colorful abstract sculptures and paintings, which plaster most of the walls and surfaces here. Gibbs is also an avid sailor and has taken up boat-building as his latest pursuit. Another forgotten Mid-Century Modern talent, Gibbs also co-designed the intimidating Long Beach Civic Center (which at the time of publication was scheduled for demolition) and much of the California State Long Beach campus, in particular the striking, corrugated-metal-clad Walter Pyramid and the elegant, glassy Psychology building. ■

186

Gibbs & Gibbs Architects Office Building

Rancho Estates

187

The largest of Cliff May's many tract housing developments, Rancho Estates is the epitome of the architect's vision for 'contemporary ranch style', a combination of Mid-Century Modern and traditional ranch house design. Part of the larger Lakewood development made famous by author D.J. Waldie in his book *Promised Land*, Rancho's seven-hundred single-story homes are all L-shaped with shallow gabled roofs, clerestory windows, concrete block walls and board-and-batten siding. Three- to four-bedroom homes, built together with May's business partner Chris Choate, were designed based on repeating, prefabricated modules and could be assembled quickly. Unlike newer residences in the area, all have front courtyards and large amounts of outdoor space, embracing the California climate and topography. Tall ceilings, large windows (on internal elevations) and clerestories helped bring this scene and copious natural light, inside. Unfortunately the model typified by Rancho Estates quickly became too complex for a small company to sustain. 'We were much too soon... and if we had come out with it a few years later, it would have been easier', said May. Larger developers like Joseph Eichler had more widespread success with Modern housing tracts, creating more structurally expressive designs than May's residences. ■

Los Angeles **Architect** Cliff May & Chris Choate **Year** 1954
Address By the corner of Studebaker Road and E Spring Street, Long Beach, CA 90808

Open to Public No **Free Entrance** No **Café/Restaurant** No
Overnight Accommodation No **Gift/Bookshop** No

Los Angeles **Architect** Raphael Soriano **Year** 1940
Address 380 Orlena Avenue, Long Beach, CA 90814

Open to Public No **Free Entrance** No **Café/Restaurant** No
Overnight Accommodation No **Gift/Bookshop** No

188

Kimpson Nixon Residence

A textbook example of Raphael Soriano's gift for gorgeous simplicity, the Kimpson Nixon Residence is defined by the two horizontal bands of windows that line the pristine white two-story structure. The second story, only half the length of the first, pops up like a boat, its constant exposure protected by deep overhangs. The International Style building's L-shape juts out in back, opening to a small landscaped patio, creating a classic example of the Southern California indoor–outdoor lifestyle. In front, a small yellow door is shaded by a tiny canopy. The light-infused interior still contains original wood paneling, wood floors and built-in cabinets and shelves. Soriano, it should be noted, designed legendary photographer Julius Shulman's splendid outdoor-oriented house in the Hollywood Hills, which, unfortunately, is not visible from the street. He also designed what's known as the 'Case Study House For 1950' in Pacific Palisades. While the recently-renovated Kimpson Nixon Residence – called 'one of the purest expressions of early Modernism in the city' by architectural historians Cara Mullio and Jennifer Volland – is in fantastic condition, many in the neighborhood have not fared as well. For instance, a Streamline Moderne next door has been completely deformed into an incomprehensible McMansion. ■

Opdahl Residence

189

Los Angeles **Architect** Killingsworth Brady Smith **Year** 1958
Address 5576 Vesuvian Walk, Long Beach, CA 90803

Open to Public No **Free Entrance** No **Café/Restaurant** No
Overnight Accommodation No **Gift/Bookshop** No

One of Los Angeles's best surprises is Long Beach's canals, along which boats scurry and unusual homes line up, row after row. There's even a nautical Christmas parade. Long Beach architects Killingsworth Brady Smith (KBS) built two of its most astounding homes here, located right around the corner from one another. The Opdahl Residence, designed for Richard and Joyce Opdahl, is set well back from the street, slowly unfolding via a stone path, making its way first through a reflecting pool, lush landscaping and a series of projecting beams. Beyond that the two-story home is completely open to the street through a double-height living room overlooked by a mezzanine of bedrooms. Sitting on the canal itself is Case Study House #25 (page 251, opposite), also known as the Frank House. A short drive away is one more Killingsworth Brady Smith secret, the Brady Residence (page 244), home to firm partner Jules Brady. You can't see much behind the entryway, but the facade is strangely special: a tall grid of solid walls, translucent glazing, exposed columns and beams and another super-tall, super-thin door. ■

Rising above the Naples Canal in Long Beach is Case Study House #25, also known as the Frank House, a pristine two-story white cube fronted by a quadrant of huge windows and a narrow, seventeen-foot-tall (five-meter) wood door. The home is accessed via a thity-five-by-fifteen-foot (ten-by-five-meter) atrium, lined by a moat dotted with square pavers and covered with a slatted wood roof. This courtyard space abuts, via tall sheets of glass, living and dining areas below and bedrooms above. The living room and master bedroom both take in expansive views of the canal, which is a popular spot for boaters, kayakers and paddle boarders. One of four Case Study Houses that Killingsworth Brady Smith designed for *Arts & Architecture* magazine, the home was commissioned by Ed Frank, owner of Frank Brothers furniture store. Frank, a classmate of Edward Killingsworth's at nearby Wilson High School, was able to fill the house with prime Mid-Century Modern furnishings, from Mies van der Rohe lounge chairs and a coffee table to a Van Keppel-Green sofa. The house is in immaculate condition, except for its rear elevation, which has been filled in with faceless stucco and blank garage doors. Around the corner, be sure to explore KBS's Opdahl Residence (page 250, opposite), a grid of square solids and voids set well back from the street and accessed, again, via a paver-lined reflecting pool. ■

Los Angeles **Architect** Killingsworth Brady Smith **Year** 1962
Address 82 Rivo Alto Canal, Long Beach, CA 90803

Open to Public No **Free Entrance** No **Café/Restaurant** No
Overnight Accommodation No **Gift/Bookshop** No

California State University Fullerton

191

Los Angeles **Architect** Howard B. Van Heuklyn **Year** 1959
Address 800 N State College Boulevard, Fullerton, CA 92831

Open to Public Yes **Free Entrance** Yes **Café/Restaurant** No
Overnight Accommodation No **Gift/Bookshop** No

Warning: Fullerton is a bleak town. But if you're hoping to become more than a casual fan of Brutalist architecture, making the trek to Cal State Fullerton's campus will separate you from the pack. Located on the site of a former citrus grove (like, sadly, so much in Orange County), the campus was planned and largely designed, by architect Howard B. Van Heuklyn, who completed academic buildings around the region. The Brutalist core, connected by wide concrete paths, is not warm and fuzzy, but it's fascinating. It centers around a quad fronted by Van Heuklyn's Pollak Library (pictured), which is wildly animated by a textured honeycomb facade, floating atop radiating columns. It's unclear why the honeycomb shape became so ubiquitious in Van Heuklyn's design (it has nothing to do with the school's mascot, an elephant named Tuffy the Titan) but it works as a unifying feature. In the immediate vicinity make sure to walk through the outdoor breezeway of the Joseph Clark Performing Arts Center and check out the similarly geometric cladding of Langsdorf Hall, McCarthy Hall and the Humanities and Social Sciences Building. ■

192

Hope International University

Located across Nutwood Avenue from California State University Fullerton (page 252, opposite), the small evangelical campus of Hope International University (HIU) is one of the largest collections of Googie architecture in existence. The complex, originally designed as a movie theater, shopping center and dorms for CSUF, was designed by none other than Eldon Davis, one of the leaders of the legendary Googie firm Armet & Davis – which designed Southern California's most famous Googie diners. Davis collaborated with Walter Beeson & Associates, which planned most of CSUF. Cal State eventually sold the complex to Pacific Christian College, which later became HIU. The centerpiece of the campus is the Darling Library (pictured), a two-level concrete-clad structure inset with stone aggregate and topped by wing-like, vaulted triangular canopies. They're supported by Y-shaped columns and evoke the typical Googie love for technology and the space age. Coincidentally, those themes and shapes translate perfectly into a message of spiritual uplift; the building's peaked roofline has been incorporated into HIU's logo. Classroom wings project from here, connected via raised walkways. Dorms and campus buildings nearby share the same Googie language, with zigzag canopies and hexagonal concrete block balconies, a shape taken from the CSUF campus across the street. ■

Los Angeles **Architect** Armet & Davis **Year** Late 1960s
Address 2500 Nutwood Avenue, Fullerton, CA 92831

Open to Public Yes **Free Entrance** Yes **Café/Restaurant** No
Overnight Accommodation No **Gift/Bookshop** Yes

Anaheim Convention Center & Arena

193

In the shadow of Disneyland's Space Mountain sits one of the most imposing forgotten buildings you'll ever see: Adrian Wilson & Associates' Anaheim Convention Center & Arena. Two two-hundred-ton (181-tonne) steel arches hold up its concrete shell dome, as if a dinosaur-sized turtle had mated with LAX's Theme Building (page 171). While it has hosted thousands of major events, including a rally for Richard Nixon and shows by bands like the Doors, few outside of Anaheim have ever seen this treasure, whose structural audacity combines the technical fluency of late Modernism with the space-age ethos of Googie. It's especially appropriate given its Disney neighbor, from where you can hear screams as ride-goers plunge into darkness. At night the arena – now overshadowed by a generic but jazzy addition by large firm HNTB – is dramatically lit in purple hues, accentuating its high-tech profile, which would be more at home in Tokyo than it is in Anaheim. Inside, the arena is much more pedestrian, so spend your time craning your neck outside instead. ■

Los Angeles **Architect** Adrian Wilson & Associates **Year** 1967
Address 800 W Katella Avenue, Anaheim, CA 92802

Open to Public Yes **Free Entrance** No **Café/Restaurant** No
Overnight Accommodation No **Gift/Bookshop** No

Los Angeles **Architect** Ladd & Kelsey **Year** 1961
Address 2241 West Coast Highway, Newport Beach, CA 92663

Open to Public Yes **Free Entrance** Yes **Café/Restaurant** No
Overnight Accommodation No **Gift/Bookshop** No

194

Stuft Shirt Restaurant

As the work of Oscar Niemeyer, Felix Candela and Eero Saarinen remind us, Expressionist Modernism can raise your pulse, not just cool your senses. But while their work has been canonized over and over, hardly anybody knows about this example, located along the Newport Beach Marina. Now occupied by luxury clothing store Amaree's, the Stuft Shirt was originally a strangely baroque restaurant designed by the underappreciated genius architecture firm Ladd & Kelsey. The white building's clam-shaped eaves, toothpick columns and wide arched floor-to-ceiling windows create a remarkable site on the water. Inside, thanks to a thoughtful renovation by Paul Davis Architects, the light-infused spaces are better than ever. Gone are the Versaille-style drapes, spider-like chandeliers, thick carpeting and other accretions added over the years and brought to the fore are an exposed concrete shell, concrete floors, frameless glass doors and a sublime feeling of light and space. This is an example of how a renovation can bring a building back to its original glory and then improve it. Designers of Mid-Century Modern architecture didn't get everything right and hindsight and new tastes can fix that, creating an enchanting combination of time periods. ■

The Arboretum (Drive-In Church)

195

Los Angeles **Architect** Richard Neutra **Year** 1961
Address 13280 Chapman Avenue, Garden Grove, CA 92840

Open to Public Yes **Free Entrance** Yes **Café/Restaurant** No
Overnight Accommodation No **Gift/Bookshop** No

Philip Johnson's Crystal Cathedral, the largest glass building in the world and an icon of postmodernism, is one of the most famous structures in Southern California. But few are aware that the cathedral's campus contains several more significant buildings, including a Mid-Century Modern church by Richard Neutra. His so-called Drive-In Church was actually the first permanent home for minister Robert Schuller's Garden Grove Community Church, an evangelical congregation that had previously rented space from the Orange Drive-In Theater. The long, narrow building was, like Johnson's edifice, filled with glazing, but in this case oriented vertically (with 620 panes of glass) along its flanks, protected by thin overhanging flat eaves. In 1968 Neutra added the campanile-like Tower of Hope – a structure that alternates between tall bands of glazing, stone and floating stair – containing offices, classrooms and a hanging belfry. Neutra's church, which became iconic for its international broadcasts of the *Hour of Power*, was replaced by Johnson's building in 1981, but it's still used for services. The complex, including its lovely arboretum, was renovated in 2014. In 2011 the Roman Catholic Diocese of Orange bought the cathedral from the financially struggling Crystal Cathedral Ministries. It's currently being renovated and converted for Catholic services. ■

195

The Arboretum (Drive-In Church)

Built for famed naturopath Philip Lovell, who also commissioned Richard Neutra's Lovell Health House in Los Feliz (page 184), the Lovell Beach House floats boldly over a residential street just steps from the ocean in Newport Beach. It is, without exaggeration, considered one of the most important structures of the Modern movement. No pressure. In order to separate the white stucco-clad home – space-challenged because of its tight site – from the road, Schindler raised it above, cantilevering its top floor (with its long strip of green ribbon windows) atop five free-standing concrete frames, which not only serve as buttresses but shape spaces below and support the home's complex external stairs. Inside, the residence's focal point is a two-story living room, an abstractly decorated hall penetrated with light from all directions, including an exceptional gridded window wall facing the ocean. You can view the house from all sides – although its rear elevation is partially obscured by other homes – including right from the beach. As you walk around the building its cubist composition changes dramatically, the interlocking forms taking on new patterns and massing, like a De Stijl painting. When you're done, take a ride on the beach's bike path – just don't expect the other houses along its length to impress you like this one. ■

Los Angeles **Architect** Rudolph Schindler **Year** 1926
Address 1242 W Oceanfront, Newport Beach, CA 92661

Open to Public No **Free Entrance** No **Café/Restaurant** No
Overnight Accommodation No **Gift/Bookshop** No

Los Angeles **Architect** George Bissell **Year** 1964
Address 31911 National Park Drive, Laguna Niguel, CA 92677

Open to Public No **Free Entrance** No **Café/Restaurant** No
Overnight Accommodation No **Gift/Bookshop** No

Horizon House

While pretty much every Modernist architecture aficionado in the world has heard of the Case Study House Program, virtually nobody is aware of a much larger, equally progressive effort: the Horizon Homes Program, sponsored by a consortium of cement companies in the early 1960s. Their goal was to show how residences (which totaled about 150 around the country) could be built cheaply and creatively with concrete and from the looks of some of the best examples, they succeeded. Almost a dozen Horizon Homes were built in Southern California and an excellent example is George Bissell's Horizon House in Laguna Niguel, a town that was one of the region's hotbeds of creative Mid-Century Modern residential design. The pie-shaped house features a rolling, cantilevered concrete roof floating above glass walls, so every room opens to rich landscaping and views. The continuous interior wraps around a curving, white central column, which contains a strange, mouth-shaped fireplace. A tall white wall blocks much of the view from the street, but you can still get a pretty good look at this entirely unique structure from the end of the driveway. Bissell, whose office was based in Newport Beach, won more than fifty local and national awards for his impressive work and he helped found the Monterey Design Conference at Asilomar, now a must-visit for California architects. ■

University of California Irvine

198

On a site that was once rolling cow pastures, unsung Modernist architect William Pereira designed one of the great unsung Modernist university campuses – University of California, Irvine. Pereira, who also master-planned the entire city of Irvine, LAX Airport and the 1933 Chicago World's Fair, put together an academic village in a park, circling around a central green. He maintained the site's hilly topography, floating heavy, sculpted concrete structures – protected via tapered and patterned fins and sunshades – above. The off-white buildings are connected via raised bridges, plinths and walkways. There are so many impressive Brutalist structures here, but a few highlights include Pereira's Langson Library (pictured, right); Pereira's Crawford Hall and Murray Krieger Hall; AC Martin's Social Sciences Tower and Kistner, Wright & Wright's Engineering Tower. In later years the school went postmodern, hiring Frank Gehry, James Stirling, Arthur Erickson, Charles Moore and Venturi Scott Brown, among others, but it's still the Modernist vocabulary that defines this place. ■

Los Angeles **Architect** William Pereira & Associates **Year** 1963
Address Irvine, CA 92697

Open to Public Yes **Free Entrance** Yes **Café/Restaurant** Yes
Overnight Accommodation No **Gift/Bookshop** No

198

University of California Irvine

University of California Riverside

199

Los Angeles **Architect** Jones & Emmons **Year** 1950s
Address 900 University Avenue, Riverside, CA 92521

Open to Public Yes **Free Entrance** Yes **Café/Restaurant** Yes
Overnight Accommodation No **Gift/Bookshop** Yes

While not as glamorous as its sister campuses at UC Irvine and UC San Diego, University of California, Riverside is a smaller-scale, unique place that's worth a visit. The campus began as a citrus research station for the University of California system in 1907, becoming an official campus in the 1950s and growing quickly in the 1960s. Los Angeles firm Allison & Rible prepared the master plan in 1955, creating a layout and a collection of buildings that is a Modernist interpretation of the California Mission style. It's like walking through a colonial Spanish village, with clusters of buildings, narrow alleys and covered passageways leading to small, shaded courtyards and gardens. Some of the Modernists who've worked on the campus are among the area's best, including Albert Frey, Jones & Emmons and William Pereira, creating understated buildings that incorporate the archways, overhangs and courtyards of colonial architecture, using materials like brick, concrete, steel and glass. Among several other subtle wonders, be sure to visit Sproul Hall, with its cantilevered waffle slab roof; the Tomás Rivera Library, with its offset, narrow window slits; and of course the 161-foot-tall (49-meter) Carillon Bell Tower, containing forty-eight brass bells, a slatted, ladder-like facade and yet another waffle roof. ■

200

Crafton Hills College

If you're driving to or from Palm Springs on the 10 Freeway, an unknown but must-stop destination is Crafton Hills College, which was planned by the legendary Palm Springs architect E. Stewart Williams. Williams, who first considered the job impossible, inserted the 523-acre (211-hectare) campus – the largest project of his career – into the steep foothills above the tiny town of Yucaipa. He decided to keep the site's natural contours and vegetation as intact as possible, so the campus's sand-colored concrete cubes and rectangles are almost all lifted above the ground, creating unique bridges, levitating walkways, and floating stairs. All this hovering is in contrast to the buildings' heavy materials, used to protect it from the harsh desert sun. Other solar protection includes deep overhangs and continuous fins. The main route through the campus is a long path starting at the center of the college, passing the library, moving under the raised laboratory and administration building (which is the complex's centerpiece), and ending at the health sciences building. Along the way you pass through grassy plazas, lovely quadrangles, and thick clusters of trees all set out over several changes in topography. ■

Los Angeles **Architect** E. Stewart Williams **Year** 1972
Address 11711 Sand Canyon Road, Yucaipa, CA 92399

Open to Public Yes **Free Entrance** Yes **Café/Restaurant** No
Overnight Accommodation No **Gift/Bookshop** No

Palm Springs

Palm Springs

201 Hotel Lautner **202** Tramway Gas Station **203** Alexander Steel Houses **204** Miller House **205** Kaufmann House **206** Edris House **207** Max Palevsky House **208** House of Tomorrow **209** Palm Springs City Hall **210** El Rancho Vista Estates **211** St. Theresa Church **212** Palm Springs Art Museum, Architecture & Design Center **213** Frey House II **214** Coachella Valley Savings and Loan (1) **215** Coachella Valley Savings and Loan (2) **216** Caliente Tropics Resort **217** Ocotillo Lodge **218** Horizon Hotel **219** Bank of America **220** Pearlman Cabin **221** Sunnylands **222** Palm Springs Palmer and Krisel Tracts

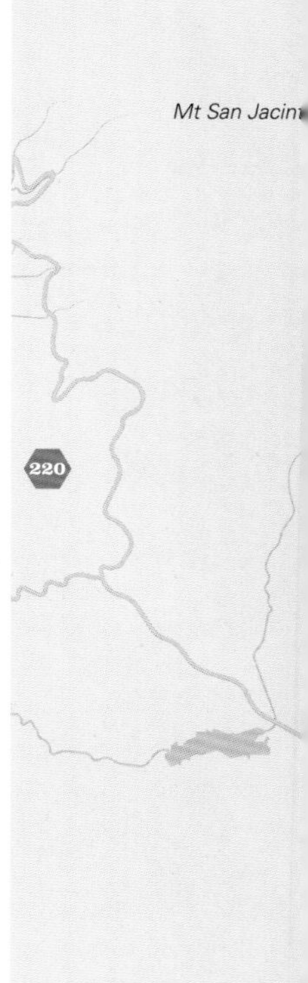

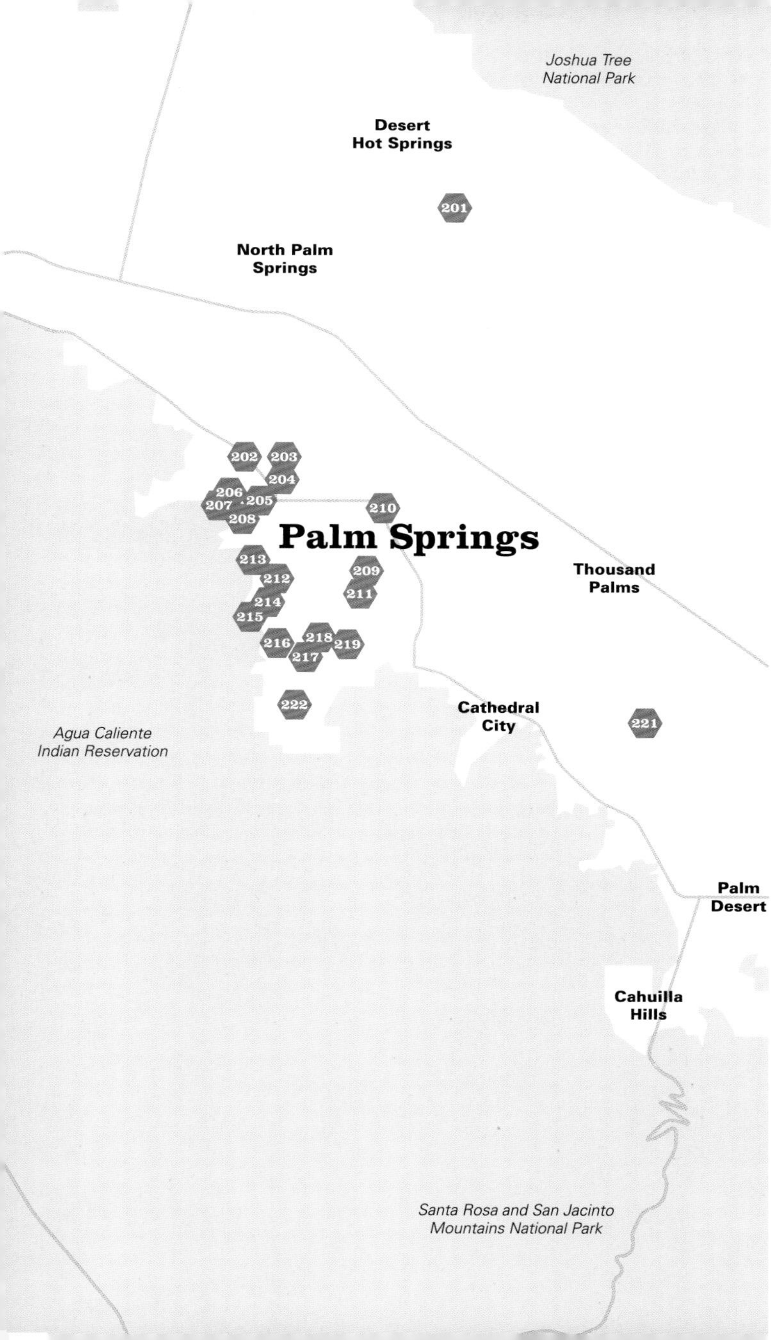

Palm Springs

Joshua Tree National Park

Desert Hot Springs

201

North Palm Springs

202 203 204 206 205 207 208 210

213 212 209 211 214 215 216 218 219 217 222 221

Thousand Palms

Cathedral City

Agua Caliente Indian Reservation

Palm Desert

Cahuilla Hills

Santa Rosa and San Jacinto Mountains National Park

Hotel Lautner

201

Palm Springs **Architect** John Lautner **Year** 1947
Address 67710 San Antonio Street, Desert Hot Springs, CA 92240

Open to Public Yes **Free Entrance** No **Café/Restaurant** No
Overnight Accommodation Yes **Gift/Bookshop** No

What is now an exclusive boutique hotel known as the Hotel Lautner was once the far less tricked-out Desert Hot Springs Motel, used by, among others, movie director Lucien Hubbard, who treated it as a getaway for his stars and starlets. The motel consisted of four units (originally intended to be part of a planned community that never happened), with separate entrances, wedge-shaped concrete roofs, exposed steel struts, angled clerestory windows and gardens walled off with horizontal-clad timber walls. Large glass walls looked into the private desert gardens without sacrificing privacy or risking sun overdoses. Gradually the motel fell into disrepair, but in 2000 artist Steve Lowe bought the property, repairing it and returning it to motel use. Then in 2008 interior designer Tracy Beckmann and furniture designer Ryan Trowbridge bought it and took four years to bring it to its current condition: an immaculate boutique property called Hotel Lautner filled with updated versions of Lautner's built-in furniture, newly paned clerestories and glass walls, richly replanted private desert gardens and enough luxury vintage furniture to start a museum. The motel's original pool is gone, but units share a small communal plunge pool and an outdoor barbecue and firepit area. ●

201

Hotel Lautner

Tramway Gas Station

It's strangely fitting that the symbol for Palm Springs architecture, forged in the car-happy mid-century, is a gas station. Albert Frey's Tramway Gas Station, a former Enco service station, now serves as the city's visitors' center. The simple staggered masonry block and glass building is topped with a soaring, white steel hyperbolic paraboloid roof. Its Erector-like underside exposed, this giant topper, propped by thin steel columns, was designed to shelter the station's gas pumps. Its pointed profile recalls the jagged mountains behind it and there's no question that it makes a powerful impression as you whiz by on your way into town. The station had been slated for demolition in 1995 but was saved at the last minute by a concerned businessman. It was purchased by the City of Palm Springs in 2002 and converted into its visitors' center in 2003. Frey also designed the A-frame Palm Springs Tramway's Lower Station, located just up the road, where brave visitors can board this unusual conveyor for a trip into the surreal mountains, where temperatures bizarrely herald snow much of the year. ●

Palm Springs **Architect** Albert Frey & Robson Chambers **Year** 1965
Address 2901 N Palm Canyon Drive, Palm Springs, CA 92262

Open to Public Yes **Free Entrance** Yes **Café/Restaurant** No
Overnight Accommodation No **Gift/Bookshop** Yes

Palm Springs **Architect** Wexler & Harrison **Year** 1962
Address Sunnyview Drive, Palm Springs, CA 92262

Open to Public No **Free Entrance** No **Café/Restaurant** No
Overnight Accommodation No **Gift/Bookshop** No

203

Alexander Steel Houses

Steel might not seem like such a good idea in the blistering hot Coachella Valley, but it was the material of choice for pioneering architects Donald Wexler and Rick Harrison, who developed a series of affordable desert homes sponsored by US Steel and built by the Alexander Construction Company. Located in a remote northern stretch of Palm Springs, the homes combined off-site and on-site assembly, taking mass-produced elements normally used in schools and industrial buildings and adapting them to trendy residences. Modular panels – consisting of a steel skin, insulated with gypsum and fiberglass – were prefabricated in Los Angeles, shipped to Palm Springs and lowered in place via crane. Large panes of glass and interior drywall were then installed. The planned tract of thirty-eight all-steel houses was never completed. Shortly after the first seven were built, the price of steel increased and the builder abandoned the project. They had fallen into disrepair, but now all seven have been beautifully renovated. They're fascinating to explore, combining economy and simplicity with a Palm Springs sense of panache: including cool-white coloring, zigzag canopies, asymetrical layouts, super-deep eaves, glass walls, exposed beams and desert landscaping. ●

Miller House

204

Palm Springs **Architect** Richard Neutra **Year** 1937
Address 2311 N Indian Avenue, Palm Springs, CA 92262

Open to Public No **Free Entrance** No **Café/Restaurant** No
Overnight Accommodation No **Gift/Bookshop** No

This small jewel box was made famous by Julius Shulman's photograph of its owner, Grace Lewis Miller, sitting in front of two tall corner windows, the vast emptiness of the desert sprawled out in front of her. The desert is no longer empty here, to say the least, but the Miller House remains a seminal regional work – a serene modern pavilion that was Neutra's first house in the area. The home and exercise studio (Miller was a teacher of the Swedish-centered Mensendieck System of Functional Exercises, a therapeutic movement technique) measures just 1,100 square feet (102 square meters), so every element is designed to conserve space. Built-in furniture lines most surfaces – cabinets and furniture serve as space dividers, bedrooms double as living spaces and large mirrors create the illusion of more space. The home is designed to tackle the harsh desert climate while also taking advantage of its spectacular, haunting vistas. Textured glass windows and solid stucco walls on the sunniest elevations provide both natural light and privacy; deep, metal-clad overhangs provide shade and plenty of operable windows and doors allow cross-ventilation. Screened porches blur the division between indoor and outdoor, while the tall floor-to-ceiling glass walls frame vistas of both the home's immediate landscaping and, of course, the desert expanses beyond. ●

The most famous residence in Palm Springs, for good reason, is Richard Neutra's Kaufmann House. The 3,800-square-foot (353-square-meter) structure was commissioned as a winter getaway by Pittsburgh department store mogul Edgar J. Kaufmann Sr., the same client who hired Frank Lloyd Wright to design Fallingwater about a decade earlier. It was immortalized by photographer Julius Shulman, whose black-and-white image of the clear glass home with its pool in the foreground and the rugged San Jacinto Mountains behind is probably his most well-known, along with the iconic image of the Stahl House in the Hollywood Hills (page 178). Shulman's eye for drama captured the essence of this building – a pristine openness that defied logic and precedent in the desert. The flat-roofed residence, edged with silver trim fascia that appears to float over large walls of glass, consists of four long wings, extending in all directions from a central living space and flowing easily from one to the next. Equally important is the landscape, which extends just as seamlessly through sliding glass doors, indoor-outdoor patios and decks and a stepped combination of grassy expanses, desert plantings and the famous pool. The only way this spectacular home disappoints is that it's not exceptional to see from the street, due to a large stone wall that provides privacy for the open space behind. ●

Palm Springs **Architect** Richard Neutra **Year** 1946
Address 470 W Vista Chino, Palm Springs, CA 92262

Open to Public No **Free Entrance** No **Café/Restaurant** No
Overnight Accommodation No **Gift/Bookshop** No

Kaufmann House

Edris House

206

Palm Springs **Architect** E. Stewart Williams **Year** 1954
Address 1030 W Cielo Drive, Palm Springs, CA 92262

Open to Public No **Free Entrance** No **Café/Restaurant** No
Overnight Accommodation No **Gift/Bookshop** No

So many homes strive to merge with their environment and so few manage to do it well. One of the best exceptions is E. Stewart Williams' Edris House, located in Palm Springs' Little Tuscany Estates. The architect was commissioned by William Edris, a prominent Seattle businessman who made a name for himself as a socialite in Palm Springs. His low-profiled home, placed at the top of a rocky outcrop, stayed true to Williams' assertion that a building should 'grow out of its site, not look like a spaceship that had just landed.' Its walls are supported with local timber, filled with local stones and shaded with an inverted triangle-shaped overhanging roof, also made of timber planks. The whole composition is meant to emulate a minimalist shelter in the rocky hills. Interior and exterior walls are quite plain and floor-to-ceiling windows are set into the walls and ceiling so one cannot see the framing. Inside, the home's main living area is focused around its fireplace, like a cave. Williams' custom-designed light fixtures reinforce the primal feeling; they are seen in, for instance an entryway planter containing projecting steel light rods that emulate natural forms. ●

Acclaimed playboy, bon vivant and master of pure Southern California Modernism Craig Ellwood brought his talents to Palm Springs late in his career when he designed the Max Palevsky House, his last residential commission. He wasn't alone: he worked closely with associate Alvaro Vallejo, who had come from Richard Neutra's office and with Palevsky himself, owner of computer company Scientific Data Systems and an avid design enthusiast who once said, 'I should have been an architect.' Importing his usual glass-dominated aesthetic to the sun-baked climate of Palm Springs took some adjustment. The inspiration was a Moroccan walled house and, with their wives, Palevsky and Ellwood took a trip to Morocco exploring several housing types. They focused on a set of desert homes in Casablanca in which three or four structures were set within a rectangular wall. The resulting white brick-clad Palm Springs residence, sited on a plateau on the southern edge of the city, contains a main house, its glass walls and sliding doors protected by bulky overhangs and a collection of separate suites, opening onto small enclosed courtyards or to a large pool area. The wall enclosing the complex contains slatted windows to protect from the sun while still maintaining views of the desert and the city below. ●

Palm Springs **Architect** Craig Ellwood **Year** 1968
Address 1021 W Cielo Drive, Palm Springs, CA 92262

Open to Public No **Free Entrance** No **Café/Restaurant** No
Overnight Accommodation No **Gift/Bookshop** No

Perched above the end of a short cul-de-sac in the foothills of Palm Springs, the House of Tomorrow, conceived by architecture firm Palmer and Krisel as an experiment in modern living, is aptly named, embodying the earnest optimism and unabashed technological obsession of the mid-century. From the street the residence takes the profile of an airplane, its orange and white wings extending from either side of a giant extended window wall. You enter by skipping up circular stone stairs through a small cascading water feature. On entering the hallway, the home unfolds, revealing a sweeping, open living room that anchors a series of free-flowing spaces (without any right angles) that seamlessly merge with the pool area in back through sliding glass windows and walls made of local stones. The project began as the home of famed Modernist developer Robert Alexander and his wife, Helene. It was later rented in 1967 by Elvis Presley and his new bride, Priscilla and is now known as the Elvis Presley Honeymoon House. The owners, who stubbornly question Palmer and Krisel's authorship, have decked it out with plenty of Elvis paraphernalia, making it a temple to the star, an ersatz Graceland West. It is part of the Alexander Construction Company's Vista Las Palmas tract, which includes great examples of Charles Dubois' distinctive Swiss Miss homes and Dean Martin's house at 1123 Via Monte Vista Drive. ●

Palm Springs **Architect** Palmer and Krisel **Year** 1960
Address 1350 Ladera Circle, Palm Springs, CA 92262

Open to Public No **Free Entrance** No **Café/Restaurant** No
Overnight Accommodation No **Gift/Bookshop** No

Palm Springs **Architect** Clark, Frey and Chambers **Year** 1952
Address 3200 E Tahquitz Canyon Way, Palm Springs, CA 92262

Open to Public No **Free Entrance** No **Café/Restaurant** No
Overnight Accommodation No **Gift/Bookshop** No

209

Palm Springs City Hall

When visitors head to Palm Springs to take in the Mid-Century Modern vibe, they generally miss out on a jewel hiding in plain sight: Albert Frey's Palm Springs City Hall, prominently located on Tahquitz Canyon Way, one of the city's main drags. True to his minimal kit-of-parts approach, Frey adorned the low-lying, linear glass and sandblasted concrete masonry building in a kaleidoscope of low-budget materials. He created a unique sun-shade with repeated metal piping, cut at angles. Green metal sun-screens shield a covered perimeter pathway, forming changing shadow patterns throughout the day. In front, a corrugated metal portico overhang contains a large circular cut-out to make room for palm trees. The jagged, stepped council chamber is separate from the rest of the building; words printed on its entry canopy read, 'The People Are The City.' Frey called this his favorite of the more than two-hundred structures he designed. He created it just after a long trip to Europe and was especially pleased with its combination of purity, simplicity and public accessibility. He was also obsessed with the shadows that its varying, textured elements created as the day changed. A quirky addition, a bronze statue of rodeo announcer and longtime Palm Springs mayor Frank Bogert on horseback, sits on the grass right in front of the building. ●

El Rancho Vista Estates

210

Palm Springs **Architect** Wexler & Harrison **Year** 1959
Address E Camino Rojos, Palm Springs, CA 92262

Open to Public No **Free Entrance** No **Café/Restaurant** No
Overnight Accommodation No **Gift/Bookshop** No

One of the many splendid Mid-Century Modern housing tracts in Palm Springs, Wexler & Harrison's El Rancho Vista Estates – located just north of the Palm Springs Airport – were conceived by developer Roy Fey, who successfully built a small real estate empire in Palm Springs. The low-lying homes (more than half by Wexler & Harrison) meant, like so many Modernist tracts, to bring the movement to the masses, include flat or butterfly roofs, down-turned eaves, decorative block walls, floor-to-ceiling glass, enclosed yards, bold colors and textured patterns. The tract of roughly seventy-five residences, spanning about one square mile (2.6 square kilometers), was severely run-down, even unsafe, two decades ago. It has since become a symbol of the power of preservation, carried out by local homeowners, new residents, the real estate community and the Palm Springs Preservation Foundation, which has helped raise awareness through tours and events. It's now one of the most beautiful Mid-Century Modern neighborhoods in the Coachella Valley. As residents continue their renovations, they bring back the original bright color schemes – from mustard yellow to mauve to turquoise – in opposition to the white that marked the original round of make-overs. Fey, often overshadowed by the Alexanders as one of Palm Springs' prime developers, named one of the streets of the development after himself, East Avenida Fey Norte. ●

El Rancho Vista Estates

St. Theresa Church

211

Palm Springs **Architect** William Cody **Year** 1968
Address 2800 Ramon Road, Palm Springs, CA 92264

Open to Public Yes **Free Entrance** Yes **Café/Restaurant** No
Overnight Accommodation No **Gift/Bookshop** No

Another unsung Palm Springs hero is William Cody, whose name sounds more like a Western hero than one of the city's most accomplished architects. He built well-regarded hotels, clubhouses, homes and libraries here, among other structures. A surprising example of Cody's exuberant style is St. Theresa Church, located on a former airfield just off the city's main drag, on Ramon Road. Surrounded by curved, fortress-like concrete walls, quiet planted courtyards and imposing, heavy doors, the church's white, upward-curving concrete roof resembles a pagoda merged with a pyramid merged with a snow-capped mountain. Large clerestory windows allow plenty of sunlight into the lofty, upturned sanctuary, which is fitted with Cody-designed red and yellow stained glass, statues, a sculptural altar and a baptismal font. The tent-like space is warmed with dark exposed wood columns, beams and pews and connected to the earth through ground-level glazed bands. Parishioners here have included Cody himself, Bob and Delores Hope, Loretta Young and Jane Wyman, while Lucille Ball and Desi Arnaz sent their children to St. Theresa School. The televised funeral of Sonny Bono took place here in 1998. ●

Palm Springs Art Museum Architecture & Design Center

Among the more than ten banks and bank complexes that E. Stewart Williams designed, one now has the honor of showcasing Palm Springs' architectural heritage: Santa Fe Savings and Loan, the home of the Palm Springs Art Museum Architecture and Design Center, which opened to the public in 2014. This beautiful single-story building, encased in floor-to-ceiling windows protected by a low overhanging roof and sliding aluminum sun-shades, has a powerful impact as a monument to Mid-Century Modern elegance – a drastic turn from the neoclassical temples that once dominated the banking world. The wide roofline is supported by thin star-profile columns, which don't obstruct the continuity of the glazed walls. The building was renovated by Los Angeles-based Marmol Radziner Architects, using Williams' original drawings and black-and-white photographs. The firm removed dividers, jettisoned carpeting to reveal original terrazzo floors, added sustainable desert landscaping and restored the anodized screens, among other things. The facility's uninterrupted exhibition spaces are a great way to take in the history of this legendary Modernist capital. More features include storage, support space, the original vault (containing a store) and a vintage teller window. ●

Palm Springs **Architect** E. Stewart Williams **Year** 1961
Address 300 S Palm Canyon Drive, Palm Springs, CA 92262

Open to Public Yes **Free Entrance** No **Café/Restaurant** No
Overnight Accommodation No **Gift/Bookshop** Yes

Frey House II

213

Palm Springs **Architect** Albert Frey **Year** 1963
Address 686 Palisades Drive, Palm Springs, CA 92262

Open to Public No **Free Entrance** No **Café/Restaurant** No
Overnight Accommodation No **Gift/Bookshop** No

Sometimes seeing a Mid-Century Modern masterpiece takes a little work. As is the case with Albert Frey's legendary Frey House II, perched in a hillside gated community overlooking Palm Springs (and therefore only viewable from below). The tiny eight-hundred-square-foot (seventy-five-square-meter) glass and steel residence – typical of Frey's preference for simple, industrial materials – sitting on a concrete platform at the edge of a cliff, blurs the line between indoor and outdoor and between man-made and natural in profound ways. The large glass walls, which open up to a small pool, are protected by the long overhang of its corrugated aluminum roof. Other protection comes from bright-yellow curtains, whose color matches the desert's *Encelia farinosa* flowers. Inside, the home is literally built around a massive boulder, which protrudes into the heart of the building, dividing the bedroom and living room. The bedroom, cantilevering off the cliff, contains one of the most remarkable desert views you'll ever see. Frey reportedly took five years to select the site, then spent another year to track the movement of the sun. Obviously it was worth it. There are few homes in the world quite like this one. ⬣

213 Frey House II

Coachella Valley Savings and Loan (1)

214

Palm Springs **Architect** E. Stewart Williams **Year** 1961
Address 499 S Palm Canyon Drive, Palm Springs, CA 92262

Open to Public Yes **Free Entrance** Yes **Café/Restaurant** No
Overnight Accommodation No **Gift/Bookshop** No

This is one of Palm Springs' most striking public buildings. Whizzing by on Palm Canyon Drive, you first notice the raised rectangular structure's inverted pre-cast concrete parabolic arches, holding up a long, overhanging flat roof. Then you take in the building's elevated concrete floor slab; wide, gently rising terrazzo stairs; curtain wall of vertical anodized-aluminum ribbed panels; long clerestory windows; and moat-like water feature in front. It looks like a building you'd see in 1960s Brazil and for good reason: its inspiration and doppelgänger, is Oscar Niemeyer's Palace of the Dawn, the Brazilian president's residence in Brasilía. Now owned by Chase Bank, the building has not been altered outside, although it has unfortunately been given the contemporary corporate treatment within. The bank is part of a collection of commercial structures on or near Palm Canyon Drive known as the Palm Springs financial district, which includes City National Bank (now Bank of America – page 289), Santa Fe Federal Savings Bank (now the Palm Springs Art Museum – page 281), Union Bank of California, Guaranty Bank and Wells Fargo. Williams, who apprenticed with Raymond Loewy, designed several of the most important buildings in Palm Springs and after his death an editorial in the *Desert Sun* said, 'If any single man can be cited for giving Palm Springs its place in architectural history, it's E. Stewart Williams.' ⬢

215

Coachella Valley Savings and Loan (2)

While E. Stewart Williams' Santa Fe Federal Savings Bank at 300 South Palm Canyon Drive has become the Palm Springs Art Museum Architecture and Design Center (page 281), don't forget Williams' other banks, which are equally impressive. Two of the best were for Coachella Valley Savings and Loan. The most famous (page 284, opposite) took on the parabolic arches and structural expression of Brasilía. But the first was at 383 South Palm Canyon Drive. The rectangular box is completely fronted by tall walls of glass and by equally tall white steel louvers hovering over a parking lot and store-front entryway on thin columns. Inside, the Mid-Century Modern time capsule, with its twenty-foot-high (six-meter) former banking floor, contains black terrazzo floors, a free-form staircase and two circular walk-in vaults. The building is now being transformed into a restored event space known as The Bank, set to open sometime in 2016, hosting cocktail parties, photo shoots and movie premieres. If you want still more of Williams' work, head to the Palm Springs Art Museum (101 Museum Drive), with its dramatic gridded Brutalist canopy, or the Frank Sinatra House, Twin Palms (1148 East Alejo Road), which is hard to see from the street, but can be booked for private tours or even rented for vacations. ●

Palm Springs **Architect** E. Stewart Williams **Year** 1955
Address 383 S Palm Canyon Drive, Palm Springs, CA 92262

Open to Public Yes **Free Entrance** Yes **Café/Restaurant** No
Overnight Accommodation No **Gift/Bookshop** No

Caliente Tropics Resort

The mid-century tiki craze is alive and well in Palm Springs, which was once flooded with Polynesian-themed hotels, restaurants and bars, but only contains a few today. The best example is the ninety-room Caliente Tropics hotel (originally called The Tropics), built by legendary developer and designer Ken Kimes, who owned forty-five motels in all, five of them with tiki themes. Caliente is by far the most elaborate of Kimes' tiki establishments and it's hard to miss its giant A-framed, Polynesian-style porte-cochere as you pass by on Palm Canyon Drive. The remainder of the property contains more A-frames, rock walls, tiki torches, island idols, tropical tchochzkes, tiki carvings and hardwood beams and surfaces organized around a central pool and lots of grass and palm trees. (All this grass makes more sense in tropical Polynesia than in water-starved Palm Springs, but who's to judge?) Guests during The Tropics' heyday included Elvis Presley, Frank Sinatra, Nancy Sinatra and Lauren Bacall, but the hotel fell into disrepair (and shuttered mainstay attractions like its colorful Congo Room steakhouse and its underground cocktail lounge, The Cellar), until it was saved in 2001, as local conservationists convinced the owners to preserve the tiki theme during a major renovation. More good news: the owners have brought back the Congo Room and the property hosts an annual convention, a yearly gathering for tiki fans worldwide. ●

Palm Springs **Architect** Ken Kimes **Year** 1964
Address 411 E Palm Canyon Drive, Palm Springs, CA 92264

Open to Public Yes **Free Entrance** No **Café/Restaurant** Yes
Overnight Accommodation Yes **Gift/Bookshop** No

Palm Springs **Architect** Palmer and Krisel **Year** 1957
Address 1111 E Palm Canyon Drive #222, Palm Springs, CA 92264

Open to Public Yes **Free Entrance** No **Café/Restaurant** Yes
Overnight Accommodation Yes **Gift/Bookshop** No

217

Ocotillo Lodge

Another Palm Springs icon immortalized by Julius Shulman, Ocotillo Lodge was a collaboration between developers George and Robert Alexander, architects Dan Palmer and William Krisel and landscape architect Garrett Eckbo. The seven-acre (three-hectare) property focuses around a curved central structure, clad in decorative brick, that meets the street with a bulky sun flap porte-cochere. The building, whose once-lovely interior has been altered, opens on its other side (via a large band of windows) to a famous keyhole-shaped swimming pool, accompanied by an outdoor bar and dining terrace. Beyond that the complex stretches out to contain rows of single-story, block-clad post-and-beam cottages and duplexes, each with its own patio accessed by sliding glass doors. All are oriented around the pool and Eckbo's oasis-like landscaping – thick with palm trees, Southwest-style plants, hedges, grassy lawns (a Mid-Century Modern staple that's now considered a no-no here due to water restrictions) and cement paving – another mid-century staple that's not as appealing today. For the Alexanders, the lodge served as a sort of bait: luring potential home owners to the area for short trips, then giving them the opportunity to check out their housing tracts, like their Twin Palms estates, just across the street. ●

Horizon Hotel

218

One of several Palm Springs getaways that have been upgraded into fancy boutique resorts, the Horizon Hotel was designed by William Cody as a private retreat with twenty guest houses for television producer and oil tycoon (who knew you could do both?) Jack Wrather and his wife, actress Bonita 'Bunny' Granville. Wrather produced, among other shows, *The Lone Ranger* and *Lassie* and also commissioned the Disneyland Hotel. Wrather's guests here included Marilyn Monroe, Ronald Reagan and many others. The four-acre (1.6-hectare) complex consists of several small bungalows, with white brick walls, exposed timber beams and floor-to-ceiling glass windows and sliding glass doors protected by especially deep overhangs (these eaves also protect exterior spaces). The units commune splendidly with their dramatic desert location, tucked up against the bulky mountains in a sea of palm trees. Once again it's all about the landscaping, as you can walk out to a private rocky patio or enjoy the glassy infinity pool or the lushly undulating common spaces. The aging property was recently restored by Los Angeles designer Steve Hermann, who had designed homes for Larry Ellison, Vera Wang and others, with upgraded surfaces, furnishings, lighting landscaping and so on. 'I wanted to take it from being a two-star to a five- or even six-star place', Hermann told *Architectural Digest*. ●

Palm Springs **Architect** William Cody **Year** 1952
Address 1050 E Palm Canyon Drive, Palm Springs, CA 92264

Open to Public Yes **Free Entrance** No **Café/Restaurant** Yes
Overnight Accommodation Yes **Gift/Bookshop** No

Palm Springs **Architect** Victor Gruen & Associates **Year** 1959
Address 588 S Palm Canyon Drive, Palm Springs, CA 92264

Open to Public Yes **Free Entrance** Yes **Café/Restaurant** No
Overnight Accommodation No **Gift/Bookshop** No

219

Bank of America

Palm Springs is one of the few places in the world where you could build a bank resembling Le Corbusier's Ronchamp Chapel in France (1955) and nobody would bat an eye. The Bank of America, formerly City National Bank, sits on a financial institution-filled stretch of Palm Canyon Drive that also includes the two Coachella Valley Savings and Loan buildings (pages 284 and 285), among others. It was designed by Victor Gruen & Associates, a firm that master-planned much of Southern California and is widely credited with inventing the shopping mall. The triangular building, indeed inspired by Ronchamp, consists of a bulky, dramatically curving white stucco crown floating atop a glassy base, shaded with aluminum louvers, alternating with blue mosaic tiles and columns. While not explicit, it's easy to connect these color choices with the city's (common) blue sky and (less common) white clouds. The well- preserved interior features terrazzo floors, marble counters, Japanese cloth wall panels and dark wood cabinetry, harkening to a time when banks were the coolest buildings in town, designed to be noticed inside and out. Indeed, it's impossible to miss this building, which conjures up reminders not just of Le Corbusier but also of *The Flintstones*; a strangely appropriate combination in a city where weird invention combines sublimity and kitsch in equal proportions. ●

Pearlman Cabin

220

Palm Springs **Architect** John Lautner **Year** 1957
Address 52820 Middleridge Drive, Idyllwild, CA 92549

Open to Public Yes **Free Entrance** No **Café/Restaurant** No
Overnight Accommodation No **Gift/Bookshop** No

Located in Idyllwild, a tiny San Jacinto Mountain hamlet near Palm Springs that's Southern California's closest approximation of the Swiss Alps, the Pearlman Cabin is one of the few John Lautner houses that you can actually spend time inside. That's a serious distinction. The circular home's roof floats over huge, angled glass walls, supported by tree trunk columns. (The glass is imbedded into these logs.) Since the home is raised on concrete columns, it doesn't disturb the local topography. Located at the top of a steep slope, it overlooks the town's pine forests and rock outcroppings, which stretch to infinity from its elevated location, so being inside is an exceptional opportunity to commune with nature. The glass facade's star-like configuration opens up the interior spaces in ways you might not anticipate, allowing trees to seemingly poke their way inside. It's been described as 'a cross between a log cabin and a treehouse' for good reason. While the living room takes in this view, bedrooms and support spaces, fronted by still curved but stucco-clad walls, are tucked away in back, sheltered from the sun and typically cozy – a Lautner speciality. The home is currently owned by Nancy Pearlman, daughter of the original owners, Carl and Agnes Pearlman, who helped in construction of the home itself and, as music lovers, were known for holding concerts in their exquisite living room. ⬢

Few places in Southern California are as profoundly weird and wonderful as Sunnylands, Walter and Leonore Annenberg's two-hundred-acre (eighty-one-hectare) estate in Rancho Mirage, just east of Palm Springs. Surrounded by a pastel-pink wall, the rolling estate is located, fittingly, just off Bob Hope Drive, Gerald Ford Way and Frank Sinatra Drive. The Annenberg family has hosted several American presidents here, including Eisenhower, Nixon, Ford, Reagan, Bush, Clinton and, more recently, Barack Obama. They also entertained the British royal family, Frank Sinatra and Sammy Davis Jr. The incongruous design style is, at heart, Mid-Century Modern, with exposed structure, deep eaves, large glass walls, waffle slab ceilings and simple trellises. But that architectural backdrop merges with the Annenberg's interesting, personal taste. Their love of Mayan architecture, for instance, influenced the bright pink pyramidal roof, Mexican lava stone walls and replica Mayan column in the porte-cochere. The flamboyant, verging on ridiculous, interior design was created by William Haines and Ted Graber, known for decorating the Reagan White House. It's resplendent with pink and yellow hues, marble floors and gaudy, Regency-style furnishings. The home also contains a world-class art collection, so it would be worth a visit even if it weren't already so fun. Make sure to also see the lovely new desert gardens and visitors' center while at Sunnylands. ●

Palm Springs **Architect** Jones & Emmons **Year** 1963
Address 37977 Bob Hope Drive, Rancho Mirage, CA 92270

Open to Public Yes **Free Entrance** No **Café/Restaurant** Yes
Overnight Accommodation No **Gift/Bookshop** Yes

Sunnylands

Palm Springs Palmer and Krisel Tracts

222

Palm Springs **Architect** Palmer and Krisel **Year** 1950s and '60s
Address Camino Real, Palm Springs, CA 92264 and surrounding streets

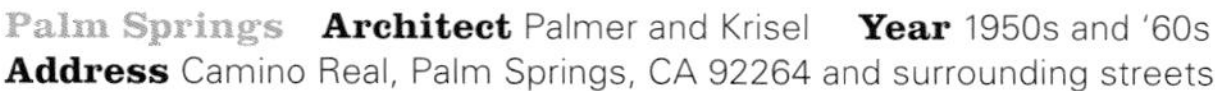

Open to Public No **Free Entrance** No **Café/Restaurant** No
Overnight Accommodation No **Gift/Bookshop** No

The dream of producing affordable, desirable housing, or 'Modernism for the Masses', came true, at least for a time, in Palm Springs through the partnership of father-and-son builders George and Robert Alexander and architects Dan Palmer and William Krisel. Over the span of about ten years, the Alexander Construction Company was able to build more than two-thousand homes in tracts around the Coachella Valley, on sites that include Twin Palms Estates, Vista Las Palmas, Racquet Club Estates, Sunmore Estates and Ramon Rise, to name just a few. Krisel and Palmer's post-and-beam homes were known for their expansive windows (shielded by overhangs), spacious open floor plans, indoor-outdoor connections, patterned-block facades and distinctive rooflines. Other notable architects soon worked for the Alexanders, including E. Stewart Williams and Donald Wexler. The Jewish Alexanders were a breath of fresh air in a conservative town whose developments had imposed restrictive covenants forbidding Jews, blacks and other minorities from owning property. Building where these rules held no sway, they opened their properties to all buyers. Their tracts, immortalized in magazines and brochures, were so successful that they helped double the size of Palm Springs and attracted owners like Dinah Shore, Dean Martin and Marilyn Monroe. ⬢

Palm Springs Palmer and Krisel Tracts

San Diego

San Diego

223 Salerno Residence **224** Scripps Green Hospital **225** Salk Institute **226** Atoll Residence **227** Bell Beach House **228** Geisel Library, University of California, San Diego **229** Scripps Institute of Oceanography **230** Forester Residence **231** La Jolla Real Estate Brokers' Association **232** Case Study House Triad Homes **233** El Pueblo Ribera Court **234** Clairemont Lutheran Church **235** North Clairemont Public Library **236** Compact Houses **237** Pacific Beach Community Congregational Church **238** Pacifica Tract Homes **239** St. Mark's Methodist Church **240** Calvary Southern Baptist Church **241** First United Methodist Church **242** Babcock Residence **243** Rigsby Residence **244** Spec Houses **245** Pearl Hotel **246** Tiki Colony, Half Moon Inn **247** Homer Delawie Residence II **248** Fifth Avenue Design Center **249** Salomon Apartments **250** Timken Museum of Art **251** Calvary Lutheran Church **252** Carlton Hills Lutheran Church **253** Fletcher Hills Presbyterian Church **254** Trinity Church

Encinitas
Solana Beach
Black Mountain Open Space
223
Del Mar
Poway
224
225
226
228
227
229
230
231
232
252
Santee
233
234
235
Mission Trails Regional Park
238
236
237
239
Pacific Beach
253
240
241
La Mesa
242
247
248
North Park
Lemon Grove
254
Spring Valley
249
251
250
245
244
246
243
San Diego
Coronado
National City
San Diego Bay
Chula Vista
Pacific Ocean
Imperial Beach

Salerno Residence

223

San Diego **Architect** Daniel Salerno **Year** 1965
Address 459 Culebra Street, Del Mar, CA 92014

Open to Public No **Free Entrance** No **Café/Restaurant** No
Overnight Accommodation No **Gift/Bookshop** No

The well-to-do, progressive coastal city of Del Mar, just north of La Jolla, was a perfect breeding ground for Mid-Century Modern architecture. Head into its hills and you'll be amazed with what you find. But never more so than when you visit the Salerno Residence, the first home local architect Daniel Salerno built for himself and his wife. Salerno liked the home's steep, oddly-shaped lot because it was much cheaper than a conventional one; besides, he loved the views and a challenge. The dark wood post-and-beam structure cantilevers dramatically over a stubby, brick base, supported only by thin steel stilts. The east side of the long, L-shaped house is mostly solid, save for a tall window wall exposing the floating, central stair. But the west side opens completely, covered with a tall and wide wall of large windows, protected by deep, flat eaves. Exploring the winding streets near this house is really fun, too. The home right across the street (460 Culebra) consists of a series of staggered wooden boxes raised on columns, carving out space for a small courtyard. Around the corner the homes range from classic Modernist to crazy futuristic. It's proof that the cluster theory of architecture (great homes, or home-owners, seem to find each other) is alive and well. ▼

Following the success of his Community Hospital on the Monterey Peninsula, Edward Durell Stone was commissioned to create several more clinics based on the concept of healing through connection to space, sunlight and nature. With its oceanside site in La Jolla – just down the street from University of Southern California, San Diego (page 304) and the Salk Institute (page 300) – Scripps Green Hospital presented the perfect opportunity to bring the outside in. Covered again with Stone's trademark geometric block relief walls, the complex consists of two bulky wings (the south for research, the north for clinical treatment) emanating from an entry plaza crammed with palm trees, its edges articulated with thin canopies. The north wing revolves around a double-height indoor courtyard, centered around a square fountain and lush plantings, topped with a pyramidal roof clad with perforated geometric tiles, creating a constellation of natural light. While there are a few narrow hallways, many spaces span floors and open up views to the outside, preventing common hospital-induced claustrophobia. The west edge of the building provides low, framed vistas of the ocean, as do many of the patient rooms, extended and protected with deep, covered balconies. Make sure to explore the complex's original buildings, because the watered-down additions, still fronted with patterned facades, don't contain the same magic. ▼

San Diego **Architect** Edward Durell Stone **Year** 1974
Address 10666 N Torrey Pines Road, La Jolla, CA 92037

Open to Public Yes **Free Entrance** Yes **Café/Restaurant** No
Overnight Accommodation No **Gift/Bookshop** No

Scripps Green Hospital

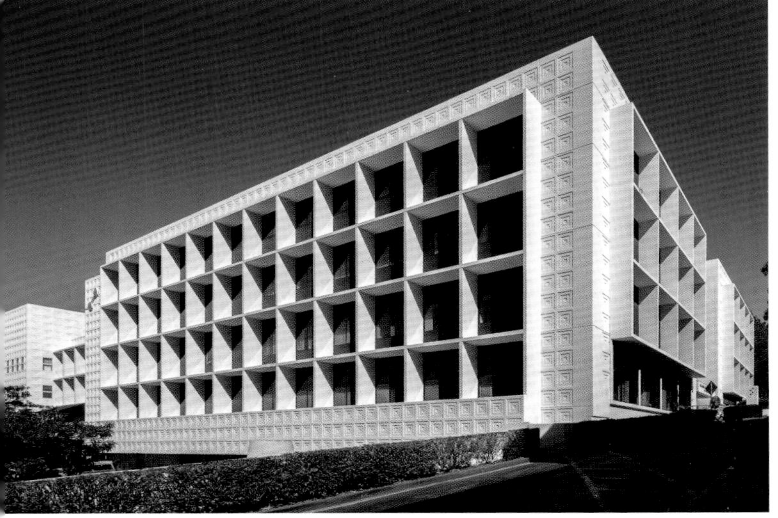

San Diego **Architect** Louis Kahn & Luis Barragán **Year** 1963
Address 10010 N Torrey Pines Road, La Jolla, CA 92037

Open to Public Yes **Free Entrance** No **Café/Restaurant** No
Overnight Accommodation No **Gift/Bookshop** No

225

Salk Institute

It's hard not to get goose bumps when you stare down the pristine vista created by Louis Kahn and Luis Barragán at the Salk Institute, a laboratory complex perched above the lush cliffs of La Jolla. This exercise in perfect symmetry is the Taj Mahal of Brutalism. Jonas Salk, developer of the Polio vaccine, asked Kahn in 1960 to 'create a facility worthy of a visit by Picasso.' Two mirror-image structures, clad in raw poured-in-place concrete and unfinished teak, line an open travertine courtyard, whose linear reflecting pool glides toward the ocean. Keeping the plaza treeless was the brainchild of Barragán, who aimed to make it 'a facade to the sky' and rarely gets the credit he deserves for his collaboration. Five angled wings on each side, joined to the base structures by floating bridges, add to the sense of syncopation. Sunken, planted light wells flood laboratories with light and warmth. There's something primal about the composition – its symmetry, its hulking masses and the way the buildings play off the central channel, the sky above and the scene in the distance – that fills you with awe. Don't confuse a derivative 1996 addition by Anshen & Allen for the real building behind it and take a walk around the compound to get a sense of the serene landscape that softens it and renders it more profound. It's fun to watch the hang gliders who throw themselves off the adjacent bluffs. As if the architecture weren't enough. ▼

Atoll Residence

Emerging from its slightly sunken site in an upscale neighborhood just around the corner from the Salk Institute (page 300) is Kendrick Bangs Kellogg's Atoll Residence. Kellogg, who adored Frank Lloyd Wright and worked in the progressive offices of Sim Bruce Richards and Dale Naegle, first studied astrophysics before switching to architecture. His fascination with outer space is clearly visible in his architecture. The Atoll is a glassy, coral island-shaped (hence the name) structure supported by white columns akin to mushrooms and topped by a shell-like copper roof, curving around its lush, back pool area that is reminiscent of *The Flintstones*. Lava block walls, a koi pond and landscaping with tropical plants like cacti and agave slither in and out of the home, making it hard to distinguish inside and outside. Kellogg is best known for his designs of the many Chart House restaurants along the California coast, which have, unfortunately, all been altered. But if you start to look at his legacy, you'll be shocked at the breadth and formal and practical originality. Organic buildings weaving in and out of their sites, through contortions of timber, concrete, glass and steel, resemble shells, eagle wings, lotus flowers, diamonds and, in the case of the Doolittle Residence in Joshua Tree, armadillos. Kellogg, who is still practicing, has completed dozens of buildings over his career and while his work is bizarre, he deserves to be recognized as one of the West Coast's masters. ▼

San Diego **Architect** Kendrick Bangs Kellogg **Year** 1978
Address 9805 Black Gold Road, La Jolla, CA 92037

Open to Public No **Free Entrance** No **Café/Restaurant** No
Overnight Accommodation No **Gift/Bookshop** No

San Diego **Architect** Dale Naegle **Year** 1968
Address 9036 La Jolla Shores Lane, San Diego, CA 92037

227

Bell Beach House

Open to Public No **Free Entrance** No **Café/Restaurant** No
Overnight Accommodation No **Gift/Bookshop** No

If any house should be a James Bond villain's lair, it's the Bell Beach House on Black's Beach in La Jolla. Attached to a cliff-hugging home above by a three-hundred-foot-long (ninety-one-meter) funicular, Dale Naegle's disc-shaped, exposed concrete-clad guest quarters hovers above a narrow, tube-shaped base, protected from the elements by a surrounding wall. Built for potato chip mogul Sam Bell, the floating residence is nicknamed the Mushroom House by locals. Its wide band of glazing allows unparalleled views of the ocean, just a few feet away and its tensioned underside looks like a moving propeller. Something like this could never be built under today's coastal restrictions. 'Dale had an amazing ability to come up with ideas', Douglas Allred, a longtime friend and business associate told the *San Diego Union-Tribune*. Be careful when you visit. It's only accessible via a walk on the beach from the south and tides in La Jolla can get very high. If you're a Naegle fan, head into the La Jolla hills to visit his Mansfield Mills Residence (7105 Country Club Drive). Much of its indoor-outdoor glory is hidden behind walls, but it's aggressively upturned roofline recalls a scud missile launcher. ▼

Geisel Library, University of California, San Diego

228

San Diego **Architect** William Pereira & Associates **Year** 1970
Address 9500 Gilman Drive, La Jolla, CA 92093

Open to Public Yes **Free Entrance** Yes **Café/Restaurant** Yes
Overnight Accommodation No **Gift/Bookshop** Yes

The campus of the University of California, San Diego is remarkable for its unprecedented collection of Brutalist buildings. The biggest concentrations are at Muir and Revelle Colleges, on the western edge of campus, where Robert Mosher, A. Quincy Jones, Robert Alexander and several others created structurally adventurous and formally inventive buildings that make heavy, board-formed concrete float, twist and dance as if it were light as a feather. All this austerity is effectively softened by rustic, eucalyptus-filled landscaping by Joseph Yamada. But the highlight of the campus is William Pereira's Geisel Library (named for Theodore Geisel, Dr. Seuss), an eight-story ziggurat-like structure whose branching structural systems resemble those of a tree. The lower two stories of the reinforced-concrete building create a pedestal for the six-story, stepped tower. Above the pedestal, bent columns anchor each of the edifice's four sides. Approaching the library via Literary Walk is one of the more dramatic architectural experiences you're likely to have. The building, while resembling a spaceship, is meant to represent a stylized version of hands holding a globe. It's all the more extraordinary paired with the Modernist treasures around it and with the sunken addition, covered with landscaping, that frames its entry. ▼

Geisel Library, University of California San Diego

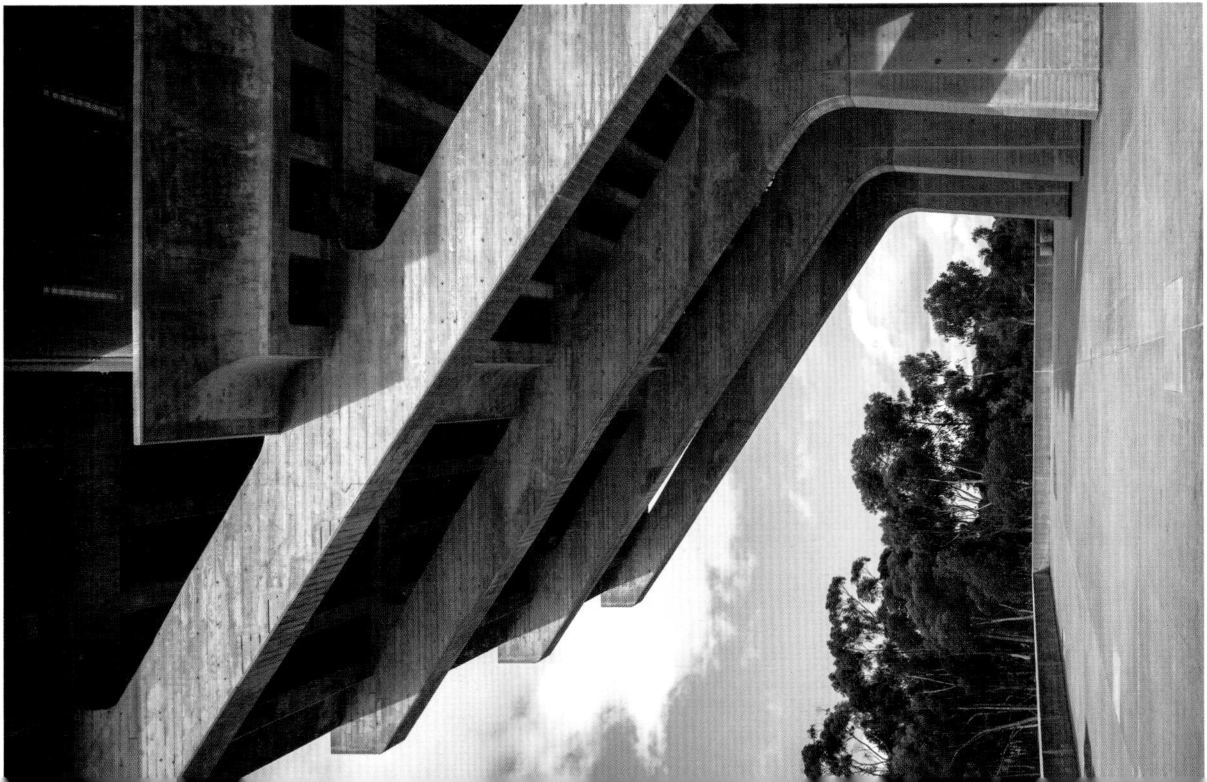

Scripps Institute of Oceanography

It's hard to get a more picturesque location than that of the Scripps Institute of Oceanography, which has been a La Jolla institution since its founding in 1903. Its campus, which hugs the beachfront north of La Jolla Shores, meanders through heavily vegetated flats, hills and even cliffs. It began with its Marine Biological Laboratory, designed by Irving Gill and grew substantially in the middle of the century. Its centerpiece and Mid-Century Modern architectural highlight, is the Judith and Walter Munk Laboratory, by Lloyd Ruocco (pictured), which serves Scripps' Institute of Geophysics and Planetary Physics. The T-shaped, redwood post-and-beam building, with its long flat roof, is perched on a cliff overlooking the ocean. Its large glass walls are edged with deep slatted eaves above long (and somewhat precarious) wooden decks below. The exterior walls of glass are rare for a science lab. Right across the street is Liebhardt & Weston's Revelle Laboratory, a series of four structures stepping down the bluffs, connected by redwood decks and glass elevators. Just down hill from there is the same firm's Eckhart Building, a sharply angled, three-story concrete building that resembles a gridded concrete structure tilted on its side forty-five degrees. ▼

San Diego **Architect** Lloyd Ruocco, and others **Year** 1963
Address 8602 La Jolla Shores Drive, La Jolla, CA 92037

Open to Public No **Free Entrance** No **Café/Restaurant** No
Overnight Accommodation No **Gift/Bookshop** No

San Diego **Architect** Russell Forester **Year** 1971
Address 2025 Soledad Avenue, La Jolla, CA 92037

230

Forester Residence

Open to Public No **Free Entrance** No **Café/Restaurant** No
Overnight Accommodation No **Gift/Bookshop** No

Russell Forester, it could be argued, was the Charles Eames of San Diego. A jack of all trades, he was obsessed with low-cost, craft-driven, modular design and he became a noted artist and designer. Of course nobody outside of San Diego has ever heard of him. His Forester Residence, along the edge of Mount Soledad, is a prototype for his philosophy and aesthetic, reusing industrial materials, off-the-shelf parts and modular elements to create a simple but lively building. Because the facade is clad with a double-height wall of gigantic windows (framed with laminate beams and exposed rivets), you can see right inside to the completely open floor plan and the red steel trusses that hold up the roof. A lofted space in the center contains utilities on the first floor and a bedroom above, while an attached studio extends outward, next to the driveway. Several of Forester's colorful, abstract art pieces peek out from the front patio. Beyond his considerable collection of residences, Forester is famed for bringing Miesian Modernism into pop culture by designing the first Jack in the Box restaurant in 1951, in San Diego's Mid-City. He went on to design dozens more. In 1976 he retired from his architectural practice to begin a full-time career as a painter and sculptor. ▼

La Jolla Real Estate Brokers' Association

Everybody loves a Modernist jewel, like Henry Hester's La Jolla Real Estate Brokers' Association, floating atop a minimalist flower garden and shaded by a thick, craggy old tree anchoring a courtyard in downtown La Jolla. The cube-shaped structure, a wing of a nondescript, L-shaped white brick building (whose only highlight is a peaceful courtyard garden), is clad on three sides by richly veined marble and on the other by glass. Inside, dark paneled walls frame a space dominated by vintage furniture that would be at home in any *Mad Men* episode. Hester, one of many University of Southern California architecture graduates in San Diego, worked with Kenneth Lind and Lloyd Ruocco before starting his own practice, partnering with, among others, William Cody, Frederick Liebhardt, Ronald K. Davis, Robert E. Jones and Fred Livingstone. He didn't limit his scope to California, working also in Arizona, New Mexico, Florida and Colorado. La Jolla, a haven for progressive politics and architecture, is blessed with a glut of Mid-Century Modern surprises, both in town and in the hills above. Around the corner, for instance, check out Kelsey and Ladd's under-appreciated Prospect Center (1020 Prospect) a four-story rectangular building floating over a glass base, with a grid of deeply projecting window boxes. ▼

San Diego **Architect** Henry Hester **Year** 1963
Address 908 Kline Street, La Jolla, CA 92037

Open to Public No **Free Entrance** No **Café/Restaurant** No
Overnight Accommodation No **Gift/Bookshop** No

232

Case Study House Triad Homes

San Diego **Architect** Killingsworth Brady Smith **Year** 1960
Address 2342, 2343 and 2329 Rue de Anne, La Jolla, CA 92037

Open to Public No **Free Entrance** No **Café/Restaurant** No
Overnight Accommodation No **Gift/Bookshop** No

Located in the breeze-filled hills above La Jolla, in a development of (oddly) French-named streets called Chateau Ville, these homes were intended as the pilot program for a large tract of houses grouped in three. But only this 'Triad' was ever built. The idea of the Triad was to produce homes with similar but individual floor plans, landscaping and exterior cladding. House A (pictured), with its redwood cladding, shallow entry reflecting pool (accessed by hopping over stone tiles) and tall ceilings is the most impressive from the street. House C, across the street, is the simplest of the three, with a rectangular plan, vertical siding and simple entry hall. But the exterior simplicity belies an outdoor-oriented residence whose living room, kitchen and master bedroom all have patios located directly off them. House B has been destroyed by a bizarre Hollywood Regency facade that will make you shudder when you see it. Like many great Mid-Century Modern homes, from the street you won't be able to observe what makes these residences so livable. Their exterior simplicity masks a spatial genius that can only be experienced from the inside. ▼

El Pueblo Ribera Court

233

San Diego **Architect** Rudolph Schindler **Year** 1923
Address 230 Gravilla Street, La Jolla, CA 92037

Open to Public No **Free Entrance** No **Café/Restaurant** No
Overnight Accommodation No **Gift/Bookshop** No

Incredibly active in Los Angeles, Rudolph Schindler built only one project in San Diego: El Pueblo Ribera Court, a complex of twelve duplexes arranged in L-shaped pairs on a residential street in La Jolla, just a block from the ocean. One of his earliest projects, it is nonetheless a resolutely modern, imaginative design whose ideas are still being emulated. He was hired by W. Llewellyn Lloyd, who asked him to design 'bungalow apartments of distinction' as beach rental properties, building them 'in a Southwest manner.' Protected from the street by tall wood and concrete walls, the complex brings the architect's mastery of indoor-outdoor living to a unique layout resembling a village or (appropriately) a native pueblo more than an apartment building. U-shaped units, with trellised roof terraces and sleeping porches above, contain concrete floors, clerestory windows and tall sliding glass doors that open to private courtyards, essentially extending their living rooms outside. The units, clad with tilt-up concrete (the concrete contained sand from the nearby beach) and redwood, are organized in varying configurations to maximize privacy and views. ▼

Pacifica Tract Homes

While Palmer and Krisel is best known for its Alexander tracts in Palm Springs, the firm designed thousands of homes throughout Southern California, including many tracts in San Diego. Working for local developers like Leonard Drogin, Irvin Kahn and Bill Starr, they built more than 1,000 properties in La Jolla, University City, Del Cerro, El Cajon, College View, Point Loma, Clairemont, Rolando and elsewhere. Located on a steeply terraced hillside of Mt. Soledad on the city's western edge is the Pacifica Tract. The glass walls, open plans and post-and-beam designs are filled with light and space and are perfectly suited to take advantage of the cool ocean breezes and views of Mission Bay, the Pacific Ocean, Coronado and even Mexico beyond. While there are very few floor plans, Palmer and Krisel created a unique appearance for each home by siting them differently and using a variety of facades. Unlike the developments in Palm Springs, the firm's San Diego homes needed less concrete block protection from the sun and were designed as permanent residences, not vacation homes. Palmer and Krisel, which kept an office in San Diego for almost fifteen years, also designed condominiums, offices, shopping centers and industrial buildings throughout the city. ▼

San Diego **Architect** Palmer and Krisel **Year** 1960
Address Pacifica Drive, San Diego, CA 92109

Open to Public No **Free Entrance** No **Café/Restaurant** No
Overnight Accommodation No **Gift/Bookshop** No

St. Mark's Methodist Church

239

San Diego **Architect** Hal Whittemore & Associates **Year** 1961
Address 3502 Clairemont Drive, San Diego, CA 92117

Open to Public Yes **Free Entrance** Yes **Café/Restaurant** No
Overnight Accommodation No **Gift/Bookshop** No

If you're going to design a cathedral-like Modernist church, why not aim high and model it after thirteenth-century La Saint-Chapelle in Paris? This was the thinking of Hal Whittemore & Associates, which designed St. Mark's Methodist's Church in San Diego's Clairemont neighborhood in 1961. Situated on the site of a former airfield (called San Diego Air Park), the soaring space is dominated – like Sainte-Chapelle – by towering, fifty-foot-tall (fifteen-meter) stained-glass window walls. Made in Germany, they showcase forty different hues; dominated by blue, but also comprising jewel-like green, red and amber. Dark wood laminated beams support the structure, joining to form wide arches. The view inside is spectacular, taking in the colorful light, the intricate, floral carved altar and pulpit, the large cross over the altar and of course the awe-inspiring height. 'Our aim in designing the sanctuary was to give expression in structure and form to the essential unity of creation and redemption', said Reverend Galal Gough at the church's opening service in 1962. The building's exterior, hovering over a stone base, resembles a shed crossed with a Bauhaus box crossed with one of the halls of Cambridge (or Hogwarts); its gridded windows hint at the light show inside. ▼

St. Mark's Methodist Church

Calvary Southern Baptist Church

240

San Diego **Architect** Robert Des Lauriers **Year** 1963
Address 6866 Linda Vista Road, San Diego, CA 92111

Open to Public Yes **Free Entrance** Yes **Café/Restaurant** No
Overnight Accommodation No **Gift/Bookshop** No

This is a classic Southern California sacred space if there ever was one. Crouched in the corner of a parking lot, just next to a Joe's 99 Cents & Up in San Diego's Linda Vista neighborhood, is Robert Des Lauriers' Calvary Southern Baptist Church, now known as Canyon Ridge Baptist Church. This remarkable circular building, with its undulating thin shell concrete roof and arched stained-glass windows, is the closest the city has to a Felix Candela edifice. (The Mexican architect is widely known as the master of thin-shell reinforced-concrete buildings, known as *cascarones*.) From above it looks like a spinning pinwheel. Founded in 1963, the church was occupied by Canyon Ridge Baptist Church in 2009. Its design is said to be modeled on a giant clam shell, which makes sense given the ocean's proximity and the common practice of using clam shells for baptism. Inside, the structural roof allows for a wide open space, dominated by the glow of the huge stained-glass windows. The underside of the roof is completely exposed. From the sanctuary it appears that you're looking up at the underside of a gargantuan white mollusk. ▼

The most astounding church you've never heard of, Reginald Inwood's First United Methodist, perches atop a steep slope in Mission Valley, its ivory-colored, thin shell concrete roof easily visible from Camino Del Rio below. The building's parabolic exterior is clad along its flanks in a wavy patterned screen that creates kinetic light patterns through colorful stained-glass windows. Indeed, this cathedral space is all about light, which arrives at all times and in all varieties. The colors become more intense as you look up. It's also about form, which you take in as you stare down the cathedral-like building's long nave through tall, rounded vaults. A vertical strip of stained glass divides the organ in two behind you and a clear grid of glass frames a pastoral slope behind the altar straight ahead. You can walk through this framed scene, which houses the church's rear memorial garden and even hike up to the parabolic bell tower above. The church moved from downtown San Diego to Mission Valley, which was being transformed from farmland into a Modernist paradise, in 1964. For another glimpse at the area's short-lived Mid-Century Modern renaissance, check out the nearby Macy's Westfield Mission Valley (1702 Camino Del Rio North), by Bill Lewis, with its unique honeycomb concrete facade and zigzag canopies. ▼

San Diego **Architect** Reginald Inwood **Year** 1960
Address 2111 Camino Del Rio S San Diego, CA 92108

Open to Public Yes **Free Entrance** Yes **Café/Restaurant** No
Overnight Accommodation No **Gift/Bookshop** No

241

First United Methodist Church

Babcock Residence

242

San Diego **Architect** Kendrick Bangs Kellogg **Year** 1957
Address 2695 Bayside Walk, San Diego, CA 92109

Open to Public No **Free Entrance** No **Café/Restaurant** No
Overnight Accommodation No **Gift/Bookshop** No

One of the finest of San Diego's many under-appreciated talents is Kendrick Bangs Kellogg, who has, over more than fifty years, built up a portfolio of some of the most adventurous buildings in the United States. In 1959 he completed what is arguably his most remarkable: the Babcock Residence in Mission Beach. The clients, Russell and Vergie Babcock, asked Kellogg, who lives just down the street, to design an A-frame with a copper roof. He went infinitely further. The home displays Kellogg's fascination with Frank Lloyd Wright (and his friendship with several Taliesen Fellows), along with San Diego's obsession with Pacific Rim art and architecture. An intricate series of interlocking copper triangles rises wing-like from a glassy A-frame base, just steps from the bay. You can see inside the entire house, which consists of a lofty living room and kitchen, with a mezzanine bedroom above. In back are timber-clad support spaces. A lovely little garden, which includes an indoor-outdoor koi pond, is sited in front. The house seems to unfold before your eyes, with layers repeating, twisting and then ripping away from each other. It's Deconstructivism decades before it came into vogue. ▼

Frank Lloyd Wright acolyte, Sim Bruce Richards, was one of the most prolific of all the city's Modernists, designing over two-hundred structures during his career. His Rigsby Residence, sited on a hillside in Point Loma, is a defining project, incorporating many of the architect's signature techniques, like dark wood siding; exposed, angular beams; and Japanese landscaping. Its zigzag roof shields triangular clerestories, which filter abundant light into the open structure and let visitors see right through the house making its roof appear to float and framing views to downtown and the San Diego Bay. Inside, gray-washed, wood-clad spaces flow seamlessly from one to the next, dominated by panoramas through tall windows to the south. Omnipresent built-in furniture and flush timber wall panels show off refined, Japanese-style joinery. Perhaps the best view of the house is from downhill – the folded roofline and large balcony projecting toward the waterfront. The new owners have replaced the original wood fence in front with a strange woven fiberglass one, but besides that, Richards' original vision is intact. This neighborhood, which reached its financial height in the mid-century, contains several superb Modernist homes to explore, from local masters like Dale Naegle, Herb Turner and Richards. ▼

San Diego **Architect** Sim Bruce Richards **Year** 1960
Address 411 San Remo Way, San Diego, CA 92106

Open to Public No **Free Entrance** No **Café/Restaurant** No
Overnight Accommodation No **Gift/Bookshop** No

Rigsby Residence

Scattered around the hills of Point Loma are some of the most adventurous Modern houses in San Diego, now known as the Spec Houses, created by maverick architects John Reed and Sim Bruce Richards. Richards, a Taliesen Fellow, bought the land with his brother John and designed them with Reed, who had worked for Lloyd Wright and Lloyd Ruocco. They built the homes on spec (thus the name), following Wright's principles of organic architecture, including proper siting, organic materials, abundant natural light and human scale. Spec House 1, otherwise known as the Triangle House because of its preponderance of angled forms, is perhaps the most spectacular: a wood-clad structure stepping off the side of a ledge, each glassy level hugging the side for dear life. Down the hill Spec House 2 (999 Gage Drive) is a classic wood post-and-beam topped by a glassy pavilion, while Spec House 3 (995 Gage Drive) (pictured), also known as the Eight-Sided Star House, consists of two interlocked square volumes offset forty-five degrees, fronted by a large glass facade and topped by a flat, dark wood roof. The team completed half a dozen spec houses in the area. Each one was sold right away, a testament to their alluring, yet still practical, designs. ▼

San Diego **Architect** John Reed and Sim Bruce Richards **Year** 1960s
Address 946 Bangor Street, San Diego, CA 92106

Open to Public No **Free Entrance** No **Café/Restaurant** No
Overnight Accommodation No **Gift/Bookshop** No

Fifth Avenue Design Center

248

Lloyd Ruocco's gift for merging sleek Modernist forms with their natural environment is on full display at the Design Center, a low-lying, flat-roofed building that steps down into a canyon in the city's wooded Hillcrest area. 'Good architecture should call for the minimum use of materials for the most interesting and functional enclosure of space', Ruocco once said, who believed no building could compete with the city's natural beauty. The split-level redwood edifice, terraced down the rear hillside, is clad in a continuous band of wood-framed glass (which can slide open completely), protected by deep, slatted overhangs. The building's L-shaped, interconnected forms frame a small paved courtyard in back. A geometric trellis accommodates flowering vines at the entry. Open interior spaces, surrounded by glass-walled offices, are designed to be flexible and collective, with walls moving easily and support spaces shared by different offices. When completed, the Design Center quickly drew architects, photographers, journalists and graphic designers and it continues to attract creative types today, as well as basic services like a florist and a hairdresser. A 1987 fire destroyed part of the building, but it was brought back with a $200,000 restoration. ▼

San Diego **Architect** Lloyd Ruocco **Year** 1949
Address 3611 Fifth Avenue, San Diego, CA 92103

Open to Public No **Free Entrance** No **Café/Restaurant** No
Overnight Accommodation No **Gift/Bookshop** No

Salomon Apartments

249

San Diego **Architect** Henry Hester **Year** 1959
Address 3200 Sixth Avenue, San Diego, CA 92103

Open to Public No **Free Entrance** No **Café/Restaurant** No
Overnight Accommodation No **Gift/Bookshop** No

Located in upscale Bankers Hill, on the northwest edge of Balboa Park, Henry Hester's Salomon Apartments are a swanky reminder of Mid-Century Modern glamour. The La Jolla-based Hester beat out Frank Lloyd Wright's son John for the commission, handed out by industrialist Irving Salomon who made his fortune at the Royal Metal Manufacturing Company. The thirty-unit apartment building combines Modernist simplicity with sculptural and ornamental flourishes. Its block-like covered balconies pop out at varied intervals to become outdoor rooms, providing enhanced shade and privacy. Other surfaces are solid (with vertical slits), clear glazed and gridded, creating a sense of tangible movement. The building was recently converted into condominiums, its glamorous interiors compromised but not destroyed. And the much simpler rear of the structure wraps around a classic, paved Mid-Century Modern pool area, its impact minimized by a security gate. Hester's career peaked at a time that photographer Julius Shulman, who shot the apartments, described as 'a good period of architecture when San Diego was just beginning to express itself in favor of Modernism.' Like many architects of the age, Hester was known as a freewheeling bon vivant, racing Formula One cars and motorcycles, flying planes and sailing out of the Coronado Yacht Club. ▼

While known to most as the site of the San Diego Zoo, San Diego's Balboa Park is one of the West Coast's great destinations. Established in 1868 and laid out on the ideals of the City Beautiful movement, the park really came to life when it hosted the Panama-California Exposition (1915–16) and the California Pacific International Exposition (1935–36). It still contains dozens of these fairs' elaborate Spanish-style buildings, but the mid-century saw some Modernist structures added to the group. Of these, the most worthy of a visit is Frank Hope's tiny Timken Museum of Art, home to the superb Putnam Foundation Collection of European and American paintings and Russian icons. The institution was founded by immigrant entrepreneur Henry Timken, who founded the Timken Roller Bearing Company. The single-story white marble and steel pavilion, wedged between the park's botanical building and the San Diego Youth Symphony, is fronted on its far ends with glass storefront doors and flanked with small gardens. Inside, a louvered skylight system brings warm well-balanced natural illumination into the traditional galleries, with their travertine floors and colorful fabric-covered walls. Hope once described it as 'an elegantly simple design both for today and for Posterity.' ▼

San Diego **Architect** Frank L. Hope & Associates **Year** 1965
Address 1500 El Prado, San Diego, CA 92101

Open to Public Yes **Free Entrance** Yes **Café/Restaurant** No
Overnight Accommodation No **Gift/Bookshop** Yes

Timken Museum of Art

Calvary Lutheran Church

Although he designed several other building types, architect Robert Des Lauriers made a name for himself as the most prolific church designer in San Diego. His Calvary Lutheran Church in the Vista Colina area of east San Diego has an ultra-thin A-frame, hyperbolic paraboloid roof that slopes up dramatically from just above the ground, like a ski jump and looks like it's launching into the heavens. Long wooden shingles accentuate the length of this roof, which rises towards a cross sitting atop an obelisk. Most of Des Lauriers' churches contain a separate element like this, like a Modernist campanile. While the building is a little ragged around the edges, it remains intact inside, where lava rock and white concrete walls echo the exterior. You enter from the rear through a tunnel-like hallway and then the building expands theatrically, pushing the eye upward. In front of the altar, thin stained-glass windows reflect colorful light deep into the space. Des Lauriers, who was a bomber pilot in World War II, has literally dozens of churches in the San Diego area. Copied widely nationwide, these designs essentially put the city's religious designs on the map. ▼

San Diego **Architect** Robert Des Lauriers **Year** 1961
Address 3060 Fifty-fourth Street, San Diego, CA 92105

Open to Public Yes **Free Entrance** Yes **Café/Restaurant** Yes
Overnight Accommodation Yes **Gift/Bookshop** No

San Diego **Architect** Robert Des Lauriers **Year** 1959
Address 9735 Halberns Boulevard, Santee, CA 92071

Open to Public Yes **Free Entrance** Yes **Café/Restaurant** No
Overnight Accommodation No **Gift/Bookshop** No

252

Carlton Hills Lutheran Church

Lutheranism, founded on the concept of reform, loves innovative architecture and in the mid-century the denomination commissioned many of the most ambitious religious structures in the country. Robert Des Lauriers' Carlton Hills Evangelical Lutheran Church is high on this list. Located in Santee, a small, hilly town about twenty minutes northeast of San Diego, the elevated building is a concrete hyperbolic paraboloid pierced along its flanks with small, geometric glazed bricks and on its corners with a system of wood louvered fins, sandwiching long, vertical bands of colorful stained glass. The thin shell, saddleback-shaped roofline tapers upward on its edges, soaring in an optimistic, space-age gesture. Inside, the towering curves and strategic glazing have a powerful effect. You feel as though you're in a textured concrete cave, punctuated by sparkling and colorful beams of light and powerful sound resonance. The louvered stained-glass windows contribute to a surreal, wedge-shaped altarpiece, emanating subtle gradients of prismatic light. When the building was under construction more than fifty years ago, the local papers called it 'revolutionary'. It went on to win an American Institute of Architects National Award of merit for its innovative design in 1959. ▼

Fletcher Hills Presbyterian Church

Several of San Diego's unusual Modernist churches were designed by Robert Des Lauriers, an architect and engineer known as 'Mr Church', who used both skills to create more than sixty structurally adventurous sacred structures here. His Fletcher Hills Presbyterian Church in El Cajon, combines – uniquely – soaring Modernist religious vernacular with a Pacific Island Tiki aesthetic. The sanctuary's eight-sided, shingle-covered, folded roof, fusing into a funnel shape, is topped by a tall cross. Exposing an underside of large clerestory stained glass windows, it hovers over a pinkish base, connected to a low-lying office and school complex, which is marked by a projecting, gridded roofline. The stained glass emits a rainbow of colors inside a fairly rustic space, with its exposed laminated beams, timber ceiling, dark wood pews, and wood-paneled altarpiece. The structure was built during a brief period when religious institutions, including churches, synagogues and mosques, were intent on advertising how progressive they were (a spirit that's sorely lost today). Besides a few modernist churches and tract homes, you won't find too much architecture in El Cajon, whose nickname (based on its Spanish name, derived from the box-like canyon it sits in, and on its numerous strip malls) is 'The Big Box'. It's become a major settlement area for displaced Iraqis, and many of its storefronts now contain excellent falafel shops. ▼

San Diego **Architect** Robert Des Lauriers **Year** 1968
Address 455 Church Way, El Cajon, CA 92020

Open to Public Yes **Free Entrance** Yes **Café/Restaurant** No
Overnight Accommodation No **Gift/Bookshop** No

Trinity Church

254

San Diego **Architect** Culver Heaton **Year** 1961
Address 3902 Kenwood Drive, Spring Valley, CA 91977

Open to Public Yes **Free Entrance** Yes **Café/Restaurant** No
Overnight Accommodation No **Gift/Bookshop** No

When touring San Diego's notable collection of Mid-Century Modern churches, you should visit Trinity Church in Spring Valley. This wonderfully expressive soaring A-frame building with a shingled bi-fold roofline dominates its hillside and bucks any thoughts that a church needs to be a solemn structure. The architect, Culver Heaton, whose practice was based in Pasadena, built more than thirty churches in his career, most of them A-frames. (If you can, check out his Chapel of the Jesus Ethic in Glendale, 336 W Colorado Street, with its bright-red steeple vault roof). This one's undoubted highlight is the entrance facade, fronted by a structural steel cross and consisting of patterned blue glass disks, hand-made in Belgium, which project fantastic colors inside. Blue glass clerestories along the sides also zoom blue light into the sanctuary. Walking inside takes your breath away. From the low-ceilinged portico you enter the sanctuary, with its exposed structural wood members. The space gains its power from the drama of its sharply sloping ceiling and the theatrical light show, bouncing blue light off the white walls. ▼

Pacific Northwest

1. University Unitarian Church
The building is open to the public as a functioning church and visits can be made Monday to Friday from 9 a.m. to 1 p.m.
All visits outside these hours must be by appointment with a minister or member of staff.
Members of the public are welcome to attend monthly art exhibitions featuring local established and emerging artists in the church's Gilmartin Gallery and the chapel.

Website uuchurch.org
Phone +1 206 525 8400

---

3. Canlis Restaurant
Open for dinner only.
Monday to Friday from 5.30 p.m. to closing and on Saturday from 5 p.m. to closing.
Closed on Sundays, Memorial Day, Independence Day, Labor Day, Thanksgiving, Christmas, and January 01 to January 06.
Smart attire required.

Website canlis.com
Phone +1 206 283 3313

---

5. Space Needle
The observation deck and shop are open from Monday to Thursday from 10 a.m. to 11 p.m., on Friday and Saturday from 9 a.m. to 11.30 p.m. and on Sunday from 9 a.m. to 11 p.m.
The Sky City restaurant at the top of the tower is open for brunch on Saturday and Sunday from 10 a.m. to 2.45 p.m., for lunch Monday to Friday from 11.30 a.m. to 2 p.m. and for dinner on Sunday to Thursday from 4.30 p.m. to 8.15 p.m. and on Friday and Saturday from 4.30 p.m. to 9.15 a.m.

Website spaceneedle.com

6. Pacific Science Center
Exhibitions are open Monday to Friday from 10 a.m. to 5 p.m., on Saturday, Sunday and holidays from 10 a.m. to 6 p.m.
The Laser Dome is open on Thursday to Sunday for evening shows and on Saturday and Sunday for matinees.
There are also daily shows in the IMAX theater.

Website pacificsciencecenter.org
Email gs@pacsci.org
Phone +1 206 443 2001

---

8. Plymouth Congregational Church
Open for church services on Sunday at 9 a.m. and 11 a.m.
The office is open Monday to Friday from 10 a.m. to 2 p.m.

Website plymouthchurchseattle.org

---

16. Veteran's Memorial Coliseum
Open to the public for ticketed events only.

Website rosequarter.com/plan-your-visit

---

18. Wells Fargo Center
As well as a branch of Wells Fargo bank, the building is home to a number of public spaces, including shops and a café, which are open during normal business hours.
The Wells Fargo & Company History Exhibit is located on the second floor of the Wells Fargo Center and is open Monday to Friday from 9 a.m. to 5 p.m.
Closed on bank holidays.
Admission is free.

Website
Wells Fargo Center
wfcportland.com/index.cfm
Wells Fargo & Company History Exhibit
wellsfargohistory.com/museums/portland
Phone +1 503 886 1102

20. Watzek House

The Watzek House is owned and run by the John Yeon Center which offers group tours of the Watzek House.
Members of the public who wish to take a tour of the Watzek House need to sign up to the mailing list to be sent information on tour dates.

Website yeoncenter.uoregon.edu/our-locations/the-watzek-house
Phone +1 503 412 3757

23. St. John the Baptist Catholic Church

The church is open for various services including Saturday Vigil Mass at 5.30 p.m., Sunday Masses at 7.30 a.m., 10 a.m., 12 midday (in Spanish), and 6.30 p.m.
Daily Mass is at 8.30 a.m.
Monday to Saturday.

Email parishoffice@sjbcatholicchurch.org
Phone +1 503 654 5449

24. Agnes Flanagan Chapel, Lewis and Clark College

The Agnes Flanagan Chapel is owned and run by the Lewis and Clark College and is only open to the public for church services, lectures, concerts, musical performances, and other events in the college's annual calendar.

Website lclark.edu/offices/spiritual_life/agnes_flanagan_chapel
Email events@lclark.edu
Phone +1 503 768 7235

25. Oregon Municipal Elevator

The elevator is open Monday to Saturday from 7 a.m. to 7 p.m. and Sunday 11 a.m. to 7 p.m. with extended opening hours from June to October.
Closed New Year's Day, Memorial Day, Independence Day, Labor Day, Thanksgiving and Christmas.

Website orcity.org/publicworks/municipal-elevator
Phone +1 503 496 1197

26. Gordon House

Guided tours start at 12 midday, 1 p.m. and 2 p.m. and must be booked in advance.

Website thegordonhouse.org
Email gordonhouse1957@frontier.com
Phone +1 503 874 6006

27. Mount Angel Library

The library is part of the Mount Angel Abbey and is open when the seminary is in session, Monday to Friday 8.30 a.m. to 5 p.m., Saturday from 10 a.m. to 4 p.m. and Sunday from 1 p.m. to 4 p.m.
The library is also open in the evenings from Sunday to Thursday from 6.30 p.m. to 9.30 p.m.
During vacation times, the library is open Monday to Friday from 9 a.m. to 4 p.m. and on Saturday from 10 a.m. to 4 p.m., except for holidays when the library is closed.
During the summer, the library is closed on Sundays.

Website mountangelabbey.org/architecture
Email info@mtangel.edu
Phone +1 503 845 3030

San Francisco

28. Sea Ranch

There are a number of properties at Sea Ranch available as vacation homes, and a number of companies that arrange rentals including Ocean View Properties.

Website stayinsearanch.com
Email info@stayinsearanch.com
Phone +1 707 884 3538

29. Marin County Civic Center

One-hour guided tours of the Civic Center are offered every Wednesday at 10.30 a.m. Reservations are not required.
Self-guided tours are also available.

Website marincounty.org/depts/cu/tours
Phone +1 415 473 3762

---

33. Hahn House

Hahn House is available for short-term rental on Airbnb.

Website airbnb.com/rooms/1677023

---

36. Weston Havens House

Ordinarily, guided tours are held on the third Sunday of every month at 10 a.m., however at the time of publication, tours have been temporarily suspended while crucial repairs and renovations to Havens House are in progress.

Website havenshouse.org
Email info@havenshouse.org

---

39. Oakland Museum of California

Open Wednesday and Thursday from 11 a.m. to 5 p.m., Friday from 11 a.m. to 10 p.m., Saturday and Sunday from 10 a.m. to 6 p.m. Closed Monday and Tuesday, as well as New Year's Day, Fourth of July, Thanksgiving, and Christmas.

Website museumca.org
Phone +1 510 318 8400

---

40. Mills College Chapel

Open during chapel hours, Sunday to Saturday from 7 a.m. to 10 p.m.

Website mills.edu/campus_life/chapel
Email chapel@mills.edu
Phone +1 510 430 2130

49. Embarcadero & Hyatt Regency

Open as a hotel to paying guests with a reservation only.

Website sanfrancisco.regency.hyatt.com
Phone +1 415 788 1234

---

52. St. Mary's Cathedral

The cathedral is open every day from the first Mass but tours are not allowed during Mass times.
Mass is held Monday to Friday at 12.10 p.m., on Saturday at 8 a.m. and 5.30 p.m. and on Sunday at 7.30 a.m., 9 a.m., 11 a.m. and at 1 p.m. in Spanish.
Guides are available in the cathedral from Monday to Friday from 10 a.m. to 12 p.m., Saturday from 11 a.m. to 1.30 p.m., and Sunday after the masses.

Website stmarycathedralsf.org
Phone +1 415 567 2020

---

53. San Francisco State University Student Union

Self-guided campus tours are available using a numbered campus map available on the university's website

Website sfsu.edu/outreach/visiting
Email outreach@sfsu.edu
Phone +1 415 338 2355

---

55. Ascension Chapel, Holy Cross Cemetery

Holy Cross periodically conducts walking tours of the grounds.

Website holycrosscemeteries.com/locations/colma
Email moreinfo@holycrosscemeteries.com
Phone +1 650 756 2060

---

57. Life House

Hahn House is available for short-term rental on Airbnb.

Website airbnb.com/rooms/664068

61. First United Methodist Church of Palo Alto

Open for church services only.

Website firstpaloalto.com
Email info@firstpaloalto.com
Phone +1 650 323 6167

62. Hanna House

Ordinarily, guided tours of Hanna House are available however at the time of publication, tours have been temporarily suspended until September 2016.

Website hannahousetours.stanford.edu
Email hannahouse@stanford.edu
Phone +1 650 725 8352

63. Foothill College

Visitors need to contact the College & Career Connections Office to arrange a guided tour.
The college can also provide visitors with a campus map for self-guided tours.

Website foothill.edu/outreach/tours
Phone +1 650 949 7813

64. First National Bank

Open during business hours for customers of the bank.
Monday to Friday from 9 a.m. to 5 p.m.
Closed Saturday and Sunday.

Website bankofthewest.com
Phone +1 408 245 4540

65. Tan's Touchless Car Wash

Open to customers of the carwash Monday to Thursday from 8 a.m. to 5 p.m., Friday and Saturday 8 a.m. to 5.30 p.m., and Sunday 9 a.m. to 5 p.m.

Website touchlesscarwash.biz
Email touchlesscarwash@gmail.com
Phone +1 408 244 8233

66. Center for the Performing Arts

Open to the public for ticketed events and performances only.

Website sanjosetheaters.org/theaters/center-for-performing-arts
Email tickets@ucsc.edu
Phone +1 831 459 2159

73. Nepenthe Restaurant

The restaurant is open Monday to Sunday and serves lunch from 11.30 a.m. to 4.30 p.m. and dinner from 5 p.m. to 10.p.m.
Closed on Thanksgiving and Christmas.

Website nepenthebigsur.com
Email ahahn@nepenthebigsur.com
Phone +1 831 667 2345

74. Wild Bird

Wild Bird is available to rent as a vacation property.

Website handpickedvillas.com
Email wildbird@handpickedvillas.com
Phone +1 424 302 5144

Los Angeles

80. California Lutheran University

Tours are offered on Tuesday, Wednesday and Thursday at 10 a.m., 2 p.m. and at 4 p.m. on Wednesday only.
Tours must be requested via the California Lutheran University website.

Website callutheran.edu

84. Congregational Church of Northridge

Tours are available by appointment only, by phoning during office hours on Tuesday, Thursday and Friday between 9 a.m. and 3.30 p.m.

Website northridgechurch.net
Phone +1 818 349 2400

88. Casa de Cadillac

Casa de Cadillac, Buick GMC Sherman Oaks is open from Monday to Friday from 8.30 a.m. to 7 p.m., Saturday from 9 a.m. to 5.30 p.m. and Sunday from 11 a.m. to 5 p.m.

Website casadecadillac.com

---

89. St. Michael & All Angels Episcopal Church

Open for church services only on Sunday at 8.30 a.m. and 10.30 a.m.

Website stmikessc.org
Email mail@stmikessc.org
Phone +1 818 763 9193

---

97. University of California, Los Angeles

The university offers various tours for prospective students as well as a self-guided walking tour.

Website admission.ucla.edu/tours

---

100. Twenty-Eighth Church of Christ, Scientist

Open for church services only.

Website 28ccs.com
Email twenty8thcl@dslextreme.com
Phone +1 310 208 8189

---

105. Eames House

Open for tours by advance reservation only on Monday, Tuesday, Thursday and Friday from 10 a.m. to 4 p.m.
Closed Wednesday, Sunday and major holidays.

Website eamesfoundation.org
Email info@eamesfoundation.org
Phone +1 310 459 9663

108. Century Plaza Tower

The towers are home to various public amenities including cafes, restaurants and shops.

Website
centurypark.net/centuryplazatowers

---

111. Norm's

Open twenty-four hours a day.

Website normsrestaurants.com/lacienega

---

112. Schindler House

Open Wednesday to Sunday from 11 a.m. to 6 p.m.
Closed Monday and Tuesday. Admission to the Schindler House is free on Friday afternoons between 4 p.m. and 6 p.m., and on International Museum Day in May and on Rudolph Schindler's birthday on September 10.

Website makcenter.org/visit
Email office@makcenter.org
Phone +1 323 651 1510

---

123. Cinerama Dome

Open to paying cinema-goers.
The café is open daily from 11.30 a.m. to 12 midnight.

Website arclightcinemas.com

---

124. Stahl House, Case Study #22

Stahl House is open for afternoon, late afternoon, and evening tours at varius times of the week.
All tours must be pre-booked and pre-paid.

Website stahlhouse.com
Phone +1 208 429 1058

131. Hollyhock House
Open for self-guided tours from Thursday to Sunday from 11 a.m. to 3 p.m. and for guided tours on Tuesday and Wednesday at 10 a.m. and 11a.m.
Guided tours can be booked in advance.

Website barnsdall.org/hollyhock-house/about
Email hollyhock@barnsdall.org
Phone +1 323 913 4030

---

134. Neutra VDL House
Open for tours on Saturday from 11 a.m. to 3 p.m.

Website neutra-vdl.org

---

136. First United Methodist Church of Glendale
Open for church services only on Sunday at 10.30 a.m.

Website glendalemethodist.org
Phone +1 818 243 2105

---

138. Art Center College
Tours of the Hillside Campus are generally only offered to prospective students, however for scheduled tours for members of the public are offered on a limited basis.

Website artcenter.edu/admissions/schedule-a-tour
Phone +1 626 396 2338

---

140. Norton Simon Museum
Open Monday, Wednesday and Thursday from 12 midday to 5 p.m., on Friday and Saturday from 11 a.m. to 8 p.m., on Sunday from 11 a.m. to 5 p.m.
Closed Tuesday, Rose Parade Day, Thanksgiving, and Christmas.

Website nortonsimon.org
Phone +1 626 449 6840

147. Beckman Auditorium
Open for ticketed events only.

Website caltech.edu/content/beckman-auditorium-1

---

149. Covina Bowl
Open Monday, Tuesday and Sunday 10 a.m. to 11 p.m., Wednesday and Thursday 4 p.m. to 11 p.m., Friday and Saturday 10 a.m. to 1 a.m.

Website bowlbrunswick.com/location/brunswick-zone-covina-bowl
Phone +1 626 339 1286

---

153. LACMA
Open Monday, Tuesday and Thursday from 11 a.m. to 5 p.m., Friday from 11 a.m. to 8 p.m., and Saturday and Sunday from 10 a.m. to 7 p.m.
Closed Wednesday, Thanksgiving, and Christmas.

Website lacma.org
Email publicinfo@lacma.org
Phone +1 323 857 6000

---

155. Mackey Apartments
Open the first Friday of each month from 11 a.m. to 6 p.m. Reservations required.

Website makcenter.org
Email office@makcenter.org
Phone +1 323 651 1510

---

156. Expert Car Wash
Open daily from 8 a.m. to 6 p.m.

Phone +1 323 938 1777

---

159. St. Basil's Church
Open for church services only.

Website stbasilchurch-la.org
Email stbasilchurchla@aol.com
Phone +1 213 381 6191

160. Founder's Church of Religious Science

Open for church services only on Sunday at 10 a.m.

Website founderslosangeles.org
Email info@founderslosangeles.org
Phone +1 213 388 9733

---

162. Dodger Stadium

Dodger Stadium provide a selection of behind-the-scenes tours.

Website losangeles.dodgers.mlb.com/la/ballpark

---

164. Music Center

The Music Center offers free guided tours of Walt Disney Concert Hall, Mark Taper Forum, Ahmanson Theater, and Dorothy Chandler Pavilion on Tuesday to Saturday at 10.30 a.m. and 12.30 p.m.
Group tours can also be arranged.

Website musiccenter.org
Phone +1 213 972 7483

---

165. Holman United Methodist Church

Open for church services only on Sunday at 8 a.m. and 11 a.m.

Website holmanumc.com
Email holman@holmanumc.com
Phone +1 323 731 7285

---

166. Westin Bonaventure Hotel

Open to guests with reservations only.

Website thebonaventure.com
Phone +1 213 624 1000

167. University of Southern California

USC offers a variety of tours including a free self-guided walking tour.

Website visit.usc.edu

---

168. Pan American Bank

Open to bank customers Monday to Thursday from 9 a.m. to 5 p.m., and Friday from 9 a.m. to 6 p.m. Closed Saturday.

Website panambk.com
Email info@panambk.com
Phone +1 877 274 6614

---

170. IBM Aerospace, Otis College of Art and Design

The Ben Maltz Gallery, part of Otis College, is open Tuesday to Friday from 10 a.m. to 5 p.m., and Saturday and Sunday from 12 midday to 4 p.m.
Closed Mondays.
Group tours can be arranged on request.

Website otis.edu
Email galleryinfo@otis.edu
Phone +1 310 665 6905

---

172. University Christian Church

Open for church services only on Sunday at 09.00, 10.15 and 11.30.

Website univcc.org
Email info@univcc.org
Phone +1 310 670 4747

---

173. St. Jerome Roman Catholic Church

Open for church services only, Monday to Saturday at 8 a.m., Saturday at 5.30 p.m. and Sunday at 7.30 a.m., 9 a.m., 11 a.m., and 5.30 p.m.

Website stjeromewestchester.org
Phone +1 310 348 8212

174. Pann's

Open to customers of the restaurant, Monday and Tuesday 7 a.m. to 3 p.m., Wednesday and Sunday 7 a.m. to 9 p.m., Thursday, Friday, and Saturday 7 a.m. to 10 p.m.

Website panns.com
Email jim@panns.com
Phone +1 310 670 1441

---

175. The Forum

Open to ticket holders for events at The Forum only.

Website fabulousforum.com
Phone +1 310 330 7300

---

176. South Bay Bank

Open to bank customers during business hours Monday to Thursday 10 a.m. to 5 p.m. and Friday 10 a.m. to 6 p.m.
Drive-up banking services are available Monday to Thursday 8.30 a.m. to 5 p.m. and Friday 8.30 a.m. to 6 p.m.

Website cbbank.com/locations/manhattan-beach-business-financial-center-3
Phone +1 310 802 4015

---

177. Chips

Open daily from 6a.m. to 8p.m. for restaurant customers.

Phone +1 310 679 2947

---

179. California State Dominguez Hills Library

The University offers a variety of tours for prospective students as well as a self-guided walking tour.

Website csudh.edu/admissions/visit-us/schedule-a-tour
Email campustours@csudh.edu
Phone +1 310 243 3673

180. Riviera Methodist Church

Open for church services only on Sunday at 10 a.m.

Website rivieraumc.com
Email office@rivieraumc.com
Phone +1 310 378 9273

---

182. Wayfarers Chapel

The chapel is open daily from 9 a.m. to 5 p.m. The Visitor's Center and gift shop is open daily from 10.00 to 17.00.

Website wayfarerschapel.org
Phone +1 310 377 1650

---

191. California State University Fullerton

The campus is open for self-guided walking tours.

Website fullerton.edu
Phone +1 657 278 2011

---

192. Anaheim Convention Center & Arena

Open to ticket holders for events at Anaheim Convention Center only.

Website anaheim.net/1117/Anaheim-Convention-Center-Arena
Phone +1 714 765 8950

---

192. Hope International University

The campus is open for self-guided walking tours.

Website hiu.edu
Phone +1 714 879 3901

---

194. Stuft Shirt Restaurant

Now home to A'maree's, a retail fashion establishment.

Website amarees.com
Email info@amarees.com
Phone +1 949 642 4423

195. Christ Cathedral
Tours are conducted Monday to Saturday at 10 a.m. and 1 p.m.
Tours for groups of fifteen or more people must be made by reservation.

Website main.alpha.christcathedralcalifornia.com
Email trudymazz@christcathedralca.org
Phone +1 949 375 5763

198. University of California, Irvine
Walking tours of the campus are offered Monday to Friday at 12 midday throughout the year.

Website campustours.uci.edu/information
Phone +1 949 824 6703

199. University of California, Riverside
The university offers a variety of tour options, including guided tours that can be scheduled in advance as well as self-guided walking tours.

Website ucr.edu/about/tours
Phone +1 951 827 1012

200. Crafton Hills College
The campus is open for self-guided walking tours.

Website craftonhills.edu
Phone +1 909 794 2161

Palm Springs

201. Hotel Lautner
Open as a hotel to paying guests with a reservation only.
Private tours are available but must be booked in advance.

Website hotellautner.com
Phone +1 760 832 5288

202. Palm Springs Visitor Center
Open daily from 9 a.m. to 5 p.m.

Website visitpalmsprings.com/overview/play/palm-springs-visitors-center/13676
Phone +1 760 778 8418

211. St. Theresa Church
Open for church services only.

Website sttheresaps.com
Phone +1 760 323 2669

212. Palm Springs Art Museum, Architecture and Design Center
Open Wednesday, Friday, Saturday, and Sunday from 10 a.m. to 5 p.m., on Thursday from 12 midday to 8 p.m.
Closed Monday, Tuesday and major holidays.
Tours available on Wednesday, Friday, Saturday, and Sunday at 11 a.m. and 2 p.m.

Website psmuseum.org
Phone +1 760 423 5260

213. Frey House II
The house is owned by the Palm Springs Art Museum and is not generally open to the public, except during Modernism Week, which occurs each February, when special tours are available.

214. Coachella Valley Bank
Open to bank customers Monday to Friday from 9 a.m. to 6 p.m., and Saturday from 9 a.m. to 4 p.m. Closed Sunday.

Phone +1 760 325 1242

215. Santa Fe Federal Savings Bank
Open to bank customers Monday to Friday from 9 a.m. to 6 p.m., Saturday 9 a.m. to 4 p.m. Closed Sunday.

Phone +1 760 325 1242

216. Caliente Tropics Resort

Open as a hotel to paying guests with a reservation only.
The lobby is open twenty-four hours a day.

Website calientetropics.com
Email reservations@calientetropics.com
Phone +1 760 327 1391

217. Ocotillo Lodge

Available to rent for overnight accommodation.

Website vrbo.com/331018

218. Horizon Hotel

Open as a hotel to paying guests with a reservation only.

Website lhorizonpalmsprings.com
Phone +1 760 323 1858

219. Bank of America

The Financial Center is open to bank customers Monday to Thursday from 9 a.m. to 5 p.m., Friday 9 a.m. to 6 p.m., and Saturday from 10 a.m. to 2 p.m.
Closed on Sunday.

Phone +1 760 864 8584

220. Pearlman Cabin

The cabin is owned by Nancy Pearlman and can be rented for photo shoots by prior arrangement.

Website nancypearlman.net
Phone +1 310 559 9160

221. Sunnylands

Admission to the Sunnylands Visitor Center and Gardens is free, and both are open Thursday to Sunday from 9 a.m. to 4 p.m. Sunnylands also offers several guided tours that require tickets.
The Historic House Tour is the only tour that takes people into the historic house.
The Bird Tour takes visitors through the estate grounds with a local birder.
The Open-Air Experience is a tour of the estate grounds with a focus on sustainability. Group tours are also available.

Website sunnylands.org
Email contact@sunnylands.org
Phone +1 760 202 2222

San Diego

225. Salk Institute

The Salk Institute offers one-hour guided tours for parties of five or less on Monday, Wednesday, and Friday at 12 midday.
Group tours are also available for parties of six or more.
All tours must be booked in advance.

Website salk.edu/events/tour-information
Email tours@salk.edu
Phone +1 858 453 4100

228. Geisel Library

University of California, San Diego's Visitor's Tour Program offers free tours on Sunday afternoons.
The tours last for two hours and start at 2 p.m.
Tours are free but must be reserved in advance.

Website ucpa.ucsd.edu/resources/tours
Phone +1 858 534 4414

234. Clairemont Lutheran Church

Open for church services only.

Website carltonhillslutheran.org
Email chlc@carltonhillslutheran.org
Phone +1 619 448 1888

235. North Clairemont Library

Open Monday, Thursday and Friday from 9.30 a.m. to 6 p.m., Tuesday and Wednesday 11.30 a.m. to 8 p.m. and on